PUBLISHED

Jane Austen: *Emma* (Revised Edition) DAVID LODGE
Jane Austen: *'Northanger Abbey' & 'Persuasion'* B.C. SOUTHAM
Jane Austen: *'Sense and Sensibility', 'Pride and Prejudice' & 'Mansfield Park'*
   B.C. SOUTHAM
Beckett: *Waiting for Godot* RUBY COHN
William Blake: *Songs of Innocence and Experience* MARGARET BOTTRALL
Charlotte Brontë: *'Jane Eyre' & 'Villette'* MIRIAM ALLOTT
Emily Brontë: *Wuthering Heights* (Revised Edition) MIRIAM ALLOTT
Browning: *'Men and Women' & Other Poems* J.R. WATSON
Bunyan: *The Pilgrim's Progress* ROGER SHARROCK
Chaucer: *Canterbury Tales* J.J. ANDERSON
Coleridge: *'The Ancient Mariner' & Other Poems* ALUN R. JONES & WILLIAM TYDEMAN
Congreve: *Comedies* PATRICK LYONS
Conrad: *'Heart of Darkness', 'Nostromo' & 'Under Western Eyes'* C.B. COX
Conrad: *The Secret Agent* IAN WATT
Dickens: *Bleak House* A.E. DYSON
Dickens: *'Hard Times', 'Great Expectations' & 'Our Mutual Friend'* NORMAN PAGE
Dickens: *'Dombey and Son' & 'Little Dorrit'* ALAN SHELSTON
Donne: *Songs and Sonets* JULIAN LOVELOCK
George Eliot: *Middlemarch* PATRICK SWINDEN
George Eliot: *'The Mill on the Floss' & 'Silas Marner'* R.P. DRAPER
T. S. Eliot: *Four Quartets* BERNARD BERGONZI
T. S. Eliot: *'Prufrock', 'Gerontion', 'Ash Wednesday' & Other Shorter Poems*
   B.C. SOUTHAM
T. S. Eliot: *The Waste Land* C.B. COX & ARNOLD P. HINCHLIFFE
T. S. Eliot: *Plays* ARNOLD P. HINCHLIFFE
Henry Fielding: *Tom Jones* NEIL COMPTON
E. M. Forster: *A Passage to India* MALCOLM BRADBURY
William Golding: *Novels 1954–64* NORMAN PAGE
Hardy: *The Tragic Novels* (Revised Edition) R.P. DRAPER
Hardy: *Poems* JAMES GIBSON & TREVOR JOHNSON
Hardy: *Three Pastoral Novels* R.P. DRAPER
Gerard Manley Hopkins: *Poems* MARGARET BOTTRALL
Henry James: *'Washington Square' & 'The Portrait of a Lady'* ALAN SHELSTON
Jonson: *Volpone* JONAS A. BARISH
Jonson: *'Every Man in his Humour' & 'The Alchemist'* R.V. HOLDSWORTH
James Joyce: *'Dubliners' & 'A Portrait of the Artist as a Young Man'* MORRIS BEJA
Keats: *Odes* G.S. FRASER
Keats: *Narrative Poems* JOHN SPENCER HILL
D. H. Lawrence: *Sons and Lovers* GAMINI SALGADO
D. H. Lawrence: *'The Rainbow' & 'Women in Love'* COLIN CLARKE
Lowry: *Under the Volcano* GORDON BOWKER
Marlowe: *Doctor Faustus* JOHN JUMP
Marlowe: *'Tamburlaine the Great', 'Edward the Second' & 'The Jew of Malta'*
   JOHN RUSSELL BROWN
Marvell: *Poems* ARTHUR POLLARD
Milton: *Paradise Lost* A.E. DYSON & JULIAN LOVELOCK
O'Casey: *'Juno and the Paycock', 'The Plough and the Stars' & 'The Shadow of a
   Gunman'* RONALD AYLING
Eugene O'Neill: *Three Plays* NORMAND BERLIN
John Osborne: *Look Back in Anger* JOHN RUSSELL TAYLOR
Pinter: *'The Caretaker' & Other Plays* MICHAEL SCOTT
Pope: *The Rape of the Lock* JOHN DIXON HUNT
Shakespeare: *A Midsummer Night's Dream* ANTONY PRICE
Shakespeare: *Antony and Cleopatra* (Revised Edition) JOHN RUSSELL BROWN
Shakespeare: *Coriolanus* B.A. BROCKMAN

Shakespeare: *Early Tragedies: 'Richard III', 'Titus Andronicus' & 'Romeo and Juliet'* NEIL TAYLOR & BRYAN LOUGHREY
Shakespeare: *Hamlet* JOHN JUMP
Shakespeare: *Henry IV Parts I and II* G.K. HUNTER
Shakespeare: *Henry V* MICHAEL QUINN
Shakespeare: *Julius Caesar* PETER URE
Shakespeare: *King Lear* (Revised Edition) FRANK KERMODE
Shakespeare: *Macbeth* JOHN WAIN
Shakespeare: *Measure for Measure* C.K. STEAD
Shakespeare: *The Merchant of Venice* JOHN WILDERS
Shakespeare: *'Much Ado About Nothing' & 'As You Like It'* JOHN RUSSELL BROWN
Shakespeare: *Othello* JOHN WAIN
Shakespeare: *Richard II* NICHOLAS BROOKE
Shakespeare: *The Sonnets* PETER JONES
Shakespeare: *The Tempest* D.J. PALMER
Shakespeare: *Troilus and Cressida* PRISCILLA MARTIN
Shakespeare: *Twelfth Night* D.J. PALMER
Shakespeare: *The Winter's Tale* KENNETH MUIR
Shaw: *Man and Superman & Saint Joan* A. M. GIBBS
Spenser: *The Faerie Queene* PETER BAYLEY
Sheridan: *Comedies* PETER DAVISON
Stoppard: *'Rosencrantz and Guildenstern are Dead', 'Jumpers' & 'Travesties'* T. BAREHAM
J. M. Synge: *Four Plays* RONALD AYLING
Swift: *Gulliver's Travels* RICHARD GRAVIL
Tennyson: *In Memoriam* JOHN DIXON HUNT
Thackeray: *Vanity Fair* ARTHUR POLLARD
Trollope: *The Barsetshire Novels* T. BAREHAM
Webster: *'The White Devil' & 'The Duchess of Malfi'* R.V. HOLDSWORTH
Wilde: *Comedies* WILLIAM TYDEMAN
Virginia Woolf: *To the Lighthouse* MORIS BEJA
Wordsworth: *The 1807 Poems* ALUN R. JONES
Wordsworth: *Lyrical Ballads* ALUN R. JONES & WILLIAM TYDEMAN
Wordsworth: *The Prelude* W.J. HARVEY & RICHARD GRAVIL
Yeats: *Poems 1919–35* ELIZABETH CULLINGFORD
Yeats: *Last Poems* JON STALLWORTHY

Issues in Contemporary Critical Theory PETER BARRY
Thirties Poets: 'The Auden Group' RONALD CARTER
Tragedy: Developments in Criticism R.P. DRAPER
Epic RONALD DRAPER
Poetry Criticism and Practice: Developments since the Symbolists A.E. DYSON
Three Contemporary Poets: Gunn, Hughes, Thomas A.E. DYSON
Elizabethan Poetry: Lyrical & Narrative GERALD HAMMOND
The Metaphysical Poets GERALD HAMMOND
Medieval English Drama PETER HAPPÉ
The English Novel: Developments in Criticism since Henry James STEPHEN HAZELL
Poetry of the First World War DOMINIC HIBBERD
The Romantic Imagination JOHN SPENCER HILL
Drama Criticism: Developments since Ibsen ARNOLD P. HINCHLIFFE
The Pastoral Mode BRYAN LOUGHREY
Three Jacobean 'Revenge' Plays R.V. HOLDSWORTH
The Language of Literature NORMAN PAGE
Comedy: Developments in Criticism D.J. PALMER
Shakespeare: *Studying Shakespeare* JOHN RUSSELL BROWN
The Gothic Novel VICTOR SAGE
Pre-Romantic Poetry J.R. WATSON

J. M. Synge
Four Plays

Riders to the Sea
The Well of the Saints
The Playboy of the Western World
Deirdre of the Sorrows

A CASEBOOK

EDITED BY

RONALD AYLING

MACMILLAN

First published 1992 by
THE MACMILLAN PRESS LTD
Houndmills, Basingstoke, Hampshire RG21 2XS
and London
Companies and representatives
throughout the world

ISBN 0-333-42383-6 hardcover
ISBN 0-333-42384-4 paperback

A catalogue record for this book is available
from the British Library.

Typeset by Footnote Graphics,
Warminster, Wiltshire

Printed in Hong Kong

To Teri

with deep love and admiration

CONTENTS

CONTENTS

ACKNOWLEDGEMENTS

The editor and publishers wish to thank the following for permission to use copyright material:

Eugene Benson, extract from *J. M. Synge* (1982), by permission of Macmillan, London and Basingstoke; Cyril Cusack, 'A Player's Reflections on *Playboy*', *Modern Drama*, 4, December (1961), by permission of Modern Drama; Errol Durbach, 'Synge's Tragic Vision of the Old Mother and the Sea', *Modern Drama*, 14:4, February (1972), by permission of Modern Drama; William Empson, extract from *Seven Types of Ambiguity* (1930) 3rd edition 1953, by permission of the estate of the author and Chatto and Windus; Donna Gerstenberger, extract from *John Millington Synge* (1964), by permission of Twayne Publishers, a division of G. K. Hall & Co., Boston; Nicholas Grene, extracts from 'Introduction' to *The Well of the Saints* (1982), by permission of Colin Smythe Limited, Publishers; Robert Bechtold Heilman, extracts from *Tragedy and Melodrama: Versions of Experience* (1968) and *The Ways of the World: Comedy and Society* (1978), by permission of University of Washington Press; T. R. Henn, 'Images, Symbols and Literary Echoes in *Riders to the Sea*', in S. B. Bushrui (ed.), *Sunshine and the Moon's Delight* (1972), by permission of Colin Smythe Limited, Publishers; Toni O'Brien Johnson, extracts from '*The Well of the Saints* and *Waiting for Godot*: Stylistic Variations on a Tradition' in Maurice Harmon (ed.), *The Irish Writer and the City* (1984), by permission of Colin Smythe Limited, Publishers; Denis Johnston, extract from *John Millington Synge* (1965). Copyright © 1965 Columbia University Press, by permission of Columbia University Press; Hugh Kenner, extract from *A Colder Eye: The Modern Irish Writers* (1983), Viking Books. Copyright © 1983 Hugh Kenner, by permission of Penguin Books Limited; Declan Kiberd, extract from 'The Fall of the Stage Irishman' in Ronald Schleiffer (ed.), *The Genres of the Irish Literary Revival* (1980), Wolfhound Press, by permission of the author; and extract from 'Brian Friel's *Faith Healer*' in Masaru Sekine (ed.), *Irish Writers and Society at Large* (1985), by permission of Colin Smythe

11

Limited, Publishers; Thomas Kilroy, extract from 'Synge and Modernism' in M. Harmon (ed.), *J. M. Synge: Centenary Papers 1971*, Dolmen Press 1972, by permission of the author; Augustine Martin, 'Christy Mahon and the Apotheosis of Loneliness' in S. B. Bushrui, *Sunshine and the Moon's Delight* (1972), by permission of Colin Smythe Limited, Publishers; Frank O'Connor, extract from 'Synge' in Lennox Robinson (ed.), *The Irish Theatre* (1939), by permission of Macmillan, London and Basingstoke; Sidney Poger, 'Brecht's *Senora Carrar's Rifles* and Synge's *Riders to the Sea*', *Canadian Journal of Irish Studies*, 10:2, December (1984), by permission of the author; Ann Saddlemyer, extract from 'Synge and the Nature of Women' in S. F. Gallagher (ed.), *Women in Irish Legend, Life and Literature* (1983), by permission of Colin Smythe Limited, Publishers, and extracts from '*Deirdre of the Sorrows*: Literature First ... Drama Afterwards' in M. Harmon (ed.), *J. M. Synge: Centenary Papers 1971*, Dolmen Press 1972, by permission of the author; Robert Welch, extract from 'The Emergence of Modern Anglo-Irish Drama: Yeats and Synge' in Masaru Sekine (ed.), *Irish Writers and the Theatre* (1986), by permission of Colin Smythe Limited, Publishers; Raymond Williams, extract from *Drama from Ibsen to Brecht* (1968), by permission of Chatto and Windus; Katherine Worth, extract from *The Irish Drama of Europe from Yeats to Beckett* (1978), by permission of The Athlone Press Limited.

Every effort has been made to trace all the copyright holders but if any have been inadvertently overlooked the publishers will be pleased to make the necessary arrangement at the first opportunity.

GENERAL EDITOR'S PREFACE

The Casebook series, launched in 1968, has become a well-regarded library of critical studies. The central concern of the series remains the 'single-author' volume, but suggestions from the academic community have led to an extension of the original plan, to include occasional volumes on such general themes as literary 'schools' and genres.

Each volume in the central category deals either with one well-known and influential work by an individual author, or with closely related works by one writer. The main section consists of critical readings, mostly modern, collected from books and journals. A selection of reviews and comments by the author's contemporaries is also included, and sometimes comment from the author himself. The Editor's Introduction charts the reputation of the work or works from the first appearance to the present time.

Volumes in the 'general themes' category are variable in structure but follow the basic purpose of the series in presenting an integrated selection of readings, with an Introduction which explores the theme and discusses the literary and critical issues involved.

A single volume can represent no more than a small selection of critical opinions. Some critics are excluded for reasons of space, and it is hoped that readers will pursue the suggestions for further reading in the Select Bibliography. Other contributions are severed from their original context, to which some readers may wish to turn. Indeed, if they take a hint from the critics represented here, they certainly will.

A. E. DYSON

INTRODUCTION

The popularity of Chekhov's plays on the English stage, now taken for granted, may make us forget the earlier vicissitudes they underwent before becoming an accepted part of the English theatrical scene. Less well known, though hardly less surprising, is Chekhov's much earlier success with Irish theatregoers, who did not have the same initial resistance to the unfamiliar ordinariness (as it seemed) of his dramatic writings. What does seem strange in hindsight, bearing in mind the specific social and cultural set-up of Ireland at the turn of the present century, was the failure of any native author remotely like Chekhov to surface at that time in either fiction or the drama. Of course, it is not to be supposed that anyone of Chekhov's particular sensibility, let alone his genius, would appear there. Yet most if not all the conditions that inspired the Russian's creative talents were actively at work in Ireland then, remaining prominent for a considerable time afterwards within that country's predominantly rural constituency in the years before and even immediately following political independence. Given the protracted nature of this way of life in Ireland, it is understandable that characteristically Chekhovian elements are to be found even today in the dramatic writings of Brian Friel, arguably the most important of contemporary Irish dramatists, and not solely in his highly regarded historical plays where he takes critical glances back to earlier and supposedly simpler times.

Friel has not only created lively 'Irish stage versions' of Chekhov's *The Three Sisters* and Turgenev's *Fathers and Sons*, but, in his own theatrical works, he has shown himself to be unusually sensitive to fluctuating group (mostly family) and individual moods and feelings and to shifting social relationships besides; he also possesses an uncanny ability to realize psychic states peculiar to a specific time and place. While Friel is always his own man with particular dramatic gifts intrinsic to himself, he can (in plays like *Living Quarters*, *Aristocrats* and *Dancing at Lughnasa*) also command a tragicomic sense akin to that of Chekhov himself in

15

recreating a past (and passing) world where sharp-edged satire
mingles with regret and even some vestiges of nostalgia.

That, as early as the first decade of the present century, an Irish
playwright of genius could be as acutely aware as was Chekhov at
the very same time of dramatic potentialities in the counterpointing
of fluctuating moods and the creation of atmosphere in setting in the
rural ambience encompassing the Big House of Anglo-Irish Ascendancy in the twilight of its power, is clearly apparent from an essay
by John Millington Synge almost certainly written at the time he
first began to wrestle with his own highly original dramatic works.[1]
That prose piece – whose suggestive title, 'A Landlord's Garden in
County Wicklow', and pervasive atmosphere invoke parallels with
Turgenev's *A Month in the Country* or the second act of *The Cherry
Orchard* – is, in turn, scathingly critical of, and then mutedly elegiac
for, the Anglo-Irish Ascendancy in its decline. Synge, much closer
than Chekhov by birth and family heritage (if not in the actual
circumstances of his upbringing) to this ruling class, was yet
fundamentally estranged from its ethos and its underlying morality.
Unlike the Russian author, Synge was temperamentally drawn to
the world outside its orbit (outside, that is, both the largely
Protestant aristocracy and the predominantly Catholic middle
class), and drawn especially to that way of life which encompassed
the social outsiders and outcasts as well as to that amoral natural
world outside human society altogether.

Synge reveals in 'A Landlord's Garden in County Wicklow' a
clear-sighted awareness of poignant Chekhovian possibilities in
the decline of his own class. That he seems not to have known the
work of the Russian author is neither here nor there; his description,
perfectly attuned to works like *The Three Sisters*, is remarkably
prescient without being sentimental. Having described the still
profuse desolation of a long neglected country demesne, Synge
comments (and his own then mostly unwritten plays immediately
come to mind): 'Everyone is used in Ireland to the tragedy that is
bound up with the lives of farmers and fishing people', going on to
add, 'but in this garden one seemed to feel the tragedy of the
landlord class also, and of the innumerable old families that are
quickly dwindling away'. Then, in the manuscript but not in the
published version, he wrote of the Ascendancy in distinctly un-
Yeatsian terms: 'Still, this class, with its many genuine qualities,
had little patriotism, in the right sense, few ideas, and no seed for

future life, so it has gone to the wall'. In the printed version, he continued:

These owners of the land are not much pitied at the present day, or much deserving of pity; and yet one cannot quite forget that they are the descendants of what was at one time, in the eighteenth century, a high-spirited and highly-cultivated aristocracy. The broken green-houses and mouse-eaten libraries, that were designed and collected by men who voted with Grattan, are perhaps as mournful in the end as the four mud walls that are so often left in Wicklow as the only remnants of a farmhouse. The desolation of this life is often of a peculiarly local kind, and if a playwright chose to go through the Irish country houses he would find material, it is likely, for many gloomy plays that would turn on the dying away of these old families, and on the lives of the one or two delicate girls that are left so often to represent a dozen hearty men who were alive a generation or two ago.[2]

Does not this description sound as though it could act as an introduction to a volume of Chekhov's writings, particularly (in the final sentence) *The Three Sisters* and *The Cherry Orchard*? Sensitive to this atmosphere of decline and decay, with its attendant and occasional splendour, Synge nonetheless found more congenial material for his own creative imagination in the (to him) more vivid everyday working lives and stories of the common folk, including those very poor farmers and fishermen to whom he had alluded earlier. Here, in creating a new subject matter for Irish drama that soon became the staple fare for the Irish dramatic movement centred in the Abbey Theatre, Synge found more empathetic material and even some characters on the outskirts of society with whom he could to some extent identify as well as sympathize. Moreover, while it is possible that he could see only the tragic dimension to the decline of his own class, where Chekhov and Friel, say, can see tragicomic possibilities inherent in this situation (neither Chekhov nor Friel create 'gloomy plays', even when writing about decline and decay), in dramatizing the boisterous life of a larger rural society Synge could encompass the robust outlook and randy folkloric humour more characteristic of Burns or Rabelais (both writers he deeply admired) or even of Yeats's much later creation, Crazy Jane, than would have been possible for him had he attempted to realize theatrically the more delicate and evanescent world that he saw poignantly symbolized in 'A Landlord's Garden in County Wicklow'. Yet, within a more sturdy even earthy form of peasant drama, Synge could also realize at certain moments something of an agonized sense of splendour in the desolation of Irish country life, seeing in it an endangered way of life in its last (and still attractive) stages – most perceptibly, perhaps, in *Riders to the Sea* and *Deirdre of the Sorrows*, where the dramas themselves enact something like a dirge or *caoine* for its passing.

Again and again in his travel writings and topographical sketches, a keen but tremulous anguish is discernible in Synge's response to people and places in Kerry, Connemara and, above all, Wicklow and the Aran Islands. On the very first page of his perceptive and poetic book entitled *The Aran Islands*, written before any of his plays and yet indispensable reading for students of them, the dramatist declared 'I have seen nothing so desolate'.[3] Elsewhere, he speaks of 'the indescribable half-plaintive atmosphere of the autumn Sundays of Wicklow',[4] asking, on another occasion, 'what has given this vague but passionate anguish to the twilights of Ireland?'[5] In such moments of personal insight we glimpse something of the playwright's close identification of his own emotional moods with the psychic states of a familiar and well-loved but often harsh environment. According to Herbert Gorman, one of James Joyce's earliest biographers, the novelist saw Synge as 'a dark tramper of a man',[6] but he can hardly have known that the playwright often affectionately signed love letters to his fiancée, 'Your old Tramp'. A hiker on foot in all weathers, Synge could see the world from the homeless vagrant's point of view, admiring the sturdy self-reliance and ingenuity of the travelling people: the tramps, bards, and storytellers (or seanachies) as well as the tinkers and gypsy-like itinerants of Ireland. Landscape and human life are, alike, wild and unpredictable and tinged with melancholy. 'In these [Wicklow] hills', he writes, 'the summer passes in a few weeks from a late spring, full of odour and colour, to an autumn that is premature and filled with the desolate splendour of decay; and it often happens that, in moments when one is most aware of this ceaseless fading of beauty, some incident of tramp life gives a local human intensity to the shadow of one's own mood.'[7] On another occasion he writes of how, in 'all tramp life', he found 'plaintive and tragic elements' to be common, 'even on the surface'.[8]

Synge possessed an instinctive understanding, then, for what we would now call Chekhovian features in Irish rural life as it was at the turn of the century, when, for seven extraordinary years from 1902 to 1908, the playwright wrote a series of plays and occasional prose writings whose very provenance – let alone complexity of expression and rapidity of maturation – would have been unthinkable in his earlier years of apprenticeship to a more precious (almost Pateresque) and certainly more bookish form of literary expression. (One thinks of early essays like 'Vita Vecchia' and 'Étude Morbide', heavily indebted to late nineteenth-century French Symbolist and Decadent practice, as well as his early apprentice play *When the Moon Has Set*, a false start for Synge in its bourgeoise drawingroom setting and appropriate but colourless language, yet one which he quickly and instinctively corrected in turning to the life and idiom of the rural peasantry. That life and language, perhaps understandably restricted to the world of the servants in *When the Moon Has Set*, was to become the dominant focus and impulse for every one of his subsequent works for the Irish theatre.) First or last, Synge's imaginative writings in no way resemble Chekhov's dramas; had they done so, it is conceivable that his plays would not have antagonized critics and public alike in the Ireland of his time. Elegies for a passing way of life need not have offended Abbey audiences; indeed, the popularity of Chekhov's plays in Ireland for what is almost certainly this aspect (which is but one of a number of interwoven threads in those works) indicates quite otherwise.

*   *   *

The story of Synge's reputation in Ireland is one of the most painful and discreditable chapters in that country's cultural history. For many years, from the hostile reception accorded his first staged play, he was unjustly reviled and traduced by critics and distrusted by theatregoers, who boycotted his plays on the Dublin stage until long after the dramatist's death in 1909; and, even then, when his reputation was high in Britain, Europe and the United States, there was little change in his native land. As late as 1971, in a volume commemorating the centenary of Synge's birth, Alan Price was forced to confirm the judgement of the Irish critic Roger McHugh that 'the best literary criticism of our modern writers in English has been written mainly by writers outside Ireland', Price adding that, in Synge criticism, 'from the Irish there is almost nothing'.[9] This state of virtual disinterest (when it was not hostility) certainly persisted until 1971, 62 years after the dramatist's death, but it was soon to change; indeed, the centenary celebrations themselves promoted in his native land radical critical revaluations whose reverberations continue to be felt in scholarly and creative writings there. In *J. M. Synge: Centenary Papers 1971* Seán O'Tuama, Seán O'Súilleabháin, Alan J. Bliss and Seumas Deane undertake positive explorations of Synge's relationship with a national literature, his skilful use of Irish folklore and, most notably, creation of a carefully and knowledgeably crafted dialect of Anglo-Irish. Subsequently, Declan Kiberd's detailed and authoritative study, *Synge and the Irish Tradition* (1979), revealed even more conclusively how sensitive was the playwright's understanding of the Irish language, how painstaking his study of early Irish literature, and how dedicated his attempts to shape and mould written and spoken forms into a new form of dialect.

Kiberd's book has profoundly affected critical perceptions of Synge's language and the complex creative processes that underlie its creation. Since its publication Kiberd and Robert Welch have refined and reinforced its linguistic and cultural discoveries. Both critics recognize that, for Synge as for Lady Gregory, extraordinary value and significance were attached to the folk-imagination (and folk-memory), which, permeating the minds and daily speech of the country people in their local worlds, formed a harmonious (if necessarily limited) world-view which native-speakers received from the consonance of language with environment, tradition, customary usage – in short, a whole way of life. As in the case of the Nigerian novelist Chinua Achebe, a full half-century later, Synge sought to construct a new form of English, growing out of a vibrant community that possessed an intuitive sense of belonging to a larger world in which physical, spiritual and even supernatural forces freely interact and are realized in an idiom responsive to all such elements.

What Welch says of Lady Gregory, in a commemorative article 50 years after her death, is apposite for Synge too:

She saw herself, in her work on Raftery, Cuchulain and Finn, as attempting to open up the lines of communication between the Irish language and the literary movement. But she also wanted to bring back *to the people* their sense of themselves in a speech, which, while English, had about it some of the realising, emphatic, and natural qualities of Irish. She had a vision (. . . we should recall Yeats's Blakean use of this word, as having to do with seeing the essential rather than the commonplace) of a community restored, where people would live in a world which was not dead and *codified*, but alive and energetic; speaking a language which could, whenever necessary, call upon the network of collaboration that obtains between people when they are truly themselves, unfettered by isolation, sadness, apathy or committees.[10]

Synge had argued: 'All art is a collaboration'. Four years after his death, Lady Gregory paid a memorable tribute to him: 'He tells what he owes to that collaboration with the people. . . . The return to the people, the reunion after separation, the taking and giving again, is it not the perfect circle, the way of nature, the eternal wedding-ring?'[11]

After years of, in turn, hostility and indifference, a new appreciation of both the uniqueness of Synge's artistry and of its communally responsive dimension is to be found abroad in his native land. Creative writers with the stature of Brian Friel, Seumas Heaney and Thomas Kilroy now acknowledge his preeminence. Irish scholarship, no longer out of step with international literary values, now freely contributes a varied and balanced series of reassessments. To the pioneering work of W. B. Yeats and T. R. Henn have more recently been added the labours of, among others, Seumas Deane, D. E. S. Maxwell, Augustine Martin, Vivian Mercier, Nicholas Grene and Anthony Roche.

That, critically, the situation has still not been entirely transformed for the better is shown by the recent publication of Denis Donoghue's collection of essays, *We Irish: Essays on Irish Literature and Society*.[12] Here, in one of the less understandable latter-day attacks (masquerading as a review of Synge's *Collected Letters*), the critic maintains that mean-spirited heritage. I say less understandable because, originally written in 1983 and revealing a knowledge of Declan Kiberd's then but recently published writings, Donoghue can reprint as late as 1986 distortions of fact and misleading innuendoes that *Synge and the Irish Tradition* had effectively dispelled a decade earlier. Donoghue is, rightly, an influential critic and his unfair strictures on the playwright's character, social values and literary worth should not go without rebuttal; ominously, they re-echo the many nationalist prejudices that bedevilled Synge's relationship with critics and political commentators in his native land throughout his creative lifetime and for many years afterwards. Declaring that the 'natural man' in Synge was 'a wearisome, fretful, petulant bore', Donoghue asserts: 'Standard English wasn't gloomy enough to express his gloom, so he invented a style called Syngesong if you don't like it and poetry if you do'.[13]

No calumny is too slight to be imagined by Donoghue: 'He had the background of a gentleman and the instincts of an aesthete: spiritualism and theosophy were more in his line than the activities of the Land League'.[14] Though Madame Blavatsky's ideas were fashionably pervasive for a while in Irish intellectual circles – and Synge took a passing interest in such matters but no more than he had evinced some years earlier in the collecting of birds' eggs and sketching rural scenes – the playwright quickly saw such fads for the effete distractions that they were. His clear-eyed rejection of them went hand in glove with his equally no-nonsense views on the high-minded but escapist aesthetic values embodied in Yeats's early verse plays, for all Synge's appreciation of their occasional poetic felicities.

Above all, it is patently wrong for Donoghue to assert: 'The truth is that Synge was never interested in political issues'. On the contrary, acutely aware of them in the Ireland of his time – how could he not be? – he was also painfully concerned by crass political intrusions into virtually every human activity there, including nationalist hostility to his own dramatic representations of past and contemporary Irish life on the Abbey stage. He was determined, nonetheless, that his own dramatic writings should neither be subordinate to nor narrowly constricted by propaganda slogans and the superimposition of black and white values then dominant in Irish nationalist politics. Political concerns in a larger human and non-doctrinaire sense, however, inform the very bedrock that under-lies the society he delineates in his drama. The debilitating effects of immigration, for instance, are everywhere apparent in the local community of *The Playboy of the Western World* that, denuded of all 'likely' or dynamic young people, tries pathetically to invent a hero worthy of reputed past glories even in what at first sight appears to be the most unlikely human material; meanwhile, the cutthroat khaki soldiery, fresh from fighting colonial wars in Kruger's South Africa, are a perceptible and threatening presence in the play's background.

Even more obtrusive, though similarly off-stage, is the manipula-tive power of the clergy in the figure of Father Reilly. Constantly invoked as the arbiter for all social and moral values, the priest's morality may not, strictly speaking, accord with what the country folk ascribe to him. As with Father Farrell in *Juno and the Paycock* – another priest, often quoted but never seen on stage – we only indirectly know of his views and possible influence in the neighbour-hood; often, what is quoted suits or favours those who invoke his name. In each case, as the thrust of the argument is towards preserving the status quo and stifling any hints of innovation or reform without prior clerical approval, we can assume that the invocations probably fairly represent both local clerical opinion and its pervasive secular acceptance. Yet there is surely an implicit suggestion in *The Playboy of the Western World*, as in Synge's other stage works, that resentment of such authoritarian rule by church and state runs as a strong undercurrent beneath the surface of the action.

We do not need evidence beyond the plays themselves to deduce such conclusions, but abundant corroboration can be found in the essays gathered together in the second volume of the playwright's *Collected Works*. Confronting the problem of emigration – 'prob-ably the most complicated of all Irish affairs' – Synge argues that 'it is important to remember that the whole moral and economic condition of Ireland has been brought into a diseased state by prolonged misgovernment and many misfortunes, so that at the present time [that is, 1905] normal remedies produce abnormal results'. Economic changes are not seen in themselves as being wholly efficacious: 'one feels that the only real remedy for emigration is the restoration of some national life to the people'.[15] Accordingly, this conviction 'makes most Irish politicians scorn all merely economic or agricultural reforms', for 'if Home Rule would not of itself make a national life it would do more to make such a life possible than half a million creameries'.[16]

Moreover, while instinctively relegating such social (and inher-ently political) concerns to the background of the dramatic action, Synge does not marginalize them. The people of his plays have a naturally free and easy attitude towards strangers (and even out-casts like the Widow Quin among themselves) that goes with a vivacious love for colourful speech and for anything out of the ordinary. The villagers give the appearance of having been cowed and conditioned to obey the authorities, however, and their inher-ently imaginative and tolerant instincts have clearly been inhibited by the powers of Church and State. Naturally, there are rebellions from time to time, however trivial and short-lived in actuality these may be, and the hero-worship spontaneously accorded Christy (with somewhat grudging admiration for the Widow Quin) is for individuals who have stood up for themselves in a society which outlaws the free spirit of independent thought and action. An alien law is invoked submissively whenever a crisis occurs, however, and it is only too appropriate that, asked by Christy's father at the end of the play why the villagers have captured and manhandled the playboy, Pegeen's father should implicate the name of God ('apologetically', it is said in a stage direction) as well as the British judicial system: 'It is the will of God that all should guard their little cabins from the treachery of law and what would my daughter be doing if I was ruined or was hanged itself?' The *treachery of the law* is a sufficiently startling as well as ambiguous a collocation to draw attention to itself; presumably, there is fear of reprisals by the authorities. The conjunction of God and the secular law echoes Joyce's bitter lines 'O Ireland my first and only love/Where Christ and Caesar are hand and glove'.[17] To find liberty, the individual must move on – a pattern found in all Synge's dramatic work and, significantly, echoed in a number of O'Casey's dramas from *Juno and the Paycock* onwards, where the political commitment (*pace* Donoghue) is often more overt. Synge's political awareness, though implicit rather than explicit, is nevertheless everywhere apparent; and the social orientation – each play being set in an economically deprived rural Ireland with the poor and politically powerless people the centre of human concern and the focus of the tragicomedy – fully and unequivocally reveals his innermost sympathies, that in some cases (as with the Tramp and Nora in *The Shadow of the Glen*) is nearer a spirit of kinship.

'Synge wanted to see local conditions improved', writes Donoghue, 'provided the peasants stayed as aesthetically winsome as they were.' This is a most unfair observation. The playwright saw clearly that the issue was more complex and more intractable than his critic is prepared to admit and he honestly believed (and the history of an independent Ireland has certainly not contradicted him) that these problems were more difficult to remedy there than elsewhere. Surely Synge's view has been borne out, again and again, in recent years and not in an Irish context alone? Whether true or not, his words have a resonance far beyond his native land or time in history; here, for instance, he is speaking of returning to a relatively barren part of Connemara on a fact-finding tour in 1905:

One's first feeling as one comes back among these people and takes a place, so to speak, in this noisy procession of fishermen, farmers, and women, where nearly everyone is interesting and attractive, is a dread of any reform that would tend to lessen their individuality rather than any very real hope of improving their well-being. One feels then ... that it is part of the misfortune of Ireland that nearly all the characteristics which give colour and attractiveness to Irish life are bound up with a social condition that is near to penury, while in countries like Brittany the best external features of the local life – the rich embroidered dresses, for instance, or the carved furniture – are connected with a decent and comfortable social condition.[18]

The dramatist does not say there should be no changes: on the contrary, he advocates a number of concrete reforms in the course of a series of articles, one of which embodies the above observation. These reforms are presented in a reasonable and temperate manner, befitting Synge's aims: writing for English readers, he embedded in his argument practical suggestions for improvement that he thought could and should be immediately implemented in what he argues was then 'the most poverty-stricken district in Ireland'. The last thing on Synge's mind is making political points or nationalist propaganda for its own sake. He wants a sympathetic response from readers in an influential and liberal-minded English newspaper with the objective of speedily promoting further improvements to a public works programme already (but imperfectly) in operation. Assuredly one of the least tendentious of playwrights, he was *not* apolitical in his occasional non-fictional writings; throughout his life, however, Synge preferred persuasive advocacy to rhetoric. His essays on the Irish Congested Districts reveal him to have been pragmatically concerned with a dilemma that, sadly, one cannot say has been resolved by more recent economic growth in an Ireland within the European Economic Community.

Synge felt something akin to an affinity with the world outside settled human society. His innate sympathies and off-beat interests, finely delineated in the occasional collection of Wicklow prose sketches (among which are to be found the article on 'A Landlord's Garden in County Wicklow'), are exemplified in a number of their titles: most notably, perhaps, in 'The Vagrants of Wicklow', 'The Oppression of the Hills' (and 'An Autumn Night in the Hills'), 'On the Road', 'The People of the Glens' and 'At a Wicklow Fair: The Place and the People'. Here, as in plays like *The Shadow of the Glen* and *The Tinker's Wedding*, we can see that he not only created figures such as tramps and tinkers to juxtapose a more imaginative and less inhibited way of life to the existing social order in Ireland – D. H. Lawrence was to do something similar with gypsy and

gamekeeper figures, before he came across the Italian peasants and
New Mexican Indians he celebrates in later writings – but, in
variously suggestive ways, came to see himself as a kind of itinerant
artist figure, in permanent exile from 'respectable' society, even
before nationalist fanatics among the primarily bourgeoise Abbey
Theatre audiences actively sought to ostracize him and his plays
from 'decent-minded' Irish society.

Quite apart from placing apparent misfits and social outcasts at
the centre of the action and, in many cases, as protagonists in his
major dramatic works (a political choice in itself, surely?), Synge
also salutes and, occasionally, clearly romanticizes their admirable
imaginative freedom, linguistic ingenuity and uninhibited comic
freemasonry; at the same time, the overriding emphasis is elegiac, in
celebrating the last imaginative gasp of a fatally endangered species
of free-living, ever-travelling and socially unencumbered people.
Mostly, the works see life from the outsiders' point of view, and this
aspect is as pronounced in Synge's own particular version of an
ancient Irish legend such as *Deirdre of the Sorrows*, in his last play
bearing that name for its title, as it is in his original adaptation of an
anecdotal folktale like that which inspired *The Shadow of the Glen*, in
his first staged one. The former's protagonist is an outsider, from
first to last; early exiled from fashionable society, Deirdre eventually
chooses death rather than what is, to her, captivity within a socially
conditioned role, that is, as passive queen to a cold and calculating
High King of a patriarchal Ireland that she has always refused to
honour or to obey. In *The Shadow of the Glen* Synge adds two
elements to Pat Dirane's folktale, told to him on Inishmaan (and
recounted in *The Aran Islands*): an exalted celebration of nature,
embodied in the Tramp and Nora, contrasted with satire at the
expense of the more materialistic values embodied in characters
such as Dan and Michael. It is a duality to be found at the heart of
all his dramas.

*   *   *

'Who else but John Millington Synge?' declared Samuel Beckett,
when asked in 1972 from which playwrights he had learned.
Quoting this retort in his book *A Colder Eye: The Modern Irish
Writers*, Hugh Kenner goes on to say: 'undistracted by the questions
that absorbed Synge's first viewers and colleagues – idiom, verisimil-
itude – he [Beckett] learned to be Synge's successor, the only one'.[19]

Kenner may well be right here, in nominating Beckett as Synge's one and only true heir, though a number of fine contemporary playwrights writing in the new literatures in English (including African authors like Wole Soyinka and J. P. Clark as well as Caribbean dramatists like Derek Walcott) have acknowledged an indebtedness to Synge's work that is clearly manifested in some of their more exciting theatrical experiments.[20] Other earlier examples have perhaps been too often taken for granted. The most recent biography of Federico García Lorca, for instance, reminds us that that poetic genius, whose plays possess distinct affinities with those of Synge, freely acknowledged to his friends his 'great enthusiasm for the Irishman's achievement'.[21] In particular, Ian Gibson argues for the inspiration of *Riders to the Sea* upon *Blood Wedding* and, specifically, similarities in speech by the mother-figures in each work. Sidney Poger's essay in the present Casebook presents a quite different form of influence, where the same play becomes the vehicle for a radical adaptation by Bertolt Brecht in one of his more didactic experiments, *Senora Carrar's Rifles*. If the result is a committed drama completely at variance with the timeless objectivity of *Riders to the Sea*, Brecht's taut one-act play still attests to the imaginative power of the older model upon a poetic Marxist sensibility.

Of course, persuasive claims have been made for other significant predecessors for Beckett's stage works. A number of influential critics – among them, Katharine Worth – have claimed W. B. Yeats as the major influence upon Beckett's dramaturgy. Beckett has spoken highly of Yeats's work, particularly his early Noh drama, *At the Hawk's Well*. *The Cat and the Moon* is another remarkable forerunner – in its grotesque crippled mimicry and its dramatic poetry arising out of farcical stage business – of Beckett's unique theatre of desolate reality. Yet, in such works, Yeats seems to be primarily in Synge's debt (especially the Synge of *The Well of the Saints*) and I am inclined to agree with D. E. S. Maxwell's judgement that, for 'all the modish invocation of Beckett as Yeats's heir, his plays occupy a different continuum'.[22] Important though *The Cat and the Moon* and *Purgatory* may be as major Synge-influenced works in Yeats's dramatic corpus, Beckett undoubtedly remains Synge's major successor, and, where a Yeatsian strain may be discerned, it is invariably that portion of Yeats's dramatic work most indebted to Synge's practice. Synge's tramp figures, simplified stage settings and stylized use of racy idiomatic speech have indeed had a lasting influence on that Irish playwright who followed

Synge's Parisian sojourn even more whole-heartedly some 30 years afterwards.

Once Beckett's dedicated theatrical practice and eventual hard-won international reputation were assured, it became impossible for his countrymen to ignore or decry Synge's drama as it had once been fashionable to do in his native land. Indeed, it may well be true that Beckett's practical example – his stage success as well as critical acclaim, that is – has almost single-handedly reversed the hostile strain towards Synge that had characterized Irish criticism of his writings for more than 60 years. In recent years, Irish critics such as Vivian Mercier, Toni O'Brien Johnson, Nicholas Grene and D. E. S. Maxwell (as well as Katharine Worth and James Knowlson among English admirers of Beckett's dramaturgy) have made illuminating revaluations of Synge in terms of Beckettian precepts. Naturally, *The Well of the Saints* – as perhaps Synge's most full-heartedly Beckettian play – has tended to be the focus for much of this revaluation. 'In *The Well of the Saints* he showed how two actors, old and battered and blind, could hold an audience by scarcely moving from where they sit', Kenner says, reminding us, furthermore: 'That was a special gratification for Yeats, who had been so exasperated by actors' restlessness he longed, he said, to imprison them in barrels.'[23]

The reminder is timely, showing implicitly another source for the Irish critical *volte face* about Synge's work: the new contemporary respect for W. B. Yeats's later *avant-garde* plays, whose direct simplicity and brutal poetic force are discernibly indebted to Synge's practice, as the remarkable growth in concrete particularity and muscular power in his verse is indebted to the small posthumously published book of Synge's poems and, especially, to the playwright's preface to that volume, where he said, prophetically, that before verse could in future be human once again, 'it must learn to be brutal'. That astonishingly prescient statement, written more than five years before the First World War began, must have had a considerable shock effect upon the older poet, who, called upon to edit Synge's verse for publication immediately following his death, first read its brief but revolutionary preface in typescript. It was not long before a profound change (not entirely surprising in the light of Yeats's earlier work, perhaps, but remarkable in its thoroughgoing execution all the same) occurred in Yeats's poetry, whose more thoroughgoing modernist starkness soon outgrew anything Synge had attempted in his verse. Still, returning to the recent critical revaluation of Synge in Ireland, we can see that Beckettian parallels and affinities are clearly of more importance than Yeatsian equivalents and, as Kenner shows conclusively in the last chapter of *A Colder Eye* that is devoted to Beckett, these parallels extend far beyond comparisons between *The Well of the Saints* and *Waiting for Godot*.[24]

*   *   *

At the time of Synge's relatively early death, friends and colleagues spoke of a projected new direction in his drama cut tragically short. In the light of conversations with him in his last months it seems that, even before he had completed *Deirdre of the Sorrows* (and death prevented its projected extensive overhaul), he was contemplating writing a play set in the Dublin slums. Fourteen years later, at the time of the Irish Civil War, Sean O'Casey's first slum tragicomedy, *The Shadow of a Gunman*, burst upon the Dublin theatrical scene and memories of Synge's final plans were re-invoked. O'Casey was then seen – misleadingly, I think – as a latterday urban Synge. Before we can credibly postulate an O'Casey-like dimension for Synge after *Deirdre of the Sorrows*, we should perhaps ask ourselves a few questions. Could Synge have found an authentic tenement idiom comparable to that created by O'Casey? Could he, in writing of an urban proletariat at an especially dynamic period (turning-point even) in recent Irish history, avoid being drawn into the contemporary political situation that became so heated from 1911 onwards? The Dublin slums were then to witness industrial and nationalist unrest – sometimes on a hideously bloody scale – for almost two decades, encompassing the 1916 Easter Rising, the Anglo-Irish War and subsequent Civil War, as well as the contentious Railway Strike of 1911 and the bitterly fought Dublin Lockout of 1913–14. For a writer commonly supposed to have little or no overt realization of political action (or even discussion) in his dramatic art, the ever-present reality of these bloody confrontations could have been a real dilemma. The aesthetic as well as social implications of any such change in theatrical orientation, if ultimately unrewarding as empty speculation in the context of Synge's actual achievement, are yet temptingly if perversely suggestive, for there's little doubt that had he pursued his

declared objectives he would, inevitably, have been involved in
events and tensions that were of immediate – and, ultimately,
momentous – political significance. In such a context, neutrality, if
theoretically not impossible, is virtually unthinkable in an Irish
context. Synge, even before 1909, was in no way neutral in any case
– and, in the light of the deterioration in Anglo-Irish relations after
1913, his anti-British proclivities were likely to have been exacer-
bated. (Many examples could be given but one of the more
illuminating is a rhetorical comparison he makes in one of his early
Aran Island notebooks, while contemplating changes then gathering
momentum in his native land: 'With this limestone Inishmaan
however I am in love. . . . How much of Ireland was formerly like
this and how much of Ireland is today Anglicized and civilized and
brutalized'.[25]) The consequences for his art, which holds a precarious but perceptible balance between various warring and increasingly incompatible social values and ways of life, could have
been incalculable. Further speculation about what might have been
is fruitless, but the context compels one to acknowledge afresh the
superb poise and balance – worthy of Chekhov himself – that is
discernible in Synge's art as we have it.

   Synge's work is remarkably unified. One of the most insistent
impressions that one receives of Synge as man and as artist, the
more one lives with his writings, is of their completeness, the
integrity everywhere apparent. His work is all of a piece; it is a
seamless whole. This is so, even in the apparent new direction for his
work that he is supposed to have spoken about towards the end of
his life. Urban slum drama, as in Gorki's *Lower Depths*, seems at first
an unlikely subject for Synge. Yet he was a man who knew Dublin
very well and its tenements, whether on O'Casey's north wall or
Synge's south side, were full of characterful individuals, many of
them with rural backgrounds and personalities little different from
the characters who people Synge's earlier dramas. Whether or not
he could capture the distinctive idiom so memorably distilled in
Joyce and O'Casey (and one cannot see why not), it is apparent
from an early and fragmentary autobiographical essay of his that he
had long nurtured a special feeling for the slums round St Patrick's
Cathedral. As a youth, even as a child, he had closely observed, with
fascination and some horror, the life and rough sport of the people in
that area known as the Liberties:

I studied the arabs of the streets. ... I remember coming out of St. Patrick's, Sunday after Sunday, strained almost to torture by the music, and walking out through the slums of Harold's Cross as the lamps were being lit. Hordes of wild children used to play round the cathedral of St. Patrick and I remember there was something appalling – a proximity of emotions as conflicting as the perversions of the Black Mass – in coming out suddenly from the white harmonies of the Passion according to St. Matthew among this blasphemy of childhood. ... I often stood for hours in a shadow to watch their manoeuvres and extraordinarily passionate quarrels.[26]

Such savagery and passionate wildness of character equate the slum dwellers with the *dramatis personae* of Synge's rural dramas. The new direction in his work, had it indeed taken place after *Deirdre of the Sorrows*, is most likely to have been of a piece with the existing peasant plays, as is *Deirdre of the Sorrows* itself, which, for all its distinctiveness in dramatizing legendary material well known to an Irish audience, realizes a tough-minded and down-to-earth peasant sensibility that similarly distinguishes each one of his pastoral writings.

NOTES

1. 'A Landlord's Garden in County Wicklow' was first published in the *Manchester Guardian* for 1 July 1907, the year in which *The Playboy of the Western World* was premièred on the Dublin stage, but in mood, psychic atmosphere and setting, it exhibits close affinities with *The Shadow of the Glen*, completed and staged in 1903. The essay, posthumously collected in the fourth volume of *The Works of J. M. Synge* (Dublin, 1910), was reprinted in the definitive edition of his *Collected Works, Volume II: Prose*, ed. Alan Price (London: Oxford, 1966), pp. 230–3.

2. *CW II, Prose*, pp. 230–1.

3. Ibid., p. 49.

4. Ibid., p. 236.

5. Ibid., p. 200.

6. Herbert Gorman, *James Joyce* (London: Bodley Head, 1941), p. 101.

7. *CW II, Prose*, p. 204.

8. Ibid., p. 204.

9. In S. B. Bushrui, ed., *Sunshine and the Moon's Delight: A Centenary Tribute to John Millington Synge 1871–1909* (Gerrards Cross & Beirut: Colin Smythe, 1972), p. 294.

10. Robert Welch, 'A Language for Healing', in *Lady Gregory, Fifty Years After*, ed. A. Saddlemyer & C. Smythe (Gerrards Cross: Smythe, 1987), p. 273.

11. Lady Gregory, *Our Irish Theatre* (Gerrards Cross: Smythe, 1972), pp. 142–3. The book was originally published in 1913.

12. 'Synge in His Letters', *London Review of Books*, 1 December 1983; reprinted in *We Irish: Essays on Irish Literature and Society* (New York: Knopf, 1986; Brighton: Harvester, 1987).

13. Ibid., p. 211.

14. Ibid., p. 210.

15. *CW II, Prose*, p. 341.

16. Ibid., p. 343.

17. 'Gas from a Burner' (1912), reprinted in *The Critical Writings of James Joyce* (London: Faber, 1959).

18. *CW II, Prose*, p. 286.

19. Hugh Kenner, *A Colder Eye: The Modern Irish Writers* (London: Penguin, 1984), p. 332. Kenner is here quoting a statement made by James Knowlson, based on conversations with Samuel Beckett.

20. Robert Hogan has written well on Synge's initial impact (more affinities than influences, really) in 'The Influence of Synge in Modern Irish Drama', *Sunshine and the Moon's Delight*, pp. 231–44. While recognizing that Synge is 'as inescapable a presence' in that drama as Shaw is to the modern English drama or O'Neill to the American, Hogan sees that presence to have receded quickly after his death.

21. Ian Gibson, *Federico García Lorca: A Life* (New York: Pantheon Books, 1989), p. 340. The testimony comes from conversations with Don Miguel Cerón Rubio.

22. D. E. S. Maxwell, *A Critical History of Modern Irish Drama 1891–1980* (London & New York: Cambridge, 1985), p. 45.

23. Kenner, p. 332.

24. The passage from Kenner's book reprinted in the present Casebook is taken from an earlier chapter in *A Colder Eye*.

25. *CW II, Prose*, p. 103.

26. Ibid., pp. 5–6. This uncompleted essay, entitled 'Autobiography' by the editor and published long after Synge's death, was written before any of his plays had been conceived.

PART ONE

Synge's Dramatic Art

D. E. S. Maxwell 'Rhetoric and Reality in Synge' (1985)

It might seem a straightforward assignment to bring Synge and Beckett within the terms of the title of this book [*Across a Roaring Hill: The Protestant Imagination in Modern Ireland*]. They are Protestant, Irish and modern. As Protestantism began in protest it might be expected to generate, as it does, protest within itself. One consequence is its proliferation of sects, each laying claim to The Truth. Another is the denial of belief, though this is not peculiar to Protestantism. In any case, it is to that denial that we must consign Synge and Beckett.

Beckett's family, like Synge's, was well-to-do Dublin Protestant. His mother, also like Synge's, was evangelically pious. While Synge returned to Ireland from his sojourn in Europe and Beckett made France his home, both men were equally exiles from the faith of their upbringing. All Synge's doings were, for his background, eccentric: studying Irish, playing the fiddle, playing the itinerant in Europe, rather aimlessly pursuing an artistic vocation in Paris. He moved in a bohemian aura. His love for the Abbey actress Maire O'Neil, ill-matched and frustrating, defied respectability. ...

Synge's commitment to an Irish artistic venture is unmistakable. He was scornful of the pieties enforced by the Victorianized, puritanical Churches, which could be relied upon to attack his plays. Yeats called them 'curious ironical' works, 'bitter condiments': Synge had his own version of a national attachment. Its imaginative energies, however, were to be native. He was, he wrote, 'prepared to stake everything on a Creative movement. ... Yeats speaks of making our theatre a copy of continental [theatres]. That is exactly what for the next ten years at least we should avoid. ... Our supply of native plays is very small and we must keep our company very small so that this little store of native work will keep it occupied.'[1]

Synge had small regard for his continental contemporaries. 'Analysts with their problems,' he wrote in the preface to *The Tinker's Wedding*, 'are soon as old-fashioned as the pharmacopoeia of Galen – look at Ibsen and the Germans.' Maeterlinck, like Mallarmé in a different camp from Ibsen and Zola, was equally reprehensible. His 'poet's dream which makes itself a sort of world, where it is kept as a dream', was as detached from 'the profound and common interests of life' as Ibsen and Zola were too much of them.[2] 'For the present,' the preface to *The Playboy of the Western World* concludes, 'the only possible beauty in drama is peasant drama.' Its vitality resided in an 'English that is perfectly Irish in essence, yet has pureness and surety of form'. Synge's plays have precedents in the classical comedy of Jonson and Molière, about which he was knowledgeable; essentially, his inspiration was an indigenous one. The places in which his people will events and feelings to their ends are Wicklow, west Kerry and the Aran Islands. Formally, as Alan Bliss has demonstrated, he forged a new poetic medium from its 'makings ... in the Anglo-Irish dialect'.[3]

The impetus was Synge's first visit to the Aran Islands in 1898. In the island talk he found what Yeats called 'more than speech, for it implied an attitude towards letters, sometimes even towards life'.[4] Ignoring or rejecting the upheavals in European culture, Synge's creative urge responded to the Aran scene, desolate and magnificent, and to a tragic joy in the islanders' endurance of a hard life. 'Isn't it a sad story to tell?' one of them wrote to him about a death in the family. 'But at the same time we have to be satisfied because a person cannot live always.' In the preface to his *Poems and Translations* Synge commended poets who 'used the whole of their personal lives as their material'. The Aran experience precipitated his own private despairs, a certain morbidity and reticence, into the impersonal, healing lament of his art. The organized Churches, which he abominated, are replaced by an almost pantheistic nature, earthy, innocent, demonic, translated into a dance of words.

Synge's theatre is certainly not Ibsen's. Yet it resembles Ibsen's to the extent that it too invades a basically realist form to enlarge its literalism. Like *The Importance of Being Earnest* – also by a kind of Protestant – *The Playboy of the Western World* depends on artifice, and in a comparable way. Both offer glances at a reality which they exclude. Synge refers to bad harvests, crippled grotesques, and a disbanded, licentious soldiery; Wilde to movements of political reform and 'acts of violence in Grosvenor Square'. None of this matters. The plays subdue it to their own events, where words have at least temporary control. Cecily courts Ernest/Algernon in her diary and it – more or less – comes to be. Jack kills off his imaginary brother and Algernon his imaginary invalid. In Wilde's version of the cross-purposes of drawing-room comedy, fiction becomes reality, though not quite as the fiction would have it. He is working in a distinctively Irish mode of matching the reality of words against literal fact. So in *The Playboy* Christy murders his father only in rhetoric, not fact, and his tale makes him a hero. When old Mahon turns up, facts make Christy again 'a Munster liar and the fool of men', until in the final reversal he masters his Da, once again by words: 'Go on, I'm saying. ... Not a word out of you.'

For Christy it is a comic victory, for Pegeen a sort of tragic defeat: '[*breaking out into wild lamentations*] Oh my grief, I've lost him surely. I've lost the only playboy of the western world'. For Pegeen, Christy has been an exotic alternative to the miserable Shawn Keogh and a marriage blessed by 'Father Reilly's dispensation from the bishops of the Court of Rome'. Christy is the antithesis not only of Shawn's timidity but of his father's grossness: snoring by a dunghill and 'shying clods against the visage of the stars', a denial of Christy's panegyric to Pegeen – 'the lovelight of the star of knowledge shining from her brow'. The onus is on language. It must be, as it is, both grandiloquent and plain speech – Pegeen counting bottles and 'in the heavens above'. We are constantly aware of gaps between the statement of words and what we see: we see a commonplace pub, hear its talk, hear transparent lies, fictions that come briefly true, are exposed, find a new truth. The drama relies on this set of agreements and differences between language and the reality around which it plays.

Christy's imaginative fiction is on the verge of bewitching the community and its local understandings: 'any girl would walk her heart out before she'd meet a young man was your like for eloquence or talk at all'. Michael James is won over totally. The beautiful love scene between Christy and Pegeen in Act III, all their former talk of 'lonesomeness' vanished, inspires him to a final prayer superbly out of place: 'A daring fellow is the jewel of the world, and a man did split his father's middle with a single clout should have the bravery of ten, so may God and Mary and St. Patrick bless you, and increase you from this mortal day'.

For the villagers, in the end, eloquence alone is not enough. 'There's a great gap', Pegeen says bitterly, 'between a gallous story and a dirty deed.' The pragmatic community rounds on Christy and displaces his poetry with its former ways – 'We'll have peace now for our drinks'. Society has no room for the artist, Christy the forger of

other worlds. He goes off not only without the lady but with the
deranged, ugly Da. Romantic comedy could not arrive at stranger
ends, nor more forcefully expose the dangerous therapies of art,
liberating and deceitful.

The Playboy's rhetoric disputes the knowledge that romantic love
is mutable, even – in a society of bartered brides – a freak, as the
artist is inescapably an alien and a fugitive. The plays revolve
around small communities of various sorts: in *The Tinker's Wedding*
a district clustered round a church, a tinkers' camp; in *The Well of
the Saints* a similar district and two blind beggars precariously on its
fringes. All are a stage for the tensions between private freedom and
agreed conventions, anarchic imagination and prudence, dream and
its compromises with actuality. The themes are consistent, their
synthesis varied.

In *The Well of the Saints* Martin and Mary Doul, successively
blind, sighted and blind again, at the climax refuse the Saint's offer
to restore sight once more. With his sight Martin has found in the
world only their own likenesses, ugly and comfortless. As their sight
dims, they come to a reconciliation, with life and between themselves, imagining 'a beautiful white-haired woman', an old man to
be dignified by 'a beautiful, long, white, silken, streamy beard'. The
world is enchanted in their now conscious limitation of it:

Isn't it finer sights ourselves had a while since and we sitting dark smelling
the sweet beautiful smells do be rising in the warm nights and hearing the
swift flying things racing in the air till we'd be looking up in our own minds
into a grand sky, and seeing lakes, and broadening rivers, and hills are
waiting for the spade and plough.

Holding to this magic, Martin strikes the holy water from the Saint's
hand. Saint and people expel them to the roads: to 'a soft wind
turning round the little leaves of the spring and feeling the sun'; and
as well to 'a slough of wet on the one side ... and a stony path with a
north wind blowing behind'. The immanence of God, to which the
Saint directs their thoughts, is far off. Martin's rejection affirms
commitment to life reduced and solaced by the blindness which can
work its imaginative miracle 'in the mind'.

When Martin's 'queer, bad talk' upsets the community it denies
him any place. When he will not resume his subservience, the early
mockery turns to violence. His fate must be to be punished: 'I'm
thinking the two of them will be drowned together in a short while,

surely'. Threatened, the community again expels the transforming intruder. *The Well of the Saints* is a fable of the shaping human spirit. Martin and Mary are creatures of the senses, making whatever more they can of sensuous perception. The play's multiplying images, of sight, sound, touch, smell, represent the reality on which imagination must work. The Saint's call to abstract, supernatural truths is the ultimate defeatist illusion. Heaven and hell are within the sensuous world, the bare, and barely endurable, recognition of 'feeling the sun' and 'a stony path'. Martin's resolution is not an escape from actuality. It is an acceptance of its dualities, fair and foul, and of the wholeness to which they may be brought.

I was the like of the little children do be listening to the stories of an old woman, and do be dreaming after in the dark night it's in grand houses of gold they are, with speckled horses to ride, and do be waking again, in a short while, and they destroyed with the cold, and the thatch dripping may be ...

The imaginative effort is to hold in poise the gold houses and the dripping thatch.

The world of Synge's plays is not a prelapsarian Eden. Rage, lust, envy, greed are just as much substance for poetic creation as innocence or exuberant joy. Holding actuality firmly in its regard, the language of the plays, and the actions, oppositions and harmonies which it develops, express an edifying meaning in experiences that might in themselves be merely disheartening. The real has a certain malleability, and the hero or heroine may take up circumstances into their view of them. So it is in *Deirdre of the Sorrows*. In Synge's last play he turned to the 'saga people', of whom he said, they 'seem very remote; one does not know what they thought or what they ate or where they went to sleep, so one is apt to fall into rhetoric'.

Deirdre is a play of autumn leading to winter intercepted, a threnody which makes celebration of life part of its lament. Time is its motif – a present time of love, as we see it in the play, intensely but briefly satisfied, with shocking rapidity a thing of the past, a memory which posterity inherits in the telling of it. Deirdre's and Naisi's is an erotic love. Synge made for it a tough rhetoric that blends carnal, natural and ecstatic. 'Flame and bright crown' find body in tangible woods and rivers, mud, the tracks and pathways of the glens, 'a gamey king' and Deirdre seven years 'spancelled' with

Naisi. Heroic myth acquires words which familiarize, while honouring, legendary grandeur.

Although never finally revised, *Deirdre* imposes a unity on the
events it records: the ageing Conchubor's love for Deirdre; her
escape to Scotland with Naisi and his brothers, Usna's sons; the
seven years of Naisi's and Deirdre's love; their return to Ireland on
Conchubor's promise of immunity and privilege; Conchubor's
treachery, the killing of Usna's sons, Deirdre's suicide: all but
Deirdre's fate foretold before her birth.

Synge firmly incorporates the prophecy but does not develop it as
in the legend, where magic and portents assist it to its fulfilment.
Here, the humans determine the outcome of love. Deirdre appeals to
the force of destiny: there's 'little power in what I'd do to change the
story of Conchubor and Naisi and the things old men foretold'. But
she is composing her own version of its concluding harmony, a
willed alliance with destiny, not mute submission.

Deirdre has a bleak sight of young love's mortality. In the play we
see only the last day, winter beginning, of her seven years with Naisi.
During it, all the events corroborate her instinct: Naisi's misgivings
that 'a day'd come I'd weary of her voice ... and Deirdre'd see I'd
wearied'; the hearty alternative offered by Conchubor's messenger,
Fergus, of stately fame; the grotesque Owen's brutish truths of
passion languishing and youth humiliated in age — 'are you well
pleased that length with the same man snorting next you at the
dawn of day?' Deirdre makes a pact with a death that will idealize
love before the attrition of time breaks its completeness. But she may
herself betray that pact. She pleads with Conchubor and almost
succeeds. Her last words to Naisi are bickering. The action questions and postpones the inevitable catastrophe. In the end, Deirdre's
suicide affirms her fidelity in a death that looks beyond the end of
life. She acts out of a sense of epic occasion:

... because of me there will be weasels and wild cats crying on a lonely wall
where there were queens and armies, and red gold, the way there will be a
story told of a ruined city and a raving king and a woman will be young
forever. ... It's a pitiful thing, Conchubor, you have done this night in
Emain, yet a thing will be a joy and triumph to the ends of life and time.

Unlike Shakespearean tragedy, *Deirdre* ends in wars and chaos just
begun. As in [Sean O'Casey's] *The Plough and the Stars*, lovers die
in a shattering world. But they defy time by consciously making

events over into legend – 'a story', as Deirdre foretells, 'will be told forever'. Again, facts become art.

It is simple to decode the stories of the plays into the events of Synge's life. The alienation of Christy and Martin; the doomed loves of Pegeen and Deirdre; the mood of transcience; the countervailing powers of imagination: all these have their analogies in Synge's experiences as man and artist. Synge raged, he tells us, against 'people who go on as if art and literature and writing were the first things in the world. There is nothing so great and sacred as what is most simple in life.'[5] His art is a defence of that sacredness in his own melancholy history. 'On the stage,' he says, 'one must have reality, and one must have joy.'[6] The language of his plays holds physical reality in its view. Nature is hazardously benign or destructive. Human nature, as the plays regard it, does not call for an honouring of peasant innocence. Impure appetites work their ways. These realities, swarming in the plays, have no final authority. Imagination and the words it beckons forth may hold sway, diverting and subduing fact. Synge's words are heroic. ...

SOURCE: extract from 'J. M. Synge and Samuel Beckett', in G. Dawe & E. Longley (eds), *Across a Roaring Hill: The Protestant Imagination in Modern Ireland* (Belfast, 1985), 25–32.

NOTES

1. Quoted in Ann Saddlemyer (ed.), *Theatre Business* (Gerrards Cross, 1982), pp. 164–80.
2. Notebook, 18 March 1907.
3. Alan J. Bliss, 'The Language of Synge', in Maurice Harmon (ed.), *J. M. Synge: Centenary Papers* (Dublin, 1972), p. 54.
4. *Uncollected Prose II* (London and Basingstoke, 1975), p. 494.
5. Quoted in David H. Greene and Edward M. Stephens, *J. M. Synge* (New York, 1959), p. 296.
6. Preface to *The Playboy of the Western World*.

Seamus Deane Synge and Heroism (1985)

Synge's career seems at first to have been dominated by a series of actual escapes and symbolic reorderings. He moved from unionism to nationalism, from respectability to the theatre, from English to Irish, from decadence (in literature) to an originary primitivism, from class to folk community, from the bourgeoisie to the peasantry, from his own ill-health to the glamorization of physical well-being and of youth. The list of transpositions could be extended but the general direction remains the same. A joyless repressive regime, linguistically anaemic, gives way to a joyful, liberating order, linguistically rich, even luxurious. The claustrophobic fears discernible in a work like *Étude Morbide* are alleviated time and again by the thought of open spaces, open and candid speech, and, above all, by the openness of a small-scale civilization like that of the West of Ireland to the European past. When Pat Dirane finished a story, Synge, who was well versed in the contemporary researches into the oral traditions of Europe, wrote: 'It gave me a strange feeling of wonder to hear this illiterate native of a wet rock in the Atlantic telling a story that is so full of European associations'.[1]

Even so, Synge never loses sight of the constrictions of peasant life. All his work recognizes the link between constriction and intensity and shows a desire to escape from the intensities of the personal life, which can become merely neurotic or worse, into the 'naturalness' of the folk life, which can retain intensity and remain communal. The psychological finesse of his autobiographical writings and of the literature of decadence (Baudelaire, Huysmans, even Zola) is, in his own view, symptomatic of an illness, a closure within the self characteristic of the late-bourgeois era. Ireland's nationalism offered an escape into health, sanity and community, but for Synge nationalism was a moment of resistance to the inevitable transformation of traditional life, not a programme of redemption for it. In this his nationalism deviates in a radical manner from that of Pearse who sought, in a new educational system and in a new ideology of cumulative rebellion, the instruments for the re-establishment of a lost cause.

In Synge, the cause is always lost. The order of things is not regenerated. Traditional Irish life, in Wicklow or in the West, is changed only to the extent that it becomes conscious of its bereavement from authentic value. In *The Playboy of the Western World*, Pegeen Mike's desolate cry of loss brings to an end the prospect of a glorious future with Christy Mahon, one which Christy had invoked by articulating a vision of pastoral romance which properly belongs to the old Gaelic past. The failure of the community to bring the past Eden into a Utopian future marks the boundary line of nationalist and romantic desire. The vagrant hero or heroine fades into legend or fantasy. The community remains; more deeply stricken, more visibly decayed. The traditional conflict between youth and age, so evident in *The Playboy*, *Deirdre of the Sorrows* and *In the Shadow of the Glen*, gives the social victory to age, the existential victory to youth. Society is not redeemed, and the traditional function of comedy remains incomplete. Synge is not writing out the failure of heroism. He is registering its failure in regard to society or, conversely, society's failure in regard to it.

This is one of the themes of Yeats and Joyce too. The hero betrayed or expelled by a community (which has itself conspired to create the idea of heroism as a means to its own salvation) is a literary trope. In it we see the suppression of its own Utopian vision of itself by a community which did not have 'courage equal to desire'. Synge himself became one of the lost heroes in Yeats's pantheon, especially after the *Playboy* riots in 1907 and the performance of *Deirdre* in 1910. In fact Yeats's search for the ideal audience is part of his interpretation of the meaning and reception of Synge's drama. The meaning was heroic, the reception base. Thus, a new audience was needed, one to which heroism would come naturally. This is not a distortion of Synge. Rather it is a true perception of the plight of the hero in his plays. Yeats's own repeated attempts to conceive of Cuchulain as a hero who could participate in the mind of the present generation, Pearse's assertion of Cuchulain's presence, and their mutual castigations on the community which could not receive these demanding exemplars, are repeated, with variations, by Joyce, O'Casey, George Moore and others. There was no audience for heroism when it became flesh.

The complexity of Synge's plays is in part focused for us by their ostensible adherence on the one hand to an oral tradition which prizes story, an institutionalized narrative, and on the other to a

written tradition which prizes textuality, a linguistic production
which calls attention to its own nature rather than to any narrative
end for which it is merely an instrument. Synge was aware of the
blend of opposites in his work. He read it sometimes as a blend of the
Irish and English elements: 'With the present generation the
linguistic atmosphere of Ireland has become definitely English
enough, for the first time, to allow work to be done in English that is
perfectly Irish in essence, yet has sureness and purity of form.'[2]
Sometimes it was a blend of the lyric and epic impulses:

Lyrics can be written by people who are immature, drama cannot. There is
little great lyrical poetry. Dramatic literature is relatively more mature.
Hence the intellectual maturity of most races is marked by a definite
moment of dramatic creation. This is now felt in Ireland. Lyrical art is the
art of national adolescence. Dramatic art is first of all a childish art ...
without form or philosophy; then after a lyrical interval we have it as mature
drama dealing with the deeper truth of general life in a perfect form and
with mature philosophy.[3]

These remarks return us to the traditional linguistic and literary
origins out of which his drama grew.

But the programme, which envisages the fusion of diverse
elements, is not identical with the plays, which enact the contradictions between them. Story is one thing and Synge's modifications of
the folk stories that supply his plays help us to understand the
inevitable difficulties of his position. Once the oral tradition is
written, it is transformed. Synge is involved in an act of translation
as much as the nineteenth-century rewriters of Irish poetry into
English. Thus the oral tradition, the story, is there as a moulding
presence, as a guarantor of universal validity, giving sanction to the
fiction but not having sanction within itself. (Joyce used *The Odyssey*
in a comparable way in *Ulysses*.) The oral hinterland lends prominence to the mode of telling the story which Synge turns into a
virtuoso performance. The balance between the 'epic' story and the
'lyric' performance, between the 'maturity' of the old tale and the
'adolescence' of the actors within it, is an expression of Synge's
desire to incorporate the present (as something that had never
happened before) into the past (as something in which the present
had happened before) in such a way that the audience would be left
to contemplate 'purity of form' or, in Yeat's words, 'an eddy of life
purified from everything but itself'.[4] In consequence, there would be
in such works something more than the disengagement from the

petty concerns of everyday life which both Synge and Yeats desired. There would be, finally, a disengagement from history, achieved by the constant relocation of the specific sequence of incidents in the frame of the universal, human condition. So the oral or mythic readings of the plays emerge: *In the Shadow in the Glen* is a rewriting of the old story of the marriage between January and May; *The Playboy* is a rewriting of the Oedipus myth; *Riders to the Sea* is a version of man's tragic struggle against the inevitability of death. Such readings would be encouraged by the almost total absence of historical references in Synge's plays and by the luxurious presence of a self-consciously 'poetic' language.

. . . So in the plays we find ourselves confronted by discontinuities. Their narrative form is oral, that of the folk-tale; their narrative mode is literary, that of the specialized language. Their background is Nature, open, wild and romantic; their foreground is Society, closed, decayed and utilitarian. The rituals of a community are invoked but the loneliness of individual heroism prevails. Mythical figures are remembered, historical detail is blurred. Love is an enchantment, marriage a travesty; lies become truths, dreams become realities; vagrancy is a virtue, settlement a vice; the heart's a wonder but there are no psychological problems; authority is pervasive but anarchy also prevails. Each play presents its own peculiar form of discontinuity, but they all have in common the story of a fantasy – Christy Mahon's fantasy about the killing of his da, Maurya's fantasy in *Riders to the Sea* about having one son pre-served, Martin and Mary Doul's fantasy in *The Well of the Saints* about their own splendid appearances – which is, first, rebuked by fact and then, in the next instant, legitimized as belonging or contributing to a higher truth than mere fact could ever reach. This double fold in the stories allows us to think of them as something more complex than exercises in a kind of cultural *bovarysme*, since they both share in and castigate illusions. Finally, the illusion must be ratified by something larger than realism. Mesmerized by an eloquence which begins in illusion but which continues after the destruction of illusion, we are forced to concede to the imagination a radical autonomy. It insists on its own truth not by ignoring fact but by including it and going beyond it. The imaginary, overtaken by the real, becomes the imaginative.

The dynamic force which makes this possible is language. People talk themselves into freedom. No longer imprisoned by sea or cottage, by age or politics, the Synge heroes and heroines chat themselves off stage, out of history, into legend. Yet they leave behind them a community more hopelessly imprisoned than ever. In one sense, we can read this as a criticism of the community's hopelessness as a receptive audience for heroism. But it is also an acknowledgement that heroism of this sort is a hopeless means of reviving the community. The central discontinuity is there. Synge's drama affirms and denies the value of the heroicizing impulse of the [Irish Literary] Revival. It produces the hero out of the 'organic' community but leaves the community empty and exhausted. The glorious language is not a signal that all is well. Self-realization involves social alienation. Those who walk away from society and those who remain within it represent two kinds of value which are not reconcilable.

An examination of the text of *The Playboy* reveals these tensions operating at the deepest level. Key-words – *lonesome, afeard, decent, sainted* – and their associated epithets, such as *queer* and *dark*, so dominate the rhythms of speech that they give it the regularity of chant. The adoption of the present habitual tense, so common in the Irish language, into the present participle in English also helps to give regularity and continuity to the speeches, allowing for a smoothness in the transitions not native to either language. 'If I am a queer daughter, it's a queer father'd be leaving me lonesome these twelve hours of dark, and I piling turf with the dogs barking and the calves mooing, and my own teeth rattling with fear.'[5] The wonderfully lubricated syntax and the grammatical nonchalance of Synge's writing certainly abet the impression of naturalness which is so important in these plays. But the ever enfolding repetitions, the picking up of one phrase by a number of speakers, the alliterative patterning ('dews of dawn', 'wonders of the western world', 'a high wave to wash him from the world'), enforce the contrary impression – of artificiality, of design. The more brilliant the artifice, the more natural it appears to be. Yet the conciliation between these things is not only a matter of cadences; it also involves meaning. The key words which generate the play's meanings provide us with no sense of final conciliation. At the simplest level we can, by their light, pick out the main movement in the play. Beginning in anonymity and squalor, Christy moves, via eloquent fiction, to fame and glory. For a moment he is offered the sidetrack temptation of the Widow Quin, notorious not famous, shrewd not glamorous. Resisting that, he is finally brought down by the reappearance of his father, only to rise again above father, above the villagers, and leave 'master of all fights from now'. Lonesomeness, tempted by decency, becomes individuality. Decency, with its saints and cardinals, popes and peelers, wakes and marriages, is left behind.

Yet it is a strange kind of decency which, for instance, demands that a dispensation be sought from Rome for the marriage of Pegeen and Shawn (because they are related) and at the same time approves of a son who boasts how he killed his father. It is an odd fact that a play which seems at one level to promote the comic idea of the subversion of adult authority and the liberation which is its consequence, should be so sparing in its references to the oppressions and dangers of authority itself. We hear of priests and of peelers and of a thousand militia '– bad cess to them! – walking idle through the land';[6] we hear of hierarchies of potentates, religious and secular, of God in his golden throne, of St Peter in his seat, and we smile at the fearful anxieties of a Shawn Keogh who is terrified at the very name of Father Reilly, the parish priest. The poverty and the limited incestuous nature of the society is hinted at on several occasions. Yet famine, eviction, military oppression and landlordism, the characteristic facts of late-nineteenth-century Irish rural existence for the peasantry are almost entirely repressed features of the text. The peasant society that Synge knew was dying because it had been atrociously oppressed – not because it had lost contact with the heroic energies which its early literature had once exhibited.

Synge aestheticizes the problem of oppression by converting it into the issue of heroism. The oppression is finally understood as self-inflicted by the community, because it insists on the lower-class realism of fact and refuses the aristocratic symbol of imaginative truth. It is strange to see this mutation of politics into literature against the background of the County Mayo which had produced Michael Davitt and the Land League, Captain Boycott and some of the worst agrarian unrest in late-nineteenth-century Ireland. The heroic figures of the Revival's imagination are social as well as literary constructs. They are leaders of their people in the sense that Lecky imagined the eighteenth-century landlord to be: 'The Irish character is naturally intensely aristocratic; and when gross oppression was not perpetrated, the Irish landlords were, I imagine, on the whole very popular, and the rude, good-humoured despotism which they wielded was cordially accepted'.[7]

This Trinity College view of Irish history was extended and enriched by Synge and by Yeats into a myth of union between peasant and aristocrat – leading to the emergence of heroism, spiritual leadership, still aristocratic in tone, Anglo-Irish in content, but frustrated by the intractable facts of a situation which Michael Davitt had more accurately described in his book *The Fall of Feudalism in Ireland* (1904). The dispossession of the landlords, the breaking of the political power of the Ascendency (urged by Burke over a century before) and the deep material and cultural impoverishment of the peasantry which was a direct result of the exercise of that power, are the central political facts of Synge's mature life. The attempt to recover a new ideal of heroism from the reintegration of the shattered Gaelic culture with the presiding English polity is no more than the after-image of authority on the Anglo-Irish retina.

It is therefore quite proper to resign ourselves to the mythic interpretations of Synge's plays. In *Riders to the Sea*, the extreme poverty of the islanders, the carefully annotated disintegration of their traditional habits, the colour symbolism of black and white, grey and red, the sheer marginality of existence, can be embraced under the aegis of Sea and Death. Maurya is the voice of humanity uttering its resignation to an incurable human plight. In her, quietism is heroic. Within this frame, every object – the clothes of the drowned Michael, the white boards for the coffin, the cake on the griddle – shines with the pathos of the human artifact in the face of the hypnotic and obliterating force of the sea.

Similarly, in *Deirdre of the Sorrows*, the betrayal of Naisi and his companions by Conchubor, already foretold, gives Deirdre the opportunity to satisfy her desire for death and for the escape from old age. The political fact is minor in contrast to the 'metaphysical' fact. As she says with her last breath: 'It's a pitiful thing, Conchubor, you have done this night in Emain, yet a thing will be a joy and triumph to the ends of life and time.'[8]

Deirdre, like Maurya and Christy, is a natural symbolist. The purity of action emerges only when it is drawn from the sheath of history. Then it glitters through all ages. But *Deirdre* is a costume drama with no image of the 'natural' to rescue it from its heavy Celtic brocade hangings. Synge's fascination with obliteration, with being open and free, closed and imprisoned, dominates the action.

NAISI: There's nothing surely the like of a new grave of open earth for putting a great space between two friends that love.

DEIRDRE: If there isn't maybe it's that grave when it's closed will make us one forever, and we two lovers have had a great space without weariness or growing old or any sadness of mind.[9]

Here again, the space that swallows the heroes up is the space that gives them legendary presence. The disappearance of the central figures into death, resignation, or the horizons beyond the cottage or village, is the precondition of that figure's abiding presence in the mind of the community. Real heroism is never in the here and now; it is always in the past of the mind. ...

SOURCE: extracts from *Celtic Revivals: Essays in Modern Irish Literature 1880–1980* (London and Boston, 1985), 52–5, 57–61.

NOTES

[Reorganized and renumbered from the original – Ed.]

1. *The Collected Works of J. M. Synge*, ed. Robin Skelton, 4 vols (London, 1962–8), vol. 2, p. 65.
2. Ibid., vol. 2, p. 384.
3. Ibid., vol. 2, p. 350.
4. *Explorations* (London, 1962), p. 154.
5. *Collected Works*, vol. 4, p. 63.
6. Ibid.
7. W. E. H. Lecky, *Leaders of Public Opinion in Ireland* (London, 1872), p. 252.
8. *Collected Works*, vol. 4, p. 269.
9. Ibid., vol. 4, p. 251.

Thomas Kilroy 'Reaction and Subversion' (1972)

The position of Synge ... within the Irish Tradition, is rather a special one, he cannot be simply accommodated within the early Abbey Theatre Movement and left there. There is a similar discomfort for those who try to associate him with the standard anthology

of modern drama, however much his stature as an artist may be
recognized. Eliot's well-known comments in *Poetry and Drama* on
Synge's language might serve as a model of the uneasy treatment
that Synge has had from modern criticism. His case, it is said, is
special, the circumstances of his achievement are local, they do not
apply beyond this. 'The language of Synge', Eliot writes, 'is not
available except for plays set among the same people.'[1] The same
might be said, and has been said, of his plots, his sense of place and
so on. Yet this cannot be the whole of the matter for Synge, with
Shaw, Yeats, Joyce and Beckett is one of the artists of permanent,
major significance born in this country in modern times.

In his Prefaces to *The Tinker's Wedding* and *The Playboy*, as
elsewhere in his occasional writings, Synge deliberately rejects
modernist drama and makes an appeal on behalf of a vital regional-
ism in literature, uncontaminated by the sterility, as Synge saw it, of
modern urban life. Yet the sensibility behind the plays is one which
constantly evokes the kind of aesthetic values that inform the best of
modern writing. This is exactly the kind of problem which faces the
modern student of Synge's work. I try to describe this sensibility as
private, intensely preoccupied with the nature of human freedom,
which is here but another way of saying human privacy, secular but
committed to the essential spirituality of human action, subversive
of the main, middle culture of which Modernism is the counter-
culture.

Robert Brustein, in his study of that title, describes the drama
from Ibsen to Genet as *The Theatre of Revolt*. He invites us in the
Foreword, if we so wish, to relate Synge to his thesis of a radical,
revolutionary drama; there are several reasons why I think we may
do so without strain.

An artist of the very first order, with a fine knowledge of classic
English and French drama and perfectly aware of contemporary
developments in the theatre elsewhere, Synge nevertheless dedicated
himself to a secluded folk culture which he knew was already
showing signs of its own demise. His treatment, however, of Irish
material is never provincial in a narrow sense; it is the product of a
rich mind which brought classical forms to bear upon the native
material. The true distinction between Synge and his Modernist
contemporaries is not a qualitative one nor even in the choice of
subject matter, for Synge's actual themes transcend his local settings, but a distinction of models, of ideal mentors. Synge looks back

to sixteenth and seventeenth century drama as his model, to Jonson, Molière and Racine. As an artist he is technically conservative while one of the very purposes of Modernism is in its progressive search for new forms to match the radical programme of the new drama.

Synge's work is a complex composite of the ideas which moved the early Abbey Theatre and the personal quality of mind of the man himself. Without him the actual achievement in dramatic literature of the Movement up to his death would be sparse indeed and would rest largely as an introduction to the development of Yeats. *The Playboy of the Western World* is the major achievement of Synge the dramatist and of the theatrical movement up to that date. Before it the theatre had had its successes, notably in the creation of a style but with this play it realized one of its fundamental aims: the production of a considerable work of literary and dramatic literature native to itself. There is about the writings of all those concerned, up to this date, an air of anticipation, the excitement of people on the verge of discovery, ready to believe that the next play would be it, the play which would give meaning to earlier experiments with Irish speech and to the methods of stage presentation which the Fays had brought to the theatre. *The Playboy of the Western World* was that play and it was this conviction which helped Yeats and Lady Gregory to defend it so vigorously, even if they had their own reservations about its language themselves.

Now *The Playboy* well illustrates that curious mixture of reaction and subversion in Synge. Firstly, it draws its detail, its ethos, from the rhythm of life of a remote corner of the West of Ireland. And, however much we may cherish this way of life for what it represents, it was already an anachronism in 1907, as is exemplified by Synge's problems in translating it to a Dublin stage. Secondly, the form of the play is that of traditional Romantic Comedy but the play ends, not in the conventional marriage, but in the ironic frustration of the lovers. Yet even here Synge has many precedents deep within the European tradition, as Berowne remarks wryly at the end of *Love's Labour's Lost*,

> Our wooing doth not end like an
> old play; Jack hath not Jill.

This traditionalism in Synge, however, does not account for the full maturity of his art and it is the other elements, less easily identified, that make him the complex artist who resists categorization. When we begin to assemble those other elements which shape his imagination we find that they act upon the traditional forms, often in a radical fashion, rather than being simply of the forms and in service to them.

The Playboy opens with Pegeen Mike laboriously writing out a colourful order for her trousseau 'to be sent with three barrels of porter' in time for her wedding to Shawneen Keogh. It ends with a pathetic cry of anguish a day later with Pegeen driven back into that loveless marriage having enjoyed briefly 'the love-light of the star of knowledge' through all the eloquence of a poet who has suddenly discovered the capacity of language. The whole force of the play is derived from that swift blossoming of the delicate, fragile, shared vision of Christy and Pegeen in Act Three, its precious, timeless innocence and its mortality before the way of the world. There are those in the play who abide by the rhythm of life about them and there are those who try to defy it. Synge reserves his sympathy for the love of Christy and Pegeen which tries to defy it but it is the rhythm from which they try to escape which is finally triumphant.

It is in this way that Synge uses the form of traditional Romantic Comedy. Shawn Keogh is a satiric representation of respectable marriage, marriage sanctioned by the Church and, more importantly perhaps, by the kind of barter system which operates as a marriage contract within the community. Both religion and the community are ridiculed in his person because as a man, as a sexual candidate he enjoys the respect of no-one. 'It's true all girls are fond of courage,' the Widow Quin taunts him,' 'and do hate the like of you.' Rather as he dismisses the young priest as irrelevant to Maurya's suffering in *Riders to the Sea*, Synge at the very beginning of this play puts aside the whole conventional, established idea of marriage. His true subject is exceptional love. In the scheme of the play respectable marriage is at the lowest end of the scale and there is a progressive ascension from that to the ecstasy of Christy and Pegeen. Between the extremes lies the wild, spirited world of Michael James and the Widow Quin, only partly touched by social respectability and only partly in touch with the kind of vision briefly enjoyed by Christy and Pegeen.

The figure of Michael James in the play rises up out of the raw earth itself, a great male voice bellowing with drink, the very voice which, significantly, interrupts the lovers' duet in Act Three. If this is a comic play about the ancient ritual of patricide it is also a play about the survival of the patriarch because while Old Mahon may have been subdued by Christy, Michael James and all he stands for continue to flourish at the end. He is indeed the true father-figure of the play and he, and not Old Mahon, is Christy's real antagonist in dramatic time in the struggle of the assertion of manhood. The lyrical style of Christy as lover could never prosper in the world of Michael James and nowhere is this more evident than in the blessing which the old man pronounces over the two, that extraordinary pagan hymn to the flesh, mixed with the shrewdness of a stock-breeder and with that ludicrous Christian apothegm tagged on at the end. Synge understood, and the play is a dramatization of it, what such a world excluded, the tenderness of passion, the poetry of love. The greatest obstacle to romance and sexual fulfilment in the play comes from the nature of the culture itself and this is one of the distinctions of the play as a Romantic Comedy.

Within this wider tradition of European Romantic Comedy Christy is but one of a whole gallery of heroes representing assertive masculine vigour, passion and romance who pit themselves against the conventions of a community. Christy, of course, fails but there are certain qualities to his make-up, peculiar to Synge, which make his final exit, even without his lover, triumphant. For, after all, the final question which the play poses, and one which continues to trouble audiences, is why Pegeen does not go along with him. She doesn't go and she realizes the horror of her choice almost at once because, ultimately, the world about her is stronger than the appeal of Christy.

Christy is one of those Synge characters (The Tramp in *In The Shadow of the Glen* being another) who comes in out of the open air, out of Nature you might say, and goes back out to it, to the open road, with a free heart at the end 'romancing through a romping lifetime from this hour to the dawning of the judgment day'. Again and again there is this evocation in Synge, particularly in his occasional writings, of a life beyond the burdens of society, a freedom and a purity of will which Synge associates with Nature, with a kind of animism of which Man is but a part. His models of this daemonic sense of life are the tramps, tinkers, wanderers and it is clear that this rôle is more than just an unconscious projection of the dramatist's own personality.

Yeats, who deeply understood the nature of Synge's genius, speaks of this facet of his personality in words which place Synge

within the mainstream of Modernism: the artist in a creative
solitude engaged in an uneasy dialogue with the world outside, the
artist questioning the very possibility of art to communicate at all.
The predicament, the abrasive relationship between the artist and
his culture, has become almost a commonplace in our century. This
passage, from the Yeats open letter of 1919 to Lady Gregory,
actually anticipates Beckett's defence of Joyce ten years later against
an identical obscurantism.[2] The issue in each case is the same: the
unwillingness or inability of the public to grant the work of art its
distinct and total self-containment or, to put it another way, the
confusing of art with journalism, sociology or history. What Yeats is
talking about, what Beckett writes about in his defence of *Work in
Progress*, is the belief, on which the most of Modern Art rests, that
art is a unique and superior medium of knowledge about human
existence and that it can only be understood and judged according
to laws of its own creating:

The outcry against *The Playboy* was an outcry against its style, against its
way of seeing; and when an audience called Synge 'decadent' – a favourite
reproach from the objective everywhere – it was but troubled by the stench
of its own burnt cakes. How could they that dreaded solitude love that
which solitude made?[3]

The position of Synge, then, is a special one both within the
particular idea of a theatre which moved the early Irish Dramatic
Movement and the wider tradition of modern European drama. ...

SOURCE: extract from 'Synge and Modernism' in *J. M. Synge:
Centenary Papers 1971*, ed. Maurice Harmon (Dublin, 1972),
170–4.

NOTES

[Reorganized and renumbered from the original – Ed.]

1. T. S. Eliot, *Selected Prose*, ed. John Hayward (Harmondsworth, 1953),
p. 74.
2. See Samuel Beckett and others, *Our Exagmination Round his Factification for Incamination of Work in Progress* (London, 1961). This is a reprint of
the 1929 edition.
3. W. B. Yeats, *Explorations* (London, 1962), p. 253.

PART TWO

Riders to the Sea

Riders to the Sea

Première: 25 February 1904, by the Irish National Theatre Society at the Molesworth Hall, Dublin.

First published in Dublin in *Samhain: An Occasional Review*, No. 3 (September 1903), 25–33; and in Boston in *Poet-Lore*, 16: 1 (Spring 1905), 1–11.

First book publication in *The Shadow of the Glen and Riders to the Sea* (London, 1905); further editions in 1907 and 1909.

Manuscript and typescript drafts are detailed by Ann Saddlemyer in Synge's *Collected Works*, Volume III (London, 1968), 234–49.

1. COMMENTS AND REVIEWS

I *W. B. Yeats* (1903)

... The two plays [printed] in this year's *Samhain* represent the two sides of the [Irish Literary] movement very well, and are both written out of a deep knowledge of the life of the people. It should be unnecessary to praise Dr Hyde's comedy [*The Poorhouse*] that comes up out of the foundation of human life, but Mr Synge is a new writer and a creation of our movement. He has gone every summer for some years past to the Aran Islands, and lived there in the houses of the fishers, speaking their language and living their lives, and his play seems to me the finest piece of tragic work done in Ireland of late years. One finds in it, from first to last, the presence of the sea, and a sorrow that has majesty as in the work of some ancient poet. ...

SOURCE: extract from *Samhain: An Occasional Review* (September 1903), p. 7.

II *Lady Gregory* (1913)

... The rich abundant speech of the people was a delight to him. ... At the time of his first visit to Coole he had written some poems, not very good for the most part, and a play [*When the Moon Has Set*] which was not good at all. I read it again after his death when, according to his written wish, helping Mr. Yeats and sorting out the work to be published or set aside, and again it seemed but of slight merit. But a year later he brought us his two plays, *The Shadow of the Glen*, and the *Riders to the Sea*, both masterpieces, both perfect in their way. He had gathered emotion, the driving force he needed from his life among the people, and it was the working in dialect that had set free his style. ...

SOURCE: 'Synge', *English Review*, 13 (March 1913), 559.

III *George Roberts* (1955)

... The rehearsals [of the Abbey Theatre première] were intensely interesting. The scene, which was laid in the Aran Islands, required different treatment from any of our other peasant plays. Synge was very particular that every detail of the properties and costumes should be correct. It was found impossible to obtain material of the right shade for the Aran Islanders' petticoats (a peculiar dark crimson) until Lady Gregory discovered in Galway a man who could dye in 'madder'. Accordingly, some homespun flannel was obtained and sent to him for dyeing. The petticoats were made under Synge's directions, in a certain way, with a broad strip of calico at the top.

The pampooties were another difficulty. Synge brought in a pair he had used in the Aran Islands to show how they were made. In the islands, the raw hide of the cow or bullock is used, but the actors were squeamish at the idea of using raw hides, so we tried to get a dried skin. I went round every tanyard in Dublin, and at last succeeded in getting a calf skin that had been prepared for a farmer who had meant to make a waistcoat from it, but changed his mind when his girl friend disapproved, and so it had been left on the tanner's hands. The members of the company, in the intervals of rehearsing, cut this up and made holes in it to make the stage pampooties.

The spinning-wheel was another trouble, until Lady Gregory again came to the rescue and sent up a large wheel from Galway. Synge himself instructed the girl how to use it.

Synge was exceedingly anxious that the 'caoine' should be as close as possible to the peculiar chant that is used in the islands, and after much searching I found the Galway woman living in one of the Dublin suburbs who consented to show two of the girls how the caoine was given. She was very nervous about it, though somewhat proud that one of what she looked on as country customs should be so eagerly sought after in the city. At the same time, she was very interested in the whole affair, wanting to know what the play was about, and saying the caoine was so terrible a thing she could hardly believe people would want to put it in a play.

At first, she tried to begin in her little parlour, but she confessed after a few moments she could not do it properly there, so she brought the two girls up to a bedroom. At first it seemed no better, until she conceived the idea that I should act the corpse. She lighted the wake candles, and then she got that note full of terror of the dead. ... She was a native Irish speaker, and the Irish cadences and rhythm of words, in conjunction with the clapping of the hands and swaying of her body, made a scene very terrible and yet beautiful to look on.

Here it may be said that there is a little too much 'composition' about the caoine in the Abbey in later years, and too little of the passionate sorrow which should inform it.

This play, like the previous one, did not win much praise in Dublin on its first performance. Some of the audience were horrified at the sight of a corpse on the stage, a few of them left the hall while the performance was going on, and the press was almost as damning as on the previous occasion of the performance of *In the Shadow of the Glen*. The adverse opinions, however, made some of us think all the more of Synge. ...

SOURCE: 'The Plays of Synge', *Irish Times* (2 August 1955), 5.

IV   *W. B. Yeats*   (1910)

... I remember saying once to Synge that though it seemed to me that a conventional descriptive passage encumbered the action at the moment of crisis, I liked *The Shadow of the Glen* better than *Riders to the Sea*, that seemed for all the nobility of its end, its mood of Greek tragedy, too passive in suffering, and had quoted from Matthew Arnold's introduction to *Empedocles on Etna* to prove my point. Synge answered: 'It is a curious thing that *Riders to the Sea* succeeds with an English but not with an Irish audience, and *The*

Shadow of the Glen, which is not liked by an English audience, is always liked in Ireland, though it is disliked there in theory'. . . .

SOURCE: extract from 'J. M. Synge and the Ireland of his Time', *Essays and Introductions* (London, 1961), 336–7.

V   *Max Beerbohm*   (1904)

. . . There is plenty of poetry in *Riders to the Sea*, modern peasants though the characters are. The theme is much the same as in Heijermans' play *The Good Hope* – a mother whose youngest son is drowned, as all her other sons have been drowned, at sea. Mr Synge . . . is content to show us the pathos of his theme: he does not, as did Heijermans, try to rouse any indignation. 'So it is, and so it must be' is his tone. It is the tone of the mother herself, whose acquiescence is deeper than the acquiescence of the mother in *The Good Hope*. She submits not merely because it were vain to rebel. To rebel is not in her nature. She has the deep fatalism of her race; and for her, the things that actually happen, for evil as for good, are blurred through the dreams that are within her. . . .

SOURCE: *Saturday Review*, 9 April 1904.

VI   *Padraic Colum*   (1926)

. . . All his work was subjective, he once told me, it all came out of moods in his own life. *Riders to the Sea* had come out of the feeling that old age was coming upon him – he was not forty at the time – and that death was making approach. And it is this sombre personal feeling that makes the play; it is odd to recall now that in Dublin quite intelligent people spoke of it as being reminiscent of Pierre Loti's *Iceland Fisherman*. James Joyce has told me that he had talked with Synge in Paris about this play: the criticism that Joyce had made of it was that it was too brief to sustain the tragic mood – 'You cannot have a tragedy in a play that lasts for twenty minutes'. I think Joyce was mistaken in this view of *Riders to the Sea*: the chanting of the *caoine* for the dead by the kneeling women brings in another temporality to the play; it adds to it, not minutes, but measurements of tragic experience. . . .

SOURCE: *The Road Round Ireland* (London and New York, 1926), 365–6.

VII *Maire Nic Shiubhlaigh* (1955)

. . . [The first production of] *Riders to the Sea* was an immediate success. . . . The story of the old woman whose sons have slowly been claimed by the sea was not altogether original – but the circumstances were of little importance. Synge's prose, his unique sense of dramatic values, made an original plot unnecessary. It was pure tragedy. There was no sentiment; every speech told. There were no unnecessary situations, no conflicting side-issues. From the moment the curtain rose, the audience was drawn inexorably towards the climax. . . .

One of the most effective passages in the play is that which introduces the *caoine* of the Aran Islands – the bitter, song-like lament of the women as they follow a coffin to a place of burial. Its inclusion is vital for the successful presentation of the piece, and the producer who dispenses with it will never achieve the effect which the author intended. Many present producers ignore its value, and in almost every case the play loses much of its tragedy; the poignancy of the climax is blunted. As Synge meant it to, it provides a strange eerie background to the final speech of Maurya, the old woman.

The custom of keening itself, at one time fairly general in Ireland, is now peculiarly western. Doubtless it is a relic of some ancient civilization, handed down with variations through the centuries. In Aran of latter years it became the practice for relatives of a dead man, or one who had been lost at sea, to hire a special party of women to sing the *caoine* before, during and after a wake, and the wealth of a family was measured by the number of singers it could afford. The lament itself has a strange savage quality about it when sung by an expert. Its effectiveness probably lies in its repetition. Over and over the women repeat the lines, softly at first, rising gradually on a sustained note to the eerie splendour of the climax. Rocking backwards and forwards to the beat of the music they seem to lose themselves in the beauty of the lilt.

As an interesting sidelight on the original production of *Riders to the Sea* . . . it may be worth adding here that the *caoine* which was sung by us in 1904 was a transcription of a genuine Aran lament. It was not composed specially for the production; it was given to two of us in rather peculiar circumstances by an old peasant woman living in Dublin. We learned it just as she sang it herself, recalling, perhaps, some island tragedy similar to the one around which Synge wrote his play.

We never learned her name, but she shared a home with her married daughter in a decaying tenement off Gardiner Street. The room, in which an entire family lived, formed a most unusual background for a woman of her upbringing. It had evidently been used as a drawing-room by the house's original tenants and had a massive marble fireplace which almost filled one whole wall. The floorboards were rotting away, and the room was filled with the usual flimsy furniture, an iron bedstead in one corner. The contrast between all this and the woman herself was startling; she was still dressed in the clothes of the Islands, the shawl and red petticoat, which her daughter said she refused to give up in favour of other garb. There was an air of poverty about the room but it was scrupulously clean. The building, of course, was one of the many Georgian mansions in that part of the city which had gradually fallen into disrepair, eventually being taken over for use as tenements.

The old woman had no English. We spoke to her in Gaelic for a time. Then she sang the *caoine*, standing, looking across the bed towards the window, her eyes closed, her arms outstretched, her head thrown back, swaying backwards and forwards with the rise and fall of the music. We had come expecting a chant or some kind of conventional lamentation. Nothing like this. It was strangely moving to see this old figure standing at the window of a crumbling tenement, looking over a city street, singing. She seemed to forget we were there. She sang:

"Tá sé imighthe uaim!
"Go deo! Go deo! Go deo!"

They were thin, piping notes. The sounds from the street outside contrasted strangely, the noise of passing vehicles. But listening, one forgot the unusual circumstances. The *caoine* seemed to possess her. Synge might have written his play around her alone; an old woman counting the loss of her sons with a bitter satisfaction. . . .

SOURCE: *The Splendid Years: Recollections of Maire Nic Shiubhlaigh as Told to Edward Kenny* (Dublin, 1955), 53–5.

2. CRITICAL STUDIES

T. R. Henn 'Images, Symbols and Literary Echoes' (1972)

I

I do not think that we realize the full ambiguity of the title of the play at our first reading; perhaps not even when we have known it through many readings and performances. On the surface it is clearly the play of the two Riders, the living man on the Red Mare, and the phantasm of the dead on the Grey Pony. One might see them as Jack Yeats did in his illustration for *The Aran Islands*; the half-wild horses, ridden by the islanders without saddle, bit or bridle, but with a halter that might be quickly knotted up out of the new rope that is hanging on the cottage wall. Behind, in depth, we may be aware of the horse as a fear-image; the chariots and horses; power and destruction; even the mysterious horses of the Bible. There are the white, red, black and pale horses – the horse of death – in Revelation (VI:2); the horses of Zecheriah (I:8 and VI:2); perhaps even the text from the prophet (Zecheriah, x:5): 'the riders on horses shall be confounded'. We should not forget Synge's extensive reading in the Bible.

Move a little into the background, and the Riders are the fishermen of the Islands, as in Norse and Homeric imagery. They are the riders who use the frail curraghs of that coast; the long high prowed boats, built of lath and tarred canvas (once of skins) that can live where no other type of boat can be launched. Over the long Atlantic rollers one does indeed have something of the sensation of riding; and, till one is accustomed to them, the fear of the sea that one encounters in them is profound. As Synge has pointed out in *The Aran Islands*, most of the fishermen of his time met (sooner or later) their death in them: usually when drunk on 'the grey poten' that was one of the few comforts of their lives. But there are other things that Synge does not mention. If one fell out of one of them the crew might refuse to rescue him, might even smash his fingers as he clung to the gunwhale; for it is ill-luck to take back anything that the Sea has tried to claim. Nor did the men of the islands learn to swim – many of that western coast refuse to do so still – believing that this skill would merely prolong the inevitable drowning. The riders of the horses and of the curraghs in which men go down to the sea are linked in the title. Odysseus, shipwrecked, rides a plank 'like a horse'.[1]

So too there is, in our background consciousness, the traditional lore of the drowned man: Clarence's dream, the famous lyric of *The Tempest*, the even more famous passage from 'Lycidas':

> Ay me! Whilst thee the shores, and sounding Seas
> Wash far away, where ere thy bones are hurld,
> Whether beyond the stormy *Hebrides*,
> Where thou perhaps under the whelming tide
> Visit'st the bottom of the monstrous world . . .[2]

Behind this and the following passages from the play is the common thought of the drowned sailor of Horace[3] and the three handfuls of dust that are the needed ritual if the grave is not to be unquiet:

How would it be washed up, and we after looking each day for nine days, and a strong wind blowing a while back from the west and south?[4]

   *   *   *

Ah, Nora, isn't it a bitter thing to think of him floating that way to the far north, and no one to keen him but the black hags that do be flying on the sea?[5]

   *   *   *

There does be a power of young men floating round in the sea, and what way would they know if it was Michael they had, or another man like him, for when a man is nine days in the sea, and the wind blowing it's hard set his own mother would be to say what man was in it.[6]

II

It is perhaps desirable to enlarge a little on the background of the play at the time of Synge's visits to the Islands. The 'desolate stony place',[7] the last outposts of man's husbandry in the Atlantic, were then the setting for the most primitive peasantry in Europe. It is not easy for the casual tourist of today to imagine the life of seventy years ago, though the mysterious forts of Dun Aengus still guard the offshore cliffs – from what invader? The horses had to be sent to the mainland, to winter on pasture that was better than the little stony

fields; or to be sold at Galway Fairs. Like the Burren, that strange
area of limestone outcrop in North Clare that lies to the southwest,
there was, as in Cromwell's description of that county 'not enough
timber to hang a man, water to drown him, or earth to bury him'.[8]
The graves in the shallow patches of soil were, like Donne's,
constantly re-used 'Some second guest to entertain'.[9] Synge gives a
macabre description of an island funeral in *The Aran Islands*: the
measuring of the coffin-space by a bramble torn from the hedge, the
throwing up of the bones from the old grave, the old woman who
recognized her husband's skull, and withdrew to a corner of the
churchyard to lament over it. These things I have seen; and without
some understanding of them we do not realize the emotional
significance of the 'fine white boards' for a coffin, Maurya's profound satisfaction that Michael has found a 'clean grave' in the Far
North.[10] Throughout the play there runs the bitter sense of loss, the
importance of ritual burial, that pre-historic man laboured so
greatly to achieve by dolmen and passage grave.

There are other depth-images that we do well to note. The 'cake'
that is turned out of the oven is the flat home-made soda bread,
baked in iron pans on the hearth; a hunk of it is commonly the sole
food for a journey for the fishermen in their curraghs. Its ritual
significance is clear; but Maurya's failure to give it to her son has in
it something of the negation of a sacrament. The meeting place is by
the spring well; we may remember, perhaps, the image from the
Psalms (LXXXIV:6): 'Who passing through the vale of misery use it
for a well'. The new rope – like all such things it comes from the
mainland, and is a thing of price – will serve for a halter for the
horses or for lowering a coffin into a grave. Each cottage will have a
tiny lamp, on or near the dresser with some crude holy picture
beside it; and close to it, the basin of holy water which now is almost
exhausted – from repeated use in tribulation and blessing. The knot
in the string that holds the bundle of clothes is 'perished with the salt
water';[11] Synge noted in *The Aran Islands* the perpetual dampness
of the salt-sodden clothes, the rheumatism that was only to be countered by the poteen, as in East Anglia the fen-dwellers fought the
dread ague with opium. And may there not be some symbolism in
the cutting of the knot by a knife bought from a stranger?[12] remem-
bering the Three Fates and the 'abhorréd shears' of 'Lycidas'.[13]
Something, but not a great deal, may be brought out in production;
the table has been used for mixing the bread-dough, and one of the

girls wipes it down hastily as Bartley's body is brought in at the doorway. It is, I think, a mistake to fill the cottage with properties not mentioned in the text, fishing-nets and so forth; or to play it against a background of the noise of waves. It is best to cultivate simplicity, and, above all to let the rhythms and cadences speak for themselves. Unless the Irish accent and its intonations are familiar, it is best not to attempt them; the stride of the speech carries the subtly-shifting advance and retreat of the action, the finely-differentiated character of the four protagonists.

III

Against some such background, of which the symbols are in the main archetypal and rooted both in tradition and in the simplicities of living, we may see the miniature tragedy. Perhaps it is the only complete one-act tragedy in any literature, for it requires no space to develop its characteristic momentum. Its conflict is the perennial one of man, driven by adventure or necessity against the Sea; itself the source of life and of death. The end comes inexorably, and this again is traditional. Dunbar's 'Lament for the Makaris' may stand to embrace them all:

> Since for the Death remeid is none,
> Best is that we for Death dispone
> After our death that live may we: –
> *Timor mortis conturbat me.*[14]

So Maurya

No man at all can be living for ever, and we must be satisfied.[15]

– set against Dante's

In la sua voluntade è nostra pace.[16]

For death and the Sea take all; but the Sea takes the young before their time, so that it acquires a new and hostile dimension, an auxiliary of Death. In it there are the constant ironic reversals. Maurya takes Michael's stick, lest she should 'slip on the big stones':

In the big world the old people do be leaving things after them for their sons and children, but in this place it is the young men do be leaving things behind them for them that do be old.[17]

Synge's anti-clerical irony is subtle and pervading; I believe that its cumulative effect gave rise to the general uneasiness of the Dublin audiences that led to the riots of 1907 over *The Playboy of the Western World*. I wonder whether there may not be an oblique reference (for the 'big stones' recur twice) to the familiar text in the Psalms (XCI: 12):[18]

[Angels] shall bear thee up . . . lest thou dash thy foot against a stone . . .

And a culminating point of irony is in the references – that seem to be emphasized, twice, intentionally – to the *young* priest:

> NORA: Didn't the young priest say the Almighty God won't leave her destitute with no son living?
> MAURYA: It's little the like of him knows of the sea . . .[19]

and we hear the intonation of scorn in the mother's voice; that changes at the last to a pathetic bewilderment:

. . . It isn't that I haven't prayed for you, Bartley, to the Almighty God. It isn't that I haven't said prayers in the dark night till you wouldn't know what I'd be saying . . .[20]

The end, in misery and even starvation in a house of three women that has lost all the breadwinners, is a benediction; thankfulness for the clean burial in the far north (clean, for a body of nine days battered by those remorseless tides is best hidden in the kindness of earth), and the white boards that will make Bartley's coffin. In her elegiac blessing of the living and the dead Maurya attains the stature of a priestess; so that the production in terms of plainsong was wholly appropriate (as in Vaughan Williams' opera):

> May the Almighty God have mercy on Bartley's soul,
> and on Michael's soul,
> and on the souls of Sheamus and Patch,
> and Stephen and Shawn [*bending her head*] . . .
> and may He have mercy on my soul, Nora,
> and on the soul of everyone is left living in the world.[21]

With those last words the death-stricken cottage on the island becomes as it were a microcosm of the world. *Who* is left alive? Let the mother, that had those hard births,[22] bless those that are living.

IV

It is a characteristic of the world's greatest literature – the Bible, Homer, Horace, Dante, Shakespeare – that one never opens the book, even in old age, without finding something that one had not seen before. So with *Riders*. It is sixty years since I first read it, and I have written of it since. I know the fishermen of those islands and that coast; I have used their craft, and maybe won even a little of their skills in them. I know, from seaward, the mercilessness of the great surf on those rocks. I have seen great actresses interpret Maurya: the greatest, perhaps, Sybil Thorndike. I thought that I had perceived the inwardness of the classic tragedy.[23]

But one thing I believe I have missed till I began to think about this little essay. Why cannot Maurya bless Bartley, give him the sacramental bread, as he passes by the spring well? For it is not the shock of seeing Michael's phantasm on the grey pony; 'something choked the words in my throat'[24] *before* she looks up, crying, to see that vision. Michael has fine clothes on him, and new shoes on his feet; we are aware, faintly, of a resurrection image.

But what was Maurya's relation to her son Michael, and why did her blessing for Bartley stick (like Macbeth's *Amen*) in her throat? We know that Macbeth could not assent to the blessing because he was not in a state of Grace. Synge sometimes hints at a mystery of the shadows, like Patch Darcy in *The Shadow of the Glen*. It is true that there are dark words before Bartley goes off on the horses, and these may be broken by the blessing at the well. One of her complaints against his going is that there will be 'no man in it to make the coffin'[25] if Michael's body is found. The white boards (paid for at a big price, and this is admirably perceptive of peasant psychology), the deep grave, seem to relate to a specially-beloved son. Michael's clothes are spread out on the table[26] beside his brother's corpse. Is Michael the beloved son, and is it for that reason that Bartley's death is received with a terrible resignation?

She's quiet now and easy; but the day Michael was drowned you could hear her crying out from this to the spring well. It's fonder she was of Michael, and would any one have thought that?[27]

Are 'sorrow's springs' exhausted; did the death of Michael numb Maurya's capacity to lament? Or does the vision of the figure on the grey pony, with fine clothes and new shoes on his feet, achieve a kind of divine resonance, as of Michael and all the angels?

V

We may praise the overwhelming power of this tiny play; its economy and reticence of statement; its images that are vécu, rooted in the reality of daily living. It has the laconic brevity of a Greek play, of which the basic myth is known to all the audience. It needs no exposition to unfold the characters. Its momentum is that of the Atlantic waves that gather their rhythms and their destructive forces out of the limitless ocean of necessity. Repeated reading, listening, seeing productions with many emphases (but with only one culmination in the high tradition, the *lusis* of lyric tragedy) may combine with some knowledge of that intricate and difficult subject, the rhythms, cadences and intonations of Anglo-Irish prose, to illuminate our understanding. That understanding embraces (but cannot exhaust) the mystery of death and loss; the women who are left to weep; and the benediction of death which must, as ever, lie between Christian resignation; and the bitter lamentation that runs through recorded literature.

SOURCE: '*Riders to the Sea*: A Note', from *Sunshine and the Moon's Delight: A Centenary Tribute to John Millington Synge 1871–1909*, ed. S. B. Bushrui (Gerrards Cross and Beirut, 1972), 33–9.

NOTES

1. *Odyssey*, XIII.
2. *Poetical Works of Milton*, II (Oxford, Clarendon Press, 1955), p. 169, ll. 154–8.
3. *Odes*, I, xxviii.
4. *C.W.*, III, p. 9.
5. Ibid., p. 17.
6. Ibid., pp. 25–7.
7. W. B. Yeats, 'In Memory of Major Robert Gregory', *Collected Poems* (London, Macmillan, 1958), p. 149.
8. This remark is usually attributed to Oliver Cromwell while on one of his punitive expeditions in the West. There are various versions.
9. 'The Relique', *The Poems of John Donne* (London, Oxford University Press, 1953), p. 62.
10. *C.W.*, III, pp. 25, 27.
11. Ibid., p. 15.
12. Steel, which is a strong protection against evil – see *The Shadow of the Glen* (*C.W.*, III, p. 41) – loses its virtue or becomes actively unlucky unless it is paid for; hence the slight inflexion of Cathleen's words in *Riders to the Sea* (*C.W.*, III, p. 15): '– the man *sold* us that knife'.

13. *Poetical Works of Milton*, II, p. 16, l. 75.

14. *The Poems of William Dunbar*, edited by W. Mackay (Edinburgh, Porpoise Press, 1932), p. 23.

15. *C.W.*, III, p. 27.

16. *Divine Comedy*, Paradiso III, l. 84.

17. *C.W.*, III, p. 13.

18. Perhaps this is far-fetched. See Synge's poem 'The Mergency Man', *C.W.*, I, p. 58.

19. *C.W.*, III, p. 21.

20. Ibid., p. 25.

21. Ibid., p. 27.

22. Cf. Euripides' *Medea* (*Collected Plays of Euripides*, trans. Gilbert Murray, London, Allen and Unwin, 1954, p. 16, ll. 250–2):

> '. . . sooner would I stand
> Three times to face their battles, shield in hand,
> Than bear one child.'

23. See the Preface to my edition of *The Plays and Poems of J. M. Synge* (London, Methuen, 1963); and to the chapter in my *Harvest of Tragedy* (London, Macmillan, 1956).

24. *C.W.*, III, p. 19.

25. Ibid., p. 9.

26. We may note, but need not stress, another sacramental suggestion. Before the coffin is made, the single work-table is the natural place for a corpse to be stretched. See also *The Shadow of the Glen* (*C.W.*, III, p. 33).

27. *C.W.*, III, p. 25.

Robert Bechtold Heilman 'Victims of Nature' (1968)

. . . The victim of nature is the subject of John M. Synge's *Riders to the Sea* (1904). On returning to it after some years, I was surprised to find how slight it is (it is, of course, only a one-acter), and how narrowly it clings to dignity and credibility; yet it has been anthologized and produced countless times, and for a half century it has had the status of at least a minor classic. Its very popularity, I believe, suggests the extent of our confusion about tragedy. It is the story of a fisherman's family on an island off the west coast of Ireland; Maurya, now an old woman, has lost a husband, a father-in-law and six sons in storms or in accidents at sea; the action of the play turns on the death of the last two sons by drowning. We see the response of several survivors to a climactic series of calamities – the daughters' concern for their mother, the grief, the sense of desolation, the sense of irony, a bowing to destiny. In examining the feelings of the survivors, Synge is neither narrow nor pat; to record the variations of their grief he finds a language that, though imagistic and unusually rhythmical, is based on plainness and understatement. This style is essential to offset a hyperbole of disasters that verges on being manipulated and false. We are moved by the survivors' foreboding, fear, courage and meditation on loss as the fate of all men; yet the play makes use of only a fraction of our total ability to be implicated. It exacts little of us. We remain fairly serene observers, sympathetic, sharing the sadness of death, but never drawn into pain such as that of incrimination.

The play is a lament; it is elegiac. When we feel an overwhelming concern for length of life, we tend to mistake elegy for tragedy, grief over the passage of things supplants contemplation of the quality of life. Death seems then not an expectable event, but a violation of order; we make it the enemy, and symbolize its hostility by pointing to its relentless, excessive attacks upon one family. In the elegiac there is a sense of the hero as victim: hence its proper relation is to disaster rather than tragedy. One of Maurya's lines is a key to all literature of disaster: 'They've all gone now, and there isn't anything else the sea can do to me'. Note the phrase, 'can do to me'. When the chief character is simply the person to whom things are done, his role as a moral agent is a small one. He is a 'whole' person, without the inner divisions or the clashing loyalties that mark the meaningful human conflicts. The dominant effect is one of pathos, and its import is limited. Naturally, this is not to say that the pathos of suffering is not a legitimate subject for literary art. It is. But if we mistake it for tragic effect, we fall short in our understanding of the whole human role, and of the modes of human failure.[1] . . .

SOURCE: extract from *Tragedy and Melodrama: Versions of Experience* (Seattle and London, 1968), pp. 38–40.

NOTE

1. It is interesting that Synge's *Deirdre of the Sorrows*, which has tinges of the tragic, is less well-known than *Riders to the Sea*. In the basic structure of the play, the lovers Deirdre and Naisi are the 'victims' of Conchubor the

King, and all of them are victims of 'fate', which has been voiced in prophecies. In dramatizing the legend, however, Synge makes the lovers act so as to assist a fate that technically they could avoid. When, after a seven-year idyl in flight, they return into the power of Conchubor, they are not simply tricked. There is even some complexity in their motives. Yet a new 'victim motif' enters into Deirdre's decision to return: life seems a 'disaster', leading to the loss of beauty and love. She cannot bear reality (the *sic transit* of all experience), she pities herself, and the sentimental intrudes – the danger in all literature of disaster. In Act III there is a recovery: Deirdre quarrels with Naisi before his death, and after his death she feels not only self-pity but guilt. Thus disaster becomes infused with the tragic: unhappiness has not merely 'happened to' them. On the other hand, this tragic is limited: like Othello, Deirdre can understand herself and her guilt only up to a point. In several lesser matters there is a remarkable parallel between Deirdre's last minutes and Othello's: Deirdre speaks of the glories of her career, reveals a hidden knife, uses the word *pitiful* twice in her final speech, stabs herself, and falls on the body of her lover.

Synge does not characteristically lean toward the 'drama of the victim'. *The Tinker's Wedding*, in which a priest refuses to marry Michael Byrne and Sarah Casey because they do not pay him enough, might easily have been given a structure very popular in modern times: the 'outsiders' victimized by 'institutions'. Synge treats the situation with comic detachment; rascality appears on both sides, and a comfortable compromise is achieved: if Michael and Sarah do not get all they have coming to them by way of ecclesiastical blessing, they manage the priest with sufficient agility and resourcefulness to ward off all they have coming to them by way of punishment for misdeeds. In *The Well of the Saints* Martin and Mary Doul might have been treated as 'victims' of blindness; or of well-meaning people who led them to a miraculous cure which would result only in disillusionment when certain facts of life were seen for the first time; or, in a different structure, as victims of a false cure which would be followed by the double disaster of a return to unwanted blindness. Synge skilfully evades these sentimental traps. Given a second chance to see, Martin and Mary choose blindness as the lesser evil, a choice which is left ambiguous – as the love of illusion, or as the hard adjustment to reality. Forty years later, dramatizing a similar theme in *The Iceman Cometh*, O'Neill omitted the ambiguity.

It is clear, then, that Synge could take situations in which human beings might be considered simply as victims of disaster and could see them in the broader perspectives of comedy or tragedy. But of all his plays (I exclude *Playboy of the Western World*) the best known is *Riders to the Sea*, which offers little more than the plain disaster. Applying the Aristotelian criterion of size, Joyce thought the work too short to be a tragedy, but called it the work of a 'tragic poet'. See Richard Ellmann, *James Joyce* (New York, 1959), p. 454.

Denis Johnston 'Orestean Dilemma' (1965)

... There are still a few old people on the Aran Islands who remember Synge, and many more who are prepared to repeat what they heard about him from their elders. Probably the most significant tribute that can be paid to his memory is the fact that on the whole they speak well of him – which is more than can be said for another visitor, Robert Flaherty, the film director, whose sentimental enthusiasms for everything about the islanders would appear at first blush to be more flattering to the ego than Synge's sardonic understanding. But however flattering it may seem, no community enjoys being pressed to assume the clothes and practices of fifty years ago for the purpose of making it seem more picturesque than it is today. Aran men do not wear funny tam-o-shanters, nor attempt to harpoon sunfish, nor fish off the top of the cliffs of Dun Aengus, and they see no point – apart from a financial one – in pretending that they do. On the other hand, *Riders to the Sea* may not be quite the sort of play that a man from Kilmurvy would write about his family, but there are many things in it that he understands. Above all, he appreciates the fact that it does not insist that he is picturesque.

The Greek analogy is legitimate here. *Riders to the Sea* has a classical unity and a completeness that makes one aware of the fact that in a sense it has ended before it begins. What happens is inevitable, and in this fact resides the real nub of its tragedy. There is no need for us to make up our minds whether or not we like the doomed Bartley, or even whether we are at all sorry for his predecessor, Michael, whose clothes are laid out on the table. It is not Bartley's death over which we grieve, nor even the death of Man. Everybody must die sooner or later – a fact which, as a rule, is a matter for congratulation rather than the reverse. 'Sooner or later' is the operative part of the statement here, and the pity of the play is that in this community the young tend to go before the old.

In the big world, says Maurya, the old people do be leaving things after them for their sons and children, but in this place it is the young men do be leaving things behind for them that do be old.

74

Riders is probably the most frequently performed of all Synge's plays – principally by amateurs, and most frequently of all in schools and colleges. It appears to present no difficulties in casting, and the sentiments to which it gives voice do not seem to offer any obvious problems either in interpretation or direction. That it does not usually manage to convey the required sensation of catharsis but merely one of depression is probably owing to the fact that both these impressions are wrong – usually as wrong as the costuming.

Riders to the Sea is not a play about a tiresome community that insists on going on with its fishing in spite of inadequate equipment and a continuing disregard for the weather reports. It is true that one son after another gets drowned, and it is not difficult to experience a certain mild irritation with Bartley – the baby of the family – who continues to wave aside all warnings, until he finishes up precisely where one would expect to find him – laid out on the table. And then one has to put up with an outburst of passionate mourning with which the performance usually ends. Without a suggestion of suspense, or some illumination of character or motivation, it is usually a pleasure when it is over. And one asks oneself how can such an expression of the obvious be put in the category of the great – except as some formal gesture of respect for peasants, for Ireland, and for Synge?

The point is, of course, that *Riders to the Sea* is a much better play than this kind of treatment suggests, and is far from easy either to cast or to perform. A superficial production of the type that has been mentioned has nothing to do with the classical form, but makes it instead into an inadequate Faust story, in which the victim goes to his predicted fate without ever having had an evening of love in return for his pains. On this basis, it would be a very much better play if Bartley were not going to the mainland to sell horses but to savour the stews of that sophisticated Babylon, the city of Galway. This would certainly give it something of the pious Christian touch that, prior to Goethe, was a necessity to any Faust story. If the production suggests that a matter of free choice is involved, and that Bartley goes on in spite of the warnings that a more sensible son would observe, it can be nothing but a Faust story. Yet whoever heard of a Faust who barters his future to attend a horse fair?

But *Riders to the Sea* is neither pious nor basically Christian. It is Orestean, and in the true Greek tradition, where no moral choice at all is offered to the characters. The sea – not the Gods – is the source of the law in this play, and there is no escape from it. The play is not trying to tell us how sad it is to have a son drowned – especially if he happens to be the last. We might be expected to know this already, and no play, classical or otherwise, can be great if it merely tells us something that we have expected from the start, without even an element of surprise in the telling.

What the play does tell us is the effect of the inevitable on these people, and what, if anything, man's answer to the Gods should be. In order to appreciate the point of the last two pages it is necessary to understand two or three unmelodramatic and very Synge-like assumptions: first, that there is no moral element whatever involved in these people pursuing the life that is theirs, whether or not it must end in death. All life ends in death, and one does not say to a dying man, 'There you are, now. This is what you get for having been born. I told you so, but you wouldn't listen'. This is a correct Faust conclusion – and it is a fatuous one without an afterlife in either heaven or hell. But nobody has any data on Bartley's final destination. The play is about him being drowned – not about his character. So it is clearly the gods whom we are up against – not a moral judgement.

The dilemma is that of Orestes, who by the law of life is bound to avenge his father. But by the law of life he must not kill his mother. What is he to do, except protest against the law of life?

So, also, Bartley must go down to the sea, and if in doing so he meets his end, there is no element of 'I told you so' about it. His mother must accept the situation. But there is an answer that she may give, an answer that is the point of the play.

They're all gone now [she says], and there isn't anything more that the sea can do to me ... I'll have no call now to be crying and praying when the wind breaks from the south, and you can hear the surf is in the east, and the surf is in the west, making a great stir with the two noises, and they hitting one on the other. I'll have no call now to be going down and getting Holy Water in the dark nights after Samhain, and I won't care what way the sea is when the other women will be keening ... it's a great rest I'll have now, and it's time, surely. It's a great rest I'll have now, and great sleeping in the long nights after Samhain, if it's only a bit of wet flour we do have to eat, and maybe a fish that would be stinking.

These expressions of human dignity under the buffetings of life are not wails of anguish, nor are they even projections of the stoicism of Job. They are man's answer to Heaven, and should be played as such. They give tongue to much the same idea that is to be found in a minor key in *Waiting for Godot*, where Vladimir protests.

> . . . we are blessed in this, that we happen to know the answer. Yes, in this immense confusion one thing alone is clear. We are waiting for Godot to come – or for night to fall. We have kept our appointment and that's an end to that. We are not saints, but we have kept our appointment. How many people can boast as much?

This is a universal answer, the significance of which we are finding extremely pertinent since the coming of the Atomic Age. Yet here it is expressed in 1903. But there is also a more special element that Synge dramatizes in the course of the play which also contains great theatrical possibilities. Bartley is drowned, but this is not by chance. He does not fall casually into the water, nor does he go down with some ship. It is the rearing of the horse behind that knocks him off the cliff. And who is riding on the rearmost horse? The ghost of his brother Michael.

Here we notice another important element of the folk attitude toward the dead themselves. In some ways it resembles the popular attitude toward the fairies that is so vividly underlined in *The Land of Heart's Desire*. In Irish eyes the fairies are not Shakespearean or Gilbertean creatures,

> Tripping hither, tripping thither,
> Nobody knows why or whither.

They are malevolent beings who steal children away with specious promises of better times. So, too, the dead want company. It is the ghostly Michael who is the killer of his younger brother – for reasons that lie deep in the Irish psychology, and are the basis of a universal fear of the dead. Count Dracula presents us with a vulgarized version of the same idea; but debased or not, the story is the same: in the half-world of the grave, there is a host of conjured spirits who would, if they could, make us like themselves.

That the dead are not to be trusted is an idea to be found even in that most sinister of spiritualistic farces – *Blithe Spirit* by Noel Coward. In Synge's play the sea is the executioner, but the horses make the occasion – the horses that must be sold at the fair but that carry the dead no less than the living. Herein we find that union of causation and denouement that is the sure sign of a well-constructed play. . . .

SOURCE: extract from *John Millington Synge* (New York, 1965), 18–22.

Donna Gerstenberger   'Riders to the Sea: The Whole Fabric'   (1964)

... The three women in the play, who are reminiscent of the three Fates of mythology, are an analogy ironic and meaningful in their *inability* to control; but Synge makes his comment effective precisely because he does not insist upon it. It is a parallel which, like many factors in the play, operates without an insistence upon a conscious awareness on the part of the audience. The three women can only endure, await the deprivation and loss which is their lot at the edge of the sea. Nevertheless, the play opens with Cathleen at the spinning wheel, spinning rapidly, as Nora brings in the shirt and stocking found on a drowned man. The clothing is identified as that belonging to their brother Michael, for Nora had dropped four stitches in the knitting of his stocking. The presence of the spinning woman and the attention given to the dropped stitches recalls the classical analogue in a persistent way throughout the play. The pattern of fate is being spun and woven as inexorably in *Riders to the Sea* as in any Classical tragedy, and Synge has provided the dramatic symbol, the stage equivalent, which is inevitable, natural and right. In the same unobtrusive manner, we have the cutting of the knot on the bundle of clothing brought from the sea. 'Give me a knife, Nora; the string's perished with the salt water, and there's a black knot on it you wouldn't loosen in a week.' The shadows of Clotho, Lachesis, and Atropos quietly rise behind the figures of Synge's fate-ridden women.

Synge's symbolism is not only Classical in origin, it is also specifically Christian in its evocation. The source of the vision that Maurya sees of the drowned Michael riding behind the son soon to die may be found in *The Aran Islands* in a story about an accident in loading horses on a hooker; in it an old woman saw her drowned son riding on one of the horses, which was caught by a young man who was, then, himself drowned in the sea. Like almost everything in *Riders to the Sea*, the raw material for this incident is present in *The Aran Islands*, but in the prose work Synge presents an unimpassioned telling which is unified, focused and given wider context for the purposes of his dramatic recreation. In Maurya's vision of

78

Bartley on the red mare, followed on the grey pony by Michael, already nine days drowned in the far north, Synge uses the Aran material to invoke wider echoes for his audience – those of the horsemen of the Book of Revelation: 'And I looked, and behold a pale horse; and his name that sat on him was Death'.

Bartley's death is for Maurya at this moment an accomplished fact, and she withholds from him the loaf which she has taken to the spring well to give him. Again, and very importantly, there is no insistence by Synge upon the pattern of meaning which is being worked out on a symbolic level, but it is operative, all the more effectively because of its inevitability on a naturalistic level. The bread is the bread of life – 'And it's destroyed he'll be going till dark night, and he after eating nothing since the sun went up, – on any level one may choose. And it is, further, the pathetic attempt of the cottage kitchen to comfort and sustain the riders to the sea – the hopeless attempt of the small world to reach into the large.

The holy water which Maurya sprinkles over Bartley's dead body and over Michael's clothes out of the sea invokes Christian symbolism placed in as ironic a context by the play as the presentation of the three Fates. The drops of holy water are themselves pathetic reminders of the implacable appetite of the waters of the sea and of the meaningless reassurance of the young priest that 'the Almighty God won't leave her destitute with no son living'. There are no sons left, and Maurya's turning of the empty cup 'mouth downwards on the table' enforces the resignation of her words: 'They're all gone now, and there isn't anything more the sea can do to me'.

Water has become, in the course of the play, perversely identified with death, not with life or regeneration. Maurya's failure to give Bartley blessing and bread occurs by the spring well, the source of lifegiving water, as opposed to the life-depriving waters of the sea, and the drops of holy water, within the context Synge has set for his play, become ironic reminders of man's frail hopes. The desolation is reminiscent of the early scene Synge draws in *The Aran Islands*, with the lonely stone crosses standing against the torrents of grey water, pitifully invoking 'a prayer for the soul of the person they commemorated', but it is a desolation particularized, given embodiment upon the stage, even in the moment Maurya reaches out with her prayer to include humanity: 'and may He have mercy on my soul, Nora, and on the soul of every one is left living in the world'. . . .

A comparison of *Riders to the Sea* with *Blood Wedding*, a consciously poetic drama by the Spanish poet García Lorca, underscores the poetic nature of Synge's play. *Blood Wedding* invites comparison, for it is, like *Riders to the Sea*, a folk tragedy and a tragedy of fate. It is also, however, a play which, like *Riders to the Sea*, transcends its origin in folk tragedy to make a large universal statement. The situations are similar also; in both plays there is the death of a male line as the result of the unyielding demands of fate, although the Lorca play (written thirty years after *Riders to the Sea*) is more complex and not so single in its effect as the Synge play, a complexity which is reflected in the multiplicity of theatrical techniques and poetic devices which Lorca uses in his tragedy of three acts and seven scenes. Yet the effect is the same as that of the one-act, one-scene play by Synge, and the conclusions of the two plays have a similar quality. In both plays the women endure; the necessary demands of life and manhood have caused the death of the men of the families in the irresistible working out of a struggle begun long before the opening curtain of either play. The neighbours are used in both plays to establish the community implications of the tragedies; and Lorca, who uses colours as persistently for symbolic meaning as Synge in *Riders to the Sea*, opens his final scene with two girls winding a red skein, an effect which serves the same comment as the similar symbolic elements in the Synge play. . . .

SOURCE: *John Millington Synge* (New York, 1964), 46–8, 51–2.

Errol Durbach Synge's Tragic Vision of the Old Mother and the Sea (1972)

Tragedy is remarkably economical in its exploitation of great visual archetypes – those stark icons which radiate behind the tragic action and illuminate the universal agony within the private grief. The literature of Western Christianity has, indeed, given dramatic expression to so few images of visual intensity that the tragedian, working within the limited imagistic range of the tradition, is often obliged to exploit an iconographical situation which has already passed into the repertory stock of all drama; and to make it radiate his particular tragic vision is, of course, the measure of his genius.

Of all such icons, the most poignant is, perhaps, that of the *Pièta* – the image of the sorrowing Mary mourning her dead Son – an icon so insistent and iterative as almost to create something of a sub-genre in modern tragedy. One thinks, most notably, of Mrs Alving torn in an agony of indecision as she confronts the raving Osvald; of the soundless cry of Mother Courage as the body of Swiss Cheese is carried onstage; of the tragic dignity of the Bridegroom's mother in Lorca's *Blood Wedding*; and, above all, of Maurya's grief in *Riders to the Sea* which extends the ritual of mourning beyond the death of one son and five more to encompass all sons of all mothers. But while the prototypical *Pièta* may be poignant and deeply moving, it is not inherently tragic. There is no conflict, no crisis. The Virgin neither precipitates the death of her Son, nor does she battle to save Him. For that which makes the sorrowing mother an essentially tragic figure is her implication – whether witting or unwitting – in the death of her child, an implication which makes the tragedy of mothers and their sons an ironic variation, as well, upon the archetypal *Kindermord*. The power of maternal love must be shown in conflict with an opposing force of equal magnitude and strength, as intense an element in the mother's being as her love, and catastrophically destructive of it. Trapped in the mesh of irreconcilable demands generated by her own intellectual, moral or passionate nature, the sorrowing mother can do little more than cry out against the implacability of fate and the Gods, or else accept her predicament as the paradigm of all tragic suffering. Mrs Alving, caught between her love and the need to conceal the rot within the Alving heritage, destroys her child as a result; and she exorcises the ghosts of her dead tradition only to find herself ensnared, once again, between the need to save her son from his heritage and the demands to her new-found freedom to help him to die. Mother Courage, to enable her children to live, ironically acquiesces in a code of greedy bourgeois mercantilism which systematically destroys them all. The mother in *Blood Wedding*, torn between devotion and the need to avenge her family's ancestral honour, consigns her only son to his inevitable death. In each case the tragedy derives from this collision within the protagonist of intense maternal love and her own firmly held moral values; and the peculiar nature of the collision determines the dramatist's tragic vision.

Synge's relationship to this tradition seems, in many respects, perfectly apparent. Not only does Maurya's name in itself suggest the prototypical Mary, but the splendidly poetic evocation of the *Pièta* in the final moments of the play – those scattered images of boards and nails and clothes and the 'broken' mother, loosened from their original content and reassembled in a wholly naturalistic idiom – makes the Aran Island cottage the site of universal mourning as the prayer for mercy finally embraces all mankind. But to see Maurya as no more than the archetypal Mother of Mercy is to deny her tragic potential. Indeed, a fairly representative view of *Riders to the Sea* as pathetic rather than tragic is expressed by Raymond Williams, who quotes from Yeats with evident approval:

Passive suffering is not a theme for poetry. In all the great tragedies, tragedy is a joy to the man who dies; in Greece the tragic chorus danced. When man has withdrawn into the quicksilver at the back of the mirror no great event becomes luminous in his mind . . . some blunderer has driven his car on to the wrong side of the road – that is all.

'In *Riders to the Sea*', Williams continues, 'the people are simply victims; the acceptance is not whole, but rather a weary resignation.'[1] It is all too tempting to see Maurya's suffering as a form of pathetic passivity, a weary resignation; for built into her struggle against the sea is an almost fatalistic sense of predetermined failure, so powerful an awareness of inevitable defeat that a mother's blessing or the gift of bread become no more than a series of unnecessary and ineffective gestures. Like her prototype, Maurya seems never to battle actively against the force that devastates her menfolk, never to resist its inevitability. But in tragedy, as Arthur Miller suggests, the tragic sufferer must at least conceive of the possibility of victory:

Where pathos rules [he says], where pathos is finally derived, a character has fought a battle he could not possibly have won. The pathetic is achieved when the protagonist is, by virtue of his witlessness, his insensitivity, of the very air he gives off, incapable of grappling with a much superior force.[2]

In many ways Maurya would seem to fit this pattern of the pathetic figure, a protagonist so drastically reduced as a viable dramatic persona and so manifestly impotent against the elemental powers that, for many critics, the central figure of the play appears to be less the sorrowing mother than her antagonist, the sea.[3]

What I should like to do in this paper is to shift the focus of

attention back to Maurya and offer a possible reading of the play as
a delicately wrought, perfectly constructed tragedy; and, in so doing,
I shall have to demonstrate, in terms of the stringent form of the
tragic *Pièta* which I have defined, Maurya's implication in the death
of her sons which converts pathos into a tragic vision of existence. I
shall also have to argue that Maurya, like Mrs Alving and Mother
Courage and the Bridegroom's mother, does more than merely
oppose some external antagonist. She becomes, in effect, her own
antagonist, embodying within her maternal function that universal
principle of destruction suggested through the pervasive symbolism
of the sea. This is not to say that Maurya *is* the sea, but to imply that
she functions as a visual presence through which the dramatist
articulates the invisible – that rhythm of the natural world, that
double movement towards both life and death of which the sea is the
most powerful metaphor in the drama. What we find in Maurya, it
seems to me, is the catastrophic collision between Maternity and
Necessity, and, ultimately, a quiet recognition that these two
opposing elements are in fact identical.

To begin, then, where any consideration of so highly symbolic a
play must begin – with the physical description of the setting:

> An island off the West of Ireland. Cottage kitchen, with nets, oilskins,
> spinning-wheel, some new boards standing by the wall, etc.[4]

The greatness of Synge, like that of Ibsen, derives partly from his
ability to convert the local and the realistic into visual metaphors of
the universal and the metaphysical. The stage-set, indeed, is an
exact replica of the kitchen which Synge describes in a passage from
The Aran Islands.

> The kitchen itself, where I will spend most of my time, is full of beauty and
> distinction. . . . Many sorts of fishing tackle, and the nets and oilskins of the
> men, are hung upon the walls or among the open rafters; . . . . Every article
> on these islands has an almost personal character, . . . and being made from
> materials that are common here, yet to some extent peculiar to the island,
> they seem to exist as a natural link between the people and the world that is
> about them –[5]

a description which in its concluding comment anticipates Synge's
dramatic realization of the macrocosmic implication in the micro-
cosmic object which transforms the stage-set of *Riders to the Sea* into
an image of Necessity.

Nets and oilskins; boards; a spinning-wheel. All the paraphernalia of peasant life, so thoroughly domestic on one level of meaning, metamorphose as the play progresses into pure 'poetry of the theatre' – dramatic symbols which, as T. R. Henn describes it, 'dissolve, coalesce, combine in tension or opposition, to give depth or contrapuntal irony'[6] to the mechanics of an apparently simple theme. The nets and oilskins, firstly, are the primary means of making at least one aspect of the sea palpable and concrete on the stage – the sea as the source of livelihood for the islanders, that rich and teeming womb which sustains life and compensates with fish and kelp for the barrenness of the rocky Aran earth.[7] Our immediate impression of the play's unseen protagonist is that of nourisher and provider; and part of the tension and 'contrapuntal irony' of the scene derives from the opposing presence of the white coffin-boards – a constant visual reminder not only of death, but of the infertile, treeless soil of the island, boards which have to be imported from Connemara to be on hand whenever needed for a burial.[8] What we have, in effect, are two carefully juxtaposed and almost conventional images of Life and Death which in their coalescence create an entirely different thematic idea. Man, in this world of barren soil, is inevitably driven to live off the teeming water; and Cathleen's remark – 'It's the life of a young man to be going on the sea' – carries with it the undertones of fatal Necessity. There is, as she well knows, no alternative for man but to live off the seemingly generous water which sooner or later will claim him as a victim.

There is, then, a form of opposition and coalescence not only between symbols, but even within a single symbol. For the nets clearly perform a counter-function, as well, to their primary connotation. Draped along the walls and rafters of the cottage, they evoke an insidious atmosphere of entrapment – a condition from which, in terms of the play's major theme, there can be no escape. Man, consigned to live off the sea, is by virtue of this fact destined to die by it. That which sustains life is, at the same time, a death-dealer. And the arbitrary rhythm of man's precarious existence in this world is the rhythm of the sea.

The spinning-wheel, however, is the first major piece of stage-property which is actually integrated into the action of the play:

[*Cathleen ... finishes kneading cake, and puts it down in the pot oven by the fire, then wipes her hands and begins to spin at the wheel. ... Nora comes in softly and takes a bundle from under her shawl.*]
CATHLEEN: [*Spinning the wheel rapidly.*] What is it you have?

NORA: The young priest is after bringing them. It's a shirt and a plain stocking were got off a drowned man in Donegal.
[*Cathleen stops her wheel with a sudden movement and leans out to listen.*][9]

The whirring of the wheel and its sudden silence generate an ominous sense of tension which is intensified by the two women, later in the play, as they search for signs of their drowned brother's identity in the clothing. The knot holding the bundle together is cut with a knife, the stitches of the stocking are meticulously counted, and the death-by-drowning of Michael is established with uncanny preciseness:

NORA: It's the second one of the third pair I knitted, and I put up three-score stitches, and I dropped four of them. ... And isn't it a pitiful thing when there is nothing left of a man who was a great rower and fisher but a bit of an old shirt and plain stocking?[10]

The 'thin-spun life' of the fated Aran fisherman is rendered all the more poignant when Maurya returns after her vision of one dead and one doomed son and Cathleen returns to her spinning, breaking off again only to look for the last time at Bartley riding the red mare over the headland.

The almost unobtrusive domestic image of the spinning women, as with all the other domestic images, helps to illuminate that other dimension of the drama in which the wheel and the weaving form part of an inexorable circle of fate slowly establishing itself as a ritualistic pattern in the formal structure of the play. 'The shadows of Clotho, Lachesis and Atropos', as Donna Gerstenberger suggests, 'quietly rise behind the figures of Synge's fate-ridden women.'[11] As women, they embody, like the sea, the principle of fate, the rhythm of destiny, the cycle of birth and inevitable death; and although one of the women is rendered effete by the destruction of all her menfolk, two daughters remain to ensure the eternal perpetuation of this cycle. Nets and wheels and boards are essential parts of the infernal machinery of the play; and it is in this sense, it seems to me, that the domestic articles of the Aran Islands exist as 'a natural link between the people and the world that is about them'.

The inclusiveness of Synge's tragic vision derives from his ability to contemplate the antinomies of existence and reconcile them by a dignified acceptance of their interrelationship as elements in a universal process, to look upon the desolation of this reality without hysteria, and to perceive a natural order in all things which finds its counterpart in the experiences of the tragic sufferer. Maurya, when the play opens, resolutely resists any recognition of the tragic axiom with which she concludes the drama – that calm acceptance of necessity and death's inevitability: 'No man at all can be living forever, and we must be satisfied'. For nine days she has been 'crying and keening, and making great sorrow in the house' for the loss of Michael; and on the tenth day she struggles vainly against Necessity for the life of her last son, feebly opposing the inevitability of which she is already assured:

> MAURYA: It's hard set we'll be surely the day you're drowned with the rest. What way will I live and the girls with me, and I an old woman looking for the grave? ... [*Turning round to the fire, and putting her shawl over her head.*] Isn't it a hard and cruel man won't hear a word from an old woman, and she holding him from the sea?
> CATHLEEN: It's the life of a young man to be going on the sea, and who would listen to an old woman with one thing and she saying it over?[12]

The querulous resistance of the old woman, who has already foreseen in the omens of wind and stars the death of her son, is countered by the daughter's defence of Bartley's apparent callousness. Cruelty and harshness are uncharitable interpretations of men whose motives are governed by inflexible circumstances. But this is clearly the last emotional appeal of a mother who has already covered her head with the cloth of mourning before the son departs, and cries out in full knowledge of his fate as he leaves:

God spare us, and we'll not see him again. He's gone now, and when the black night is falling I'll have no son left me in the world ... [*Maurya takes up the tongs and begins raking the fire aimlessly without looking around.*][13]

The ritual of mourning is completed as Maurya rocks herself among the ashes of the scattered fire, the shawl over her head; and it is with a sense of predetermined defeat and reluctance that she allows herself to be persuaded to intercept Bartley on his way with the redemptive and restorative gifts of blessing and bread.

Once again, the antinomial imagery establishes itself as a visual element in the drama as the old woman sets out with the staff of life in one hand and the staff of death, the drowned Michael's stick, in the other. And at the spring well, the source of life and vitality, the prophetic vision of death upon the pale horse renders her incapable of restoring life to her doomed son. The mother, herself the source of life, womblike as the sea, unwittingly consigns her lastborn to his drowning, powerless to resist the operation of a universe in which the very fact of birth consigns all living to inevitable death. What the course of events serves to impress upon Maurya is her own implication in universal process, in the double ritual of birth and death which is an ineluctable contingency of motherhood. For this is the nature of her revelation at the spring well – not that of death alone, but of death as an inextricable element in the whole cycle of life:

> MAURYA: [*Starts so that her shawl falls back from her head and shows her white tossed hair* . . .] I've seen the fearfullest thing any person has seen since the day Bride Dara seen the dead man with the child in his arms . . . I went down to the spring well, and I stood there saying a prayer to myself. Then Bartley came along, and he riding on the red mare with the grey pony behind him. [*She puts up her hands, as if to hide something from her eyes.*] The Son of God spare us, Nora! . . . I looked up then, and I crying, at the grey pony, and there was Michael upon it. . . .[14]

The first stage direction is an important one. Although the old woman returns shaken and keening, she slowly begins coming to terms with the nature of what she has seen, and its implications. Her shawl is jerked from her head, and from that moment her mourning and her keening cease, resumed now by the daughters and the chorus of women. But the gesture that casts the shawl aside does more than change the key of Maurya's grief from the minor one of weak and regretful lamentation to the major key of fearful revelation and a dignified acceptance of necessity – it also reveals that one concrete visual correlation of the old woman with the sea: her white, tossed hair. If, like the sea, she is the womb of life, she is also, like the sea, the natural source of her children's death as well. The whiteness of death, of the coffin boards, of the surf and the rocks against which Bartley is dashed are all subsumed in the old woman's spray-like hair as she confronts, for the first time in the drama, the interrelationship of life and death as a single process. Dead men bear living children in their arms and the grey spectre of doom runs behind the red pony of youthful strength and vitality. To accept this as a vision of existence is to acknowledge the principle of necessity, to emerge from a state of submissive defeat in the face of an overwhelming force to one of dignity and triumph in confronting reality with recourse to neither pathos nor hysteria.

The entire play moves, it would seem, towards a synthetic vision of existence in which images of life and death intermingle in a series of diverse variations. The dead are clothed in fresh garments, while the living wear the clothes of the dead; bread baked for the doomed man is finally eaten by those who fashion his coffin; the halter for the red horse of vitality is the same rope needed to lower the coffin into the grave; and the pain occasioned by the mother's loss of her children calls naturally to mind the pain of bearing them:

> MAURYA: I've had a husband, and a husband's father, and six sons in this house – six fine men, though it was a hard birth I had with every one of them and they coming into the world – and some of them were found and some of them were not found, but they're gone now the lot of them. . . .[15]

And then begins Maurya's long elegaic account of the death of son after son, the fourth corpse carried home while the last child is still a baby on the knee:

> I was sitting here with Bartley, and he a baby lying on my two knees, and I seen two women, and three women, and four women coming in, and they crossing themselves and not saying a word. I looked out then, and there were men coming after them, and they holding a thing in the half of a red sail, and water dripping out of it. . . .[16]

As she speaks, the cyclical pattern of fate begins to establish itself again, that sense of inexorable repetition in which the central ritual of the play is uttered and enacted simultaneously. For her words are underscored by the action which they describe, the past asserting its eternal presence as the chorus of keening women drift onstage followed by the men with the sail-enshrouded body of Bartley. The baby on the knee becomes, as time compresses, the corpse on the table. And yet, once again, the rituals of birth and death seem almost indistinguishably superimposed upon each other. The drab grey stage suddenly becomes vibrant with the colour of life as the keening women kneel in front of the table with their red petticoats over their heads – the mourning and the bright colour combining in ironic tension to create the most impressive visual moment in the play: the shape on the plank, the water dripping from it, the scrap of red sail covering it, the surrounding impression of redness, the moaning women, and the pain-stricken mother – an image, perhaps, of some primitive sacrificial ritual, the iconographical *Pièta*. But the same elements which constitute the rites of death may also constitute, by a slight shift of the visual angle, the rites of childbirth as well.

The scene encompasses all aspects of the maternal function in a complex organic unity; and facing the reality of this function as an aspect of universal process, Maurya experiences a sense of almost triumphant freedom. Nine days of keening have culminated in the tenth day of acceptance, followed by that curious sense of satisfaction which the contemplation of tragic reality provides for the sufferer. Once again Maurya finds herself able to bless, and the words that choked in her throat at the spring well are finally spoken as the blessing of the Universal Mother upon all her sons:

They're all together this time, and the end is come. May the Almighty God have mercy on Bartley's soul, and on Michael's soul, and on the souls of Sheamus and Patch, and Stephen and Shawn [*bending her head*]; and may He have mercy on my soul, Nora, and on the soul of every one is left living in the world.[17]

All men are riders to the same unappeasable sea; and to accept Maurya's blessing is to share in the tragic experience of the play – an experience not of 'the futility of human life,'[18] but of the inevitability of death which comes to all. And if the final, muted line of the play – 'No man at all can be living for ever, and we must be satisfied' – seems too axiomatic, almost, for utterance, the great ingenuity of dramatic craftsmanship which gives it force and substance, and the splendour of Maurya's growth towards a confrontation of this Necessity make *Riders to the Sea* a perfectly conceived and exquisitely wrought tragedy of the Sorrowing Mother and her fated sons.

SOURCE: *Modern Drama*, 14 (February 1972), 363–72.

NOTES

1. Raymond Williams, *Drama from Ibsen to Eliot* (Harmondsworth, 1964), p. 177.
2. Arthur Miller, 'Tragedy and the Common Man,' reprinted in *The Play and Reader*, eds John, Bierman and Hart (Englewood Cliffs, N.J., 1966), p. 232.
3. Cf. Thomas F. Van Laan, 'Form as Agent in Synge's *Riders to the Sea*', *Drama Survey*, Vol. 3, no. 3, Feb. 1964, p. 363. 'It is this focus upon a protagonist mightier than the human, this attempt to glimpse things vaster than the individual that constitutes the primary reason for the suppression of personality in *Riders to the Sea*. By sacrificing the development of character Synge makes the antagonist the central figure of the play.'

4. J. M. Synge, *Plays, Poems and Prose* (London, 1959), p. 29. All quotations from Synge derive from this edition.

5. Ibid., p. 254.

6. T. R. Henn, ed., *Riders to the Sea* and *In the Shadow of the Glen* (London, 1961), p. 82.

7. Cf. 'The land is so poor that a field hardly produces more grain than is needed for seed the following year. . . .' *Aran Islands*, p. 282.

8. Cf. ' "She's nearly lost," said the old woman; "she won't be alive at all tomorrow morning. They have no boards to make her a coffin, and they'll want to borrow the boards that a man below has had this two year to bury his mother, and she still alive." ' *Aran Islands*, p. 297.

9. *Riders to the Sea*, p. 19.

10. Ibid., p. 25.

11. Donna Gerstenberger, *John Millington Synge* (New York, 1964), p. 47.

12. *Riders to the Sea*, p. 22.

13. Ibid.

14. Ibid., pp. 26, 27.

15. Ibid., p. 27.

16. Ibid., pp. 27–8.

17. Ibid., p. 30.

18. Cf. Van Laan, p. 360.

Sidney Poger Brecht's *Senora Carrar's Rifles* (*Die Gewehre Der Frau Carrar*) and Synge's *Riders to the Sea* (1984)

Bertolt Brecht's deviation from his dramatic theory in *Senora Carrar's Rifles* suggests the powerful influence of an outside source. Brecht acknowledges in a note that his play used an idea of Synge's (*'Unter Benutzung einer Idee von J. M. Synge'*), which could mean anything, such as, he used a suggestion by Synge which had never been developed enough for the stage, or, he based his play closely on Synge's play *Riders to the Sea*.[1] Johannes Kleinstück calls the connection vague, with only the incident when Juan's body is brought in copied directly. 'The rest is different from anything Synge could have thought or written as one might expect.'

Kleinstück argues that no one has ever challenged Brecht's assertion that he borrowed from Synge, and he argues that the similarities simply show how little the plays resemble each other.[2]

Brecht, however, borrows much more from *Riders to the Sea* for his own play than Kleinstück allows. The central figure of each play is a mother with a son whom she wishes to protect. The character of each mother's life is dominated or determined by a great outside impersonal force, one natural (the sea), one historical (the war). A particular irruption of that force into the lives portrayed kills the son and, through the finality of that act, provides a relief and resolution of the mother's doubts, fears and sorrows. In each play the son dies during the course of the action; in each play the mothers are surrounded by similar lesser characters such as the priest and the keening women, similar symbols, bread, for instance, carry thematic weight, and similar important actions, such as bearing in the son's body, take place. This bare resumé in itself suggests considerable indebtedness. An examination of the two plays may show us how far this indebtedness extends so we can see that, although Brecht did not follow Synge's spirit, he was influenced in important ways by *Riders to the Sea*.

During the 1930s, Bertolt Brecht turned from his ambitious early plays and the success of *The Threepenny Opera* to didactic plays or *lehrstueck*, plays to be put on by 'worker's choirs, amateur theater groups, school choirs and school orchestras'.[3] These plays would teach the members of their audience the right way to act by involving them in the production and as members of the panel of judges. In his most successful didactic piece *The Measures Taken*, for example, a group of five agitators sent on a mission into China is almost betrayed by the kindly and humane acts of one of their number. With his permission, they shoot him and throw his body into a chalk pit to remove all traces of his existence rather than be betrayed by further precipitate humane actions which he would not be able to suppress. This cantata of soloists and chorus represents the dilemma of an agent caught between the humanity of the individual and the necessities of history and the state. While it is an effective dramatic work, its primary purpose is to teach the audience what to do by having them issue the judgement. The agitators describe the murder of their comrade and their deposit of his body. The chorus balances the gains of revolution against the loss of one life:

And your work was successful
You have spread
The teaching of the classics
The ABC of communism:
To the ignorant, instructions about their situation
To the oppressed, class consciousness
And to the class conscious, the experience of revolution.
In yet another country the revolution advances
In another land the ranks of the fighters are joined
We agree to what you have done.[4]

This didacticism was a major part of Brecht's theory of epic or non-Aristotelian drama which has had so profound an effect on modern drama. But he stepped back from this kind of drama to write *Senora Carrar's Rifles*, which was first produced in October, 1937, in Paris, 'dedicated to the heroic fight for freedom of the Spanish people'.[5] Brecht's play is one of his most popular in terms of production, having had 54 separate productions in the German Democratic Republic alone between 1947–1967.[6] *Senora Carrar's Rifles* is Brecht's least epic play, having a traditional structure, a climax, straight prose dialogue, and an absence of stylization. Deviating from Brecht's dramatic theory, it seems a betrayal of what Brecht the dramatist was trying to achieve through the rest of his writings, both for the stage and about it. Or the play seems a potboiler, written under the pressure of events to serve a particular war as did the American movies produced during World War II which still light up the late-night television screens.

Brecht's idea is based on Synge's *Riders to the Sea*, a play about the complex relationships between the people of the Aran Islands and the sea with which they live. When the play begins Maurya has already lost her husband, her husband's father and four sons to the merciless sea: she has, she thinks, only two sons left, unaware that one of the two has already drowned and his clothing had been sent to the house to confirm the identity of the body. All these men lost their lives in order to maintain their family's existence: without their going to sea, the rest of the family would starve. Going to sea is what a man must do to feed his family as well as to fulfil himself. Going to sea is as inevitable as death, which often comes from the sea. Nature both gives and takes away. Bartley, her last son who is about to sail over to Galway for the horse fair and is knocked into the sea by his horse and drowned, is another of those who have been killed through nature and supernatural necessity, a necessity which is present throughout the play. This last death releases Maurya from her constant concern, and she is free of doubts, of listening for storms and signs of danger, for her care for her family is now no longer necessary. 'It's a great rest I'll have now, and great sleeping in the long nights after Samhain.' She calls on God to have mercy 'on the soul of everyone [who] is left living in the world'.

Riders to the Sea expresses an integrated view of peasant life which Synge gained from his periods of residence on the Aran Islands. This is a play, not of a single event, but of a continuous struggle. The play presents the seamless garment of time, the past extending into the present, which is responsible for much of the play's effect. The daughters, Cathleen and Nora, spin and cut the thread holding the bundle like two Greek fates cutting short Michael's life by confirming the identity of his body. But, if their actions in the play echo those of the Fates, their role in the play does not. They remain as part of the action, sorrowing for their brothers and providing for Maurya in her sorrow. But they see only the limits of that sorrow.

> NORA: [*in a whisper to Cathleen*]. She's quiet now and easy; but the day Michael was drowned you could hear her crying out from this to the spring well. It's fonder she was of Michael, and would any one have thought that?
> CATHLEEN: [*slowly and clearly*]. An old woman will soon be tired with anything she will do, and isn't it nine days herself is after crying and keening, and making great sorrow in the house?[7]

Maurya accepts finally because she has lost all those who could have been lost to the sea. Cathleen and Nora, however, cannot accept as she can, for they still have their own lives to live, their own husbands and sons who will set out to sea.

This rough summary of Synge's play provides a structure which Brecht borrowed. In Brecht's play there is at least a hint of the spinning and cutting of Cathleen and Nora in Senora Carrar's baking of bread, the sign of life. Nature, however, presents no threat; indeed, it provides an apparent refuge. If Juan can be kept fishing, his mother thinks, he can be kept safely out of the war. The rifles, hidden under the floorboards, can be used to protect the family if the war ever should come their way, but their being kept hidden is a sign that the family can be kept out of the war. But Juan is killed and, since the sea is calm and the night clear, there can be no doubt about the motives for the killing. The lamp from the boat can easily be seen from the window of the house and the fisherman who witnesses the

killing would have heard any challenge from the patrol boat or
Juan's cursing of the soldiers which might have called down their
wrath.

Into this scene, like the sea in Synge's play, comes the war, the
overwhelming force which destroys all before it. Senora Carrar has
lost her husband to the war. The neighbours whisper it is because
she encouraged him to go to the front that she now so vigilantly
protects her two sons. She bitterly accuses her husband of having
run away from life, like others who have run off to America. But the
children from the village taunt the boys with their cowardice
because they have not followed their father. Through the window
the children chant:

> Juan is chicken
> Scared to be hurt
> Hides from the war
> In Mamma's skirt.[8]

Juan's girl friend Manuela breaks off their relationship because he
does not come to the meetings and, with his neighbours, go off to the
front.

Teresa Carrar must meet three adversaries in her fight to keep her
sons at home: the wounded man, a worker (her brother) who has
come back from the front to secure the rifles and who is a great
arguer and propagandist and the teacher in the play, and the Padre
who along with Teresa Carrar suffers the brunt of the worker's
lectures. The wounded man comes to her for rebandaging his
wound. She is more generous in her ministrations than we might
expect, using a whole skirt out of her meagre store to bandage his
arm. She warns him that she has limits: she will have nothing left to
bandage his other arm. The wounded man laughs, promising more
care in the next war. This man represents those from the village who
have done what they all support; he has done so unthinkingly. Now
he is accepted back home to resume his earlier activities. This man
stands between Teresa Carrar and her brother, who has come back
from the front but must return to take up his duties once again.

The priest represents those who stay behind even though they
sympathize with the workers at the front. He takes care of the
children whose parents are away fighting, he shares everything with
his parish to keep its members functioning, but he declares himself
governed absolutely by the commandment: Thou shalt not kill. In

Riders to the Sea, Maurya depends on the young priest to stop
Bartley, but he has already declared that he would not do so,
shifting any responsibility for the results onto God: 'I won't stop
him,' he says to Nora, 'but let you not be afraid. Herself does be
saying prayers half through the night, and the Almighty God won't
leave her destitute ... with no son living'. His weak hope is not
enough to save Bartley as Brecht's priest's heroic but inconsequen-
tial efforts cannot save Spain.

The worker accuses the priest of praying to a God who isn't
listening. The priest prays for his daily bread but won't do anything
to break Franco's blockade which successfully keeps the bread from
getting through. By preaching that the workers shall not kill, the
priest disarms them for the struggle and Franco's forces kill them.
The priest, argues the worker, is thus a participant in the war, on the
side of Franco. Those who are not with us, the worker argues, are
against us.

The priest leaves in some confusion, which reflects Senora Carrar's
mood. He has not successfully upheld her position, as she expected
he would, that, if one withdraws from the action and goes peacefully
about her work, she will be spared. She still wants to believe this,
trying to keep both her sons at home until, when Juan's body is
brought in, she realizes that to remain at home is to fight on the
wrong side.

The worker has the last word. Unlike the wounded man, he will
go back to the fighting. He does not, like the priest, use beautiful
words to hide reality, but thinks clearly and realistically, like a
participant, not a spectator. Unlike his sister, he does not so
overvalue human life that he loses all other values in trying to
protect it. When her husband was killed, Teresa Carrar confessed
she wanted to hang herself, but the priest saved her. Since she now
helps Franco by not fighting or releasing her three rifles, her brother
declares, 'It'd be better if you'd hang yourself, Teresa'.

All these arguments, however, do not sway her. What causes her
conversion is not logic or truth but the death of her son. Maurya
gives in to the inevitable logic of a symbiotic life with the sea; Teresa
Carrar gives in to the brutality of a gratuitous killing. While the
worker and the fisherman discuss why Juan was killed, she, in her
new-found knowledge and insight, knows. He was killed because of
his shabby cap which marked him as a poor man. Now she has
changed to see things clearly and rationally. As Maurya is moved by

Bartley's death to acceptance and a noble passivity, Teresa Carrar is moved by Juan's death to defiance and revolution. Not only does she send her brother and her younger son to the front with the rifles, she herself accompanies them to fight against Franco.

Synge's play is powerful largely because it comes out of the lives of the people whom it describes. It comes out of a long religious, cultural and linguistic tradition. While the presence of death is overpowering, the beauty of ceremony and acceptance blend with it to create the play's texture. Its strength is also in its Aristotelian cathartic sense. We suffer with Maurya, about whom the play revolves, and we sympathize with her relief as well as acknowledge the truth of her final declaration: 'No man at all can be living forever, and we must be satisfied'. These are all of a piece. The inevitability of death receives a sanction through its closeness to the spiritual world. Maurya, who knows better than the priest and her daughters, declares herself past suffering; she will wait with patience for the end of her own life. Her daughters admire, but they cannot attain Maurya's noble acceptance; they still have their own lives to lead.

Brecht has changed Synge into a political figure; he wished to write what Synge might 'have written if he had been a communist or a social reformer',[9] almost as if Brecht thought that being a writer during the Irish literary renaissance made Synge automatically a member of the IRA. Although Brecht's play can be effective on the stage – Teresa Carrar's conversion because of her son's death after stubbornly upholding her arguments can be made impressive by the actress taking the part – yet that conversion seems almost accidental, not growing out of an inevitable fate. The didactic tone of the play may convince the audience to support the workers, yet the conversion does not come from logic, as in the *lehrstueck*, but from the impetus of a brutal murder. The symbols are there, the conversion is there, but the audience is left separated from the decision. The tone of the play and the arguments put forth by the worker militate against an emotional involvement as they pretend to a cool rationality but insist on that emotional climax.

In some ways Brecht's play seems old fashioned while Synge's does not. The life struggle in the Aran Islands is a real, ongoing and eternal struggle, summed up in the wisdom of Maurya's closing lines. Brecht's conclusion seems part of its own time. We have learned a great deal since the Spanish Civil War about revolution and about who can be trusted, and Brecht's conclusion does not ring true. A healthier feeling of scepticism about the Spanish Civil War – perhaps that of George Orwell's *Homage to Catalonia* – seems truer.

Perhaps the handling of bread in both plays is significant. Maurya, who has not blessed Bartley before his departure, is sent out by her daughters to meet him on the road, ritually blessing him, and give him the bread which they had baked for his journey. Disturbed by a vision, Maurya can neither bless Bartley nor give him the bread. She comes back to her house with the bread in her hands, to await the return of his body. Passive and suffering nobility mark the conclusion of the play.

Teresa Carrar has had bread baking in the oven throughout the play. When she goes off at the end to join the troops in place of her dead son, she rolls the bread in a cloth and takes it with her. She is forging a new communion. She does not accept as Maurya does, but she is moved to action. It is this difference between suffering and action which separates Synge's play from Brecht's but their similarities in development argue the depth of the influence of *Riders to the Sea* on *Senora Carrar's Rifles*.

SOURCE: *Canadian Journal of Irish Studies*, 10 (December 1984), 37–43.

NOTES

1. Johannes Kleinstück, 'Synge in Germany' in *A Centenary Tribute to John Millington Synge, 1871–1909: Sunshine and the Moon's Delight*, S. B. Bushrui, ed. (New York, 1972), p. 275.
2. Kleinstück, pp. 275–6.
3. Klaus Volker, *Brecht Chronicle* (New York, 1975), p. 57.
4. Bertolt Brecht, *The Measures Taken* from *The Jewish Wife and Other Short Plays*, translated by Eric Bentley (New York, 1965), p. 108.
5. Volker, p. 81.
6. Claude Hill, *Bertolt Brecht* (Boston, 1975), p. 89.
7. J. M. Synge, *Riders to the Sea* in *Collected Works* III, edited by Ann Saddlemyer (London, 1968), p. 25.
8. Bertolt Brecht, *The Guns of Carrar*, translated by George Tabori (New York, 1971), p. 11.
9. Kleinstück, p. 276.

PART THREE

The Well of the Saints

The Well of the Saints

Première: 4 February 1905, by the Irish National Theatre Society at the Abbey Theatre, Dublin; revived by the Abbey company on 14 May 1908 with a revised third act.

First published in a limited edition: *The Well of the Saints: A Play in Three Acts*, being Vol. I of the Abbey Theatre Series (London: A. H. Bullen; Dublin: The Abbey Theatre, 1905). The edition printed in *Plays of John M. Synge* (London: Allen & Unwin, 1932) was the first one to embody the version of the third act revised in 1908. The text printed in *Collected Works*, Vol. III (London: OUP, 1968) by Ann Saddlemyer notes manuscript and typescript drafts (262–74) and records alterations in Synge's copy of the first edition; she did not have access to the prompt-book or the accompanying typescript embodying the 1908 revisions, which are made use of in the separate edition of the play published in 1982 in the Irish Dramatic Texts series by Catholic University of America Press (Washington, D.C.) and Colin Smythe (Gerrards Cross, Bucks). The latter edition was edited with a long introduction and notes by Nicholas Grene, whose remarks on the textual provenance of this version may be found on pp. 26–8.

1. COMMENTS AND REVIEWS

I *Padraic Colum* (1926)

... He once talked to me about a medieval French farce that had suggested the plot of *The Well of the Saints* to him. In the farce two beggars accidentally run into the relics of a saint, and are cured of their blindness. They are disgusted, for the cure leads to the loss of their livelihood. ...

SOURCE: *The Road Round Ireland* (London & New York, 1926), 367.

II *W. B. Yeats* (1904)

... Mr Synge has written us a play in three acts called *The Well of Saints*, full, as few works of our time are, of temperament, and of a true and yet bizarre beauty. ...

SOURCE: programme note reprinted in *Plays and Controversies* (London, 1923), 84.

III *W. B. Yeats* (1905)

... When the Norwegian National movement began, its writers chose for their maxim, 'To understand the saga by the peasant and the peasant by the saga'. Ireland in our day has rediscovered the old heroic literature of Ireland, and she has rediscovered the imagination of the folk. My own preoccupation is more with the heroic legend than with the folk, but Lady Gregory in her *Spreading the News*, Mr Synge in his *Well of the Saints*, Mr Colum in *The Land*, Mr Boyle in *The Building Fund*, have been busy, much or little, with the folk and the folk-imagination.

Mr Synge alone has written of the peasant as he is to all the ages; of the folk-imagination as it has been shaped by centuries of life among fields or on fishing-grounds. His people talk a highly coloured musical language, and one never hears from them a thought that is of to-day and not of yesterday. ... Mr Synge is the most obviously individual of our writers. He alone has discovered a new kind of sarcasm, and it is this sarcasm that keeps him, and may long keep him, from general popularity. ...

SOURCE: programme note reprinted in *Plays and Controversies* (London, 1923), 140–2.

IV   *J. M. Synge*   (1905)

... I should be very glad to have it [*The Well of the Saints*] translated into German but – as you will see – it will not be easy to render adequately a great part of the dialogue which depends for its effect on the peculiar colour-quality of the dialect I have used. I imagine in the German 'Volkslieder' one would get a language that would be pretty nearly what is needed. ...

SOURCE: letter to Max Meyerfeld dated 26 May 1905.

V   *W. G. Fay*   (1935)

... And now the Abbey Theatre was launched on its voyage of fame. It was not a rich adventure. We had only a matter of forty pounds in cash in hand to keep us afloat, but, thanks to Miss Horniman, we were worthily housed and free from debt, and could fairly boast of being the only endowed theatre in the English-speaking world. We faced the future with confidence, not to say hardihood, and the measure of it was that for our very next production (February 1905) we trailed our coats in front of the Dublin public by presenting a full-length play by Synge. This was *The Well of the Saints*, in my opinion his best play. He gave himself a large enough canvas on which to paint the picture in his mind. He had felt what all writers of one-act plays must feel sooner or later, that the concentration demanded by a short play allows one to give only the headings and suggestions of what ought to be full scenes, if truthfully developed. As for the story, a great deal of research has gone in trying to find out the source of it; but to me this has always seemed to be a waste of time, though it may be interesting. All good dramatists have taken their plots from where they could find them. Shakespeare used Italian *novelle*; Wilde got the theme of *Lady Windermere's Fan* from *The Family Herald*; and Arnold Bennett, as he once told me, had a box full of old Spanish plays that he dipped into now and again when he was short of ideas. Whether the idea of *The Well of the Saints* came from *The Maid of Malines* or *Marianiela* is immaterial. In any case those who knew Synge knew that in his travels through the back mountains of Wicklow and Kerry, as well as during his sojourn in the Aran Islands, he had collected enough stories for many plays without having recourse to foreign soil.

When one is producing a difficult play like this it is not easy to remain objective, to see it from the point of view the audience will take on the first night. It is only after years of experience with all kinds of plays and all kinds of audiences that one acquires the working knowledge of crowd psychology that enables one to tell, while a play is still in rehearsal, whether it is likely to offend or not. That is the most one can do. There is no way of foretelling success. The most experienced producers and actors can be deceived, and are so every day. But one can at least discern any factor that will militate against success and try to eliminate it before the public sees the play. Here, I believe, the author has to be consulted, and authors are notoriously obstinate. I never could get either Yeats or Synge to understand that if you write plays to be acted, not read by the fireside, there are certain rules that you cannot break without destroying the sympathy between the stage and auditorium. The rules I refer to are not technical but psychological. For example, as *The Well of the Saints* took shape, I realized that every character in the play from the Saint to Timmy the Smith was bad-tempered right through the play, hence, as I pointed out to Synge, all this bad temper would inevitably infect the audience and make them bad-tempered too. I suggested that the Saint anyway might be made into a good-natured easy-going man, or that Molly Byrne might be made a lovable young girl, but Synge would not budge. He said he wanted to write 'like a monochrome painting, all in shades of the one colour'. I argued that all drama depended on contrast and on tension. All in vain. We had to agree to differ.

One technical trouble we had to overcome was that Synge had not yet acquired the art of breaking up his dialogue into short speeches, without which it is impossible for the actors to get pace. Many of his speeches were very long. They took a cruel lot of practice before we could get them spoken at a reasonably good pace and without at the same time losing the lovely lilt of his idiom. Take, for example, the Saint's speech at the end of the first act. 'May the Lord – who has given you sight – send a little sense into your head the way it won't be – on you two selves you'll be looking,' etc. Worse still for the actors is Martin's speech in Act III when he enters blind. 'The divil mend Mary Doul – for putting lies on me – and letting on she was grand. The divil mend the ould saint for letting me see it was lies,' etc.

The Well of the Saints had very much the same reception as *In the Shadow of the Glen*. As before, few of our public knew what to make of it. Was it a piece of harsh realism or was there something else behind it? The lyrical speeches were beyond them, and there was the old suspicion that most of the plays we produced were intended in some way to debunk the saintly Irish character. Who, for example, would be trusting Mr Yeats? Hadn't he always something up his sleeve? If it wasn't the birds of Angus Oge it might be a political rabbit of some kind. Then, Synge, of course, had heard of a man

called Boccaccio and a story about the Widow of Ephesus. In short
the play was admired and enjoyed by those who were capable of
regarding it simply as a play without reading into it a criticism of the
Irish people or an attack on their religion. But these were too few.
The great majority, thinking of religion and themselves, abominated
the play on both counts. It had a bad Press and we lost money and
audience over it. . . .

SOURCE: *The Fays of the Abbey Theatre: An Autobiographical Record*
by W. G. Fay & Catherine Carswell (London & New York, 1935),
166–9.

VI   *Freeman's Journal*   (1905)

. . . This is the third of Mr Synge's contributions to the repertoire of
the Irish National Theatre; and his point of view as a dramatist is
pretty clearly defined. The point of view is not that of a writer in
sympathetic touch with the people from whom he purports to draw
his characters. To begin with, he knows nothing of Irish peasant
religion. The widow in *Riders to the Sea*, who consoles herself with
the thought that her prayers to Providence may cease, leaves off her
praying just when the Irish peasant's prayers would really begin.
The wife in *The Shadow of the Glen* shows never a trace of the
conscience that even the vagabond carries somewhere in Ireland.
With Martin Doul – the principal character, in fact, the only
character in *The Well of the Saints* – religion is only a decayed
mythology, useful for incantation or imprecation, but having no
further concern with soul or body. Behind this representation of the
popular religion is the subtle irony of the latterday French school
satirizing a Providence that has ceased to be paternal, and is
shadowed forth merciless as the Destiny of the Greek drama. Such a
presentation of the peasant religion, lacking in reverence and
expressed in a jargon of profane familiarity, is an artistic blunder
and a constant offence. Again Mr Synge is as preoccupied with the
sex problem as any of the London school of problem playwrights. . . . Add to all this, or rather a result of all this, Mr Synge's
leading characters repel sympathy. . . .

The analysis of the blind man's feelings and frenzies is not without power; and in the dialogue beauty of thought and felicity of phrase are not lacking. The monologue of the lonely blind man after darkness has fallen upon him a second time is quite searching in its pathos. But the roughness of the peasants' passion is exaggerated, the ferocity of their rage excessive, and the hell-wrath of their imprecations repulsive. Here and there are touches of cynicism that make an ugly impression, and help to deepen the conviction that as a painter of Irish life and manners Mr Synge is either too incredulous of its main health or too much attracted by the problems suggested by unhealthy elements that no society is free from to give a typical picture. ...

SOURCE: extract from anonymous review in *The Freeman's Journal* (Dublin: 6 February 1905), 5.

VII   *George Moore*   (1905)

I should like to call the attention of the readers of *The Irish Times* to an important event which has just happened in Dublin, and which very likely may be overlooked by them and to their great regret hereafter. The event I allude to is of exceeding rarity, it happens occasionally in Paris. I have never seen in London any play written originally in English that I can look upon as dramatic literature. I have not forgotten Oscar Wilde's plays – that delicious comedy *The Importance of Being Earnest* – but however much I admire them I cannot forget that their style is derived from that of Restoration comedy, whereas Mr Synge's little play seems to me to be of a new growth. Its apparent orthodoxy reminds us of the painters who worked in the latter half of the 15th century. Filippo Lippi and Botticelli did not accept religious superstitions as easily as the monk of Fiesole. There are other points of comparison between Mr Synge's writings and these pictures, but I must reserve my explanation for another occasion. In your paper I would call attention to the abundance and the beauty of the dialogue, to the fact that one listens to it as one listens to music and the ease with which phrase is linked into phrase. At every moment the dialogue seems to lose itself, but it finds its way out. Mr Synge has discovered great literature in barbarous idiom as gold is discovered in quartz, and to do such a thing is surely a rare literary achievement. ...

SOURCE: extract from letter published in *The Irish Times* (13 February 1905), 6.

VIII *James Agate* (1917)

... Synge's *The Well of the Saints* was beautiful to read, and proves extraordinarily stimulating on the stage. In this little play Synge shows the power, common to all great creative work, of transfiguring his material, of seeing things and making us see things as though they were newly created. The words used last night are possible peasant utterance, but we are not to suppose that the author took a victoria to see the peasants, as one French realist said of another, or that the play is a verbatim transcript of the jottings of a note-book. The talk of these poor folk comes to us through the artist, that saving wall between us and a so-called realism. The theme is brutal enough for any realist – the healing by a saint of a pair of blind beggars, the man's revulsion at the revealed ugliness of his wife, his desire for the first beautiful woman he sees, her contempt and rejection of him, the old couple's miserable compromise. Zola would have given you every cut of their soiled feet, every horror of their rags, every dark place in their souls. Synge walks the road in fellowship with them. His is creative work, and the angels of heaven, the pigsty, the common muck of the road, the passions of men and women are all assimilated with equal zest and given back to us with the old relative value as between each other, but of new and equal loveliness in his exquisite and self-conscious prose. Take this description of a dirty day:

When I was roused up and found I was the like of the little children do be listening to the stories of an old woman, and do be dreaming after in the dark night that it's in grand houses of gold they are, with speckled horses to ride, and do be waking again in a short while, and they destroyed, with the cold and the thatch dripping, maybe, and the starved ass braying in the yard.

Every word in this passage leads you unfalteringly to that amazing last line, the 'starved ass braying in the yard', at which the picture flashes complete. Or again:

> A little drop of water is enough to make the blind see as clear as the grey hawks do be high up, on a still day, sailing the sky.

It is the artist, not the peasant, taking you through these successive degrees of intensity of expression:

> Whitish yellow hair does be soon turning the like of a handful of thin grass you'd see rotting, where the wet lies, at the north of a sty.

This startles one as though the words had been newly made to fit the thing expressed. It is English as elaborately found, for all its artlessness, as Flaubert's French.

And Synge does for his people what he has done for their speech. The theme is no longer ignoble, squalid, mean. When Martin Doul, inarticulate poet in real life, articulate only when he speaks through Synge, leaves the church healed, and makes his way to the beautiful Molly Byrne, shrinking instinctively from the hag in whom he does not recognize his wife, the audience laughed a little – audiences always laugh a little – although the thing is pitiful. His belief in the continued loveliness of his wife has been the blind old man's comfort. The lie always comfortably maintained by the village is exposed, and Martin is torn between loathing of his wife and desire of the beautiful woman. Zola would have shown the animal; Synge shows the poison of disillusion, the inveterate poet in the man going out to the first loveliness he has known, and, perhaps strongest of all, the horror of old age and the imminence of decay. 'It's a few sees the old women rotting for the grave.' It would be a mistake to imagine that the play is all high tragedy or even tearful. There is extraordinary comic bite to much of it and a deal of honest laughter. Merciful darkness falls upon the old couple again, and they realize, he that he will have a glorious white beard, she that she will have soft white hair the way there won't be the like of her in the seven counties of the east. 'Sight's a queer thing for upsetting a man', they decide, declining the offer of a second healing. They are inveterate romantics. 'The idea of' their hair contents them. What would they do with their sight, 'the way we'll see our grey hairs falling each day and turning dirty in the rain'? They are content with their unknown kingdom, the kingdom of the blind; the humming of bees, sweet smells, and the warm night, the sense of flying things racing in the air, the gentle wind, and the sunshine. Synge's blind folk pray for these as seeing people pray for daily bread. ...

SOURCE: extract from 'The Irish Players', *Buzz, Buzz! Essays on the Theatre* (London, 1917), 153–6.

2. CRITICAL STUDIES

W. B. Yeats Preface to the First Edition of *The Well of the Saints* (1905)

... Mr Synge, indeed, sets before us ugly, deformed or sinful people, but his people, moved by no practical ambition, are driven by a dream of that impossible life. That we may feel how intensely his Woman of the Glen [in *The Shadow of the Glen*] dreams of days that shall be entirely alive, she that is 'a hard woman to please' must spend her days between a sour-faced old husband, a man who goes mad upon the hills, a craven lad and a drunken tramp; and those two blind people of *The Well of the Saints* are so transformed by the dream that they choose blindness rather than reality. He tells us of realities, but he knows that art has never taken more than its symbols from anything that the eye can see or the hand measure.

It is the preoccupation of his characters with their dream that gives his plays their drifting movement, their emotional subtlety. In most of the dramatic writing of our time, and this is one of the reasons why our dramatists do not find the need for a better speech, one finds a simple motive lifted, as it were, into the full light of the stage. The ordinary student of drama will not find anywhere in *The Well of the Saints* that excitement of the will in the presence of attainable advantages, which he is accustomed to think the natural stuff of drama, and if he see it played he will wonder why act is knitted to act so loosely, why it is all like a decoration on a flat surface, why there is so much leisure in the dialogue, even in the midst of passion. ... While I write, we are rehearsing *The Well of the Saints*, and are painting for it decorative scenery, mountains in one or two flat colours and without detail, ash-trees and red salleys with something of recurring pattern in their woven boughs. For though the people of the play use no phrase they could not use in

110

daily life, we know that we are seeking to express what no eye has ever seen.

SOURCE: preface to the first edition of *The Well of the Saints*, reprinted in *Essays and Introductions* (London, 1961), 304–5.

Katharine Worth 'Drama of the Interior' (1978)

... *The Well of the Saints* is Synge's most grotesque treatment of the self-dramatizing process; of all the plays it pushes the hardest towards incongruity and absurdity, forcing us into uneasy relation with its dreamers and non-dreamers alike. We are made to see clearly the formidable obstacles in the way of the dream; the poverty of the physical materials it is built from and the lack of real support from the bleakly literal-minded villagers. Synge exposes this physical poverty to our view for a long, slow spell; in the static opening scene that so impressed Yeats there is nothing to look at but the weatherbeaten, blind beggar of fifty and his ugly, blind wife, sitting under a stone cross, ludicrously talking about her yellow hair and fine white skin and the jealousy she arouses in the young women. It is a sculptural scene, a grotesquely comic version of the statuesque grouping of the blind figures in *The Sightless*, we might assume, for Maeterlinck is strongly echoed elsewhere in the play; his beautiful blind girl with her marvellous pre-Raphaelite hair is surely in the background of the Douls' final vision of themselves:

... a face would be a great wonder when it'll have soft white hair falling around it, the way when I'm an old woman there won't be the like of me surely in the seven counties of the east.
... a beautiful, long, white, silken, streamy beard, you wouldn't see the like of in the eastern world.

Maeterlinck of course keeps us confined to the viewpoint of the blind, but Synge characteristically pushes the action to prickly and in the end violent oppositions between the modes of perception experienced by the sighted and the sightless. He holds the balance between them with a ruthless impartiality that cuts out any danger of sentimentality. Immediately after the cure, when Martin goes looking for his wife among the prettiest girls and the villagers mock him, our sympathy must be with the blind pair, and yet they repel pity, partly by their unattractive lack of pity for each other, but, more importantly, by the disdain which they are able to feel for their tormentors. It is not just a defensive reflex but a real disdain for the 'seeing' world which is so bounded by the facts of the flesh. 'Ah, you're thinking you're a fine lot', he says, 'with your giggling, weeping eyes, a fine lot to be making game of myself, and the woman I've heard called the great wonder of the west . . .'. The fearful appropriateness of that image, the 'giggling, weeping eye', attacks us as well as the stage audience. We have laughed and felt pity, looked in fact with the same eye as the villagers, and now we are told that this eye is an inferior one, unable to look into the rich inner world the sightless ones inhabited at the beginning of the play, and to which they return at the end.

Synge takes trouble to establish that the Douls are neither monsters nor simpletons; they are not unaware of facts nor free from doubts; at the beginning Martin is hankering after the sweet voices of the girls he cannot see and questioning whether Mary with her cracked tones can really be a beauty. His acceptance of the Saint's cure can be seen as a momentary faltering of his will, a weariness with holding up by the force of imagination the golden landscape he and Mary inhabit. He relaxes, as it were, into ordinary seeing, but it turns out a bitter experience; for the whole of the second act he is occupied in drawing contrasts between the two ways of perception, always to the disadvantage of the visible world. Now he seems able to see only ugly things; raw, beastly days, grey clouds, people with red noses, and, always, those weeping and watering eyes; 'the like of your eyes, God help you, Timmy the Smith'. In a way it is easy to dismiss this as sour grapes; the first disillusionment, forcing him to see himself as others see him, was a terrible blow, not easy to surmount. It may be true too, as the Saint suggests (and critics have often agreed with him), that the Douls suffer because they are so self-centred and aesthetically narrow; they should be turning their minds outwards, forgetting about 'the faces of men' and learning to look at nature and the splendour of the spirit of God 'till you'll be living the way the great saints do be living, with little but old sacks, and skin covering their bones'.

The Saint, however, has small grip on ordinary reality himself. He too is busy converting raw nature into material for a glorious vision and he can often seem naïvely unaware of simple facts, as Mary observes when she is told of his idea that young girls are best fitted to carry the holy water, being 'the cleanest holy people you'd see walking the world'. 'Well', she says, sitting down and laughing to herself, 'the Saint's a simple fellow, and it's no lie'. She finds him absurd as the villagers find the Douls absurd and indeed the sensible, laughing attitude to vision and imagination is very strong and persuasive throughout the play. Synge piles up the odds against the chance of our taking the Douls' vision seriously: there is their physical grotesqueness, often exuberantly comic, as in the scene where their bodies stick out behind bushes while they think themselves out of view; the incongruity of their overweening self-assurance; their cruelty towards each other. It is important to the whole effect that we, like the villagers, should see them as comic, sometimes pitiable, sometimes unsympathetic and remote. Only then can we appreciate the full force of the extraordinary power they have to make a self-contained, inner world of rich possibilities in contrast to which the factual world of the sighted, sensible people is intolerably narrow and constrained.

Because the odds against them are so enormous, it is peculiarly perturbing when their inner world forces itself into a position of superior reality. It happens first when Martin, earning his living by tedious chores for Timmy the Smith, courts Timmy's sweetheart, Molly Byrne, and actually succeeds in moving the hard, unimaginative beauty from her first contemptuous indifference to interest and even a kind of fascination: Synge describes her as 'half-mesmerised'. The romance is on the edge of bathos, as Synge makes plain; Molly is cruelly pleased, even when he is praising her charms, to remind him of his own physical shabbiness and the shock it gave him. And yet, even with so cool an audience, Martin is able not only to charm, but to invest his rhetoric with troubling implications for those who put their faith entirely in the visible world. He uses images of sight and blindness with increasing mastery. What does a woman want, he cries in a last passionate appeal, but to be seen by a man who can truly 'see' her:

You'd do right, I'm saying, not to marry a man is after looking out a long while on the bad days of the world, for what way would the like of him have fit eyes to look on yourself, when you rise up in the morning and come out of the little door you have above in the lane, the time it'd be a fine thing if a man would be seeing, and losing his sight, the way he'd have your two eyes facing him, and he going the roads, and shining above him, and he looking in the sky, and springing up from the earth, the time he'd lower his head, in place of the muck that seeing men do meet all roads spread on the world.

Synge's strange language is at its least life-like here: the queer, bony structure, the intricately linked phrases, the alien word order, which one can well believe the Abbey actors had trouble mastering, almost defy us to take it as the ordinary speech of common men. And it is appropriate in that way, for Martin is by no means a common man, but one of extraordinary gifts; with so much against him, he can still make an impression on coarse-fibred Molly, while later, in the scene when he is preparing to reject a second cure, he momentarily persuades one of the incredulous and angry villagers that there is something in his account of what ordinary seeing is: 'He's right, maybe, it's lonesome living when the days are dark'. The word 'dark', normally in the play (as in Irish usage) a synonym for 'blind', has more the sense here of dull or drear, and implies support for Martin's view, that without imagination there is nothing to the world and its sights. A Maeterlinckian equation between sight and insight develops. Martin connects Molly's villainy with her enjoyment of physical sight, and she, reversing the meanings, calls on the Saint to leave the obdurate tramp to his darkness: 'If it's that is best fitting to the blackness of his heart'. A violent opposition between these views comes to a violent climax when Martin asserts the supremacy of the inner eye by the act which so astounds and affronts the villagers and the Saint, his deliberate refusal of the second, permanent cure for his physical blindness:

> SAINT: [*coming close to Martin Doul and putting his hand on his shoulder*] Did you never set eyes on the summer and the fine spring in the places where the holy men of Ireland have built up churches to the Lord, that you'd wish to be closed up and seeing no sight of the glittering seas, and the furze is opening above, will soon have the hills shining as if it was fine creels of gold they were, rising to the sky?
> PATCH RUADH: That's it, holy father.
> MAT SIMON: What have you now to say, Martin Doul?
> MARTIN DOUL: [*fiercely*] Isn't it finer sights ourselves had a while since and we sitting dark smelling the sweet beautiful smells do be rising in the warm nights and hearing the swift flying things racing in the air [*Saint draws back from him*], till we'd be looking up in our own minds into a grand sky, and seeing lakes, and broadening rivers, and hills are waiting for the spade and plough.

Martin has taken the word 'dark' in the sense used by the others and transformed it to his own. The saint draws back, we might notice, at the phrase 'swift flying things racing in the air', as though he had scented black magic. And it *is* a kind of black magic the blind man has effected: he has almost persuaded at least one or two of the sighted that it is they who might be living in the real dark and disturbed us into thinking hard about this idea by the extraordinarily aggressive act of refusing the healing water. He refuses it for his wife too – in the later part of the play she is a more passive figure, willing to follow the strongest persuasion – and this tyranny no doubt sets up in us, as in the stage audience, some hostility towards him. It is certainly not possible, at this fierce ending, to patronize the sightless ones: our position as sighted beings has been too seriously undermined by the powerful words that have reduced the faculty of sight to an image of 'giggling, weeping eyes'.

There is also a call on our admiration, for at the other pole his words have power to extend, enlarge, enrich. Indeed Synge puts his weight behind the rightness of the final choice, which includes the forcing of Mary, by showing how with the return of the physical blindness, a kind of inner light is restored. After all the bitter recriminations, the almost total estrangement of husband and wife during their period of sight, affection and tenderness return:

MARTIN DOUL: [*throwing himself down on the ground clinging to Mary Doul*] I'll not come, I'm saying, and let you take his holy water to cure the blackness of your souls today.
MARY DOUL: [*putting her arm round him*] Leave him easy, holy father, when I'd liefer live dark all times beside him, than be seeing in new troubles now.

The play ends with a piece of striking visual symbolism: the Douls groping their way out, to the 'south' of their imagining – which to Timmy the Smith's mind is likely to be their death by drowning – and the others lining up for the wedding procession of Molly and Timmy, to the sound of the Saint's bell. Two ways of life, and we are left divided between them, far from knowing clearly where our sympathies lie, critical of the Douls as of the villagers, sure of one thing only, that the inner eye has a terrifying power to create its own reality.

The well which gives the play its title and which has so haunted the imagination of Yeats and Beckett, is a well never to be seen with mortal eye. Synge makes it seem infinitely distant in Timmy's opening account, a green and ferny well on an island, where there is a grave of four beautiful saints; a drop of its water is 'enough to cure the dying, or to make the blind see as clear as the grey hawks do be high up, on a still day, sailing the sky'. A powerful image of vision that clearly fastened in Yeats's mind to surface some years after in *At the Hawk's Well*. Yeats got his well on to the stage as a square of blue cloth, having by then acquired a technique for representing inner landscape in terms of scenic symbolism. Synge did not have this, and in any case it is characteristic that he should prefer to work through totally ordinary and commonplace visible objects. There *is* a well in *The Well of the Saints* but it is quite prosaic, simply part of the setting of the second act, a village roadside with a forge, broken wheels lying about and 'a well near centre, with board above it, and room to pass behind it'. Insidiously this contrast between the ordinary visible well and the magical world we hear of serves to remind us that the holy water and the well and all that goes with it are things of the mind and indeed that everything is; the characters are in a way blind by their own will.

At the far end of the shadowy road the Douls go out on at the end of the play, one seems to see coming to meet them the pathetic and alarming figure of Lucky, his long white hair falling round him, leading the blind Pozzo, or the Rooneys, that strange old married pair [in *All that Fall*], clumping along, the blind man's stick tapping, listening to the country sounds which they sardonically enumerate. . . .

A place where it seems natural to begin in thinking of what is especially modern and influential in Synge is that bare roadside scene in *The Well of the Saints*. Scenes like these are naturalistic enough and it is obviously possible in production to stress the naturalism: this is indeed what is most often done. But his landscapes should not be made too real; they have a local habitation and a name – County Mayo, the Wicklow hills, the Aran islands – but little particularity; the direction in *The Well of the Saints* is typical: 'Some lonely mountainous district on the east of Ireland, one or more centuries ago'. . . . [T]he art of producing Synge must be to strike on the stage the fine balance he himself maintains between that full-blooded, solid reality and the equally powerful impression that life is some kind of fantastic illusion, a conjuring trick performed in a dark space. A high degree of stylization is needed; certainly it is essential if a production is to accommodate and make us take seriously grotesque incidents like the scene in *The Well of the Saints* when the Douls shelter in the briars, their behinds sticking out, convinced they can't be seen, spinning the images of their future. ...

SOURCE: extracts from *The Irish Drama of Europe from Yeats to Beckett* (London, 1978), 128–36.

Nicholas Grene 'Alternative Visions in *The Well of the Saints*' (1982)

... Synge took great pains not to sentimentalize the blind beggars and their situation. Nothing would have been easier, or more intolerable, than a pathetic image of the couple cherishing their beautiful illusion. The play opens in an ironic minor key with the tone of the relationship that of mild marital squabbling, rather than any more eye-catching form of happiness. The illusion of beauty is comic rather than pathetic in the complacent words of Mary Doul:

I've heard tell there isn't anything like the wet south wind does be blowing upon us, for keeping a white beautiful skin – the like of my skin – on your neck and on your brows, and there isn't anything at all like a fine skin for putting splendour on a woman.

We are made aware of the inversion of the blind viewpoint – 'the seeing is a queer lot, and you'd never know the thing they'd do'. We are not encouraged to identify with the plight of the beggars as outsiders but rather observe with detached amusement their self-satisfied contempt and distrust for the 'seeing rabble below'. Initially at least, ours is an ironic vantage-point on the home-made world of their own in which Martin and Mary live.

However, a common strategy in Synge's drama is to set up a comic perspective and then to shift the mode of the drama away from comedy. Such a shift is central to *The Well of the Saints*. The comedian habitually distances us from feeling, suspends our capacity for sharing pain or suffering. Such a technique of ironic distance is there in the opening scenes of *The Well of the Saints*, never more than in the gallows humour of Martin and Mary's speculations on the 'wonder' Timmy has promised them.

Maybe they're hanging a thief above at the bit of a tree? I'm told it's a great sight to see a man hanging by his neck, but what joy would that be to ourselves, and we not seeing it at all?

But as the prospect of their cure approaches, we find ourselves no longer immune from sympathy; our detachment is eroded. In this development of discomfort the scene with Molly and the girls is crucial. In the context of Molly's heartless and inane mockery of Martin in the Saint's cloak, the beggars take on a new dignity:

> MOLLY BYRNE: . . . Isn't that a fine holy-looking saint, Timmy the smith? [*Laughing foolishly.*] There's a grand handsome fellow, Mary Doul, and if you seen him now, you'd be as proud, I'm thinking, as the archangels below, fell out with the Almighty God.
>
> MARY DOUL: [*with quiet confidence going to* MARTIN DOUL *and feeling his cloak*] It's proud we'll be this day surely.

The foolish laughter of Molly is laughter we cannot share and our feelings go out to the vulnerability of Martin and Mary.

While at work on the play, Synge drew up a plan showing the changing mode of its various parts, and the final scene of Act I he marked 'tragic' (see *Plays* I, Appendix C, p. 264). It is the more tragic because of the moment of ecstasy which follows Martin's cure. A dramatic off-stage cry breaks into the aimless arguments of the villagers – 'Oh, glory be to God, I see now surely. . . . I see the walls of the church, and yourself, holy father, and the great width of the sky'. There is a terrible tragic irony in the words of wondering delight with which he greets Molly Byrne, mistaking her for his wife:

Oh, it was no lie they told me, Mary Doul. Oh, glory to God and the seven saints I didn't die and not see you at all. The blessing of God on the water, and the feet carried it round through the land, for it's grand hair you have [*she lowers her head a little confused*], and soft skin, and eyes would make the saints, if they were dark awhile and seeing again, fall down out of the sky.

The people's reaction is one of painful embarrassment and it is to escape the intolerable burden of sympathy that they join in the jeering taunts as Martin searches ever more desperately for Mary in a cruel game of ex-blind-man's-buff. By the time she appears, cured in her turn, they have hardened themselves to laugh at the beggars' mutual disillusionment. The slanging-match which follows, with all its grotesque hyperbole, could in fact almost be comic, were it not for the intensity of feeling which its expresses. Martin and Mary take their tragedy tragically. Anyone can be hurt and humiliated; only a few can make of that humiliation a significant betrayal.

Yet the move from comedy to tragedy is never made once and irrevocably in a Synge play. After the dramatic moment of tragic loss at the end of the first act, Martin is once again seen in a comic light at the beginning of the second. Like the traditional comic beggar, he has little enthusiasm for hard labour, and there is a splendid vituperative edge to his grumbles at his taskmaster, Timmy the smith, who insists on his stripping off for work:

Oh, God help me! [*He begins taking off his coat.*] I've heard tell you stripped the sheet from your wife and you putting her down into the grave, and there isn't the like of you for plucking your living ducks, the short days, and leaving them running round in their skins, in the great rains and the cold.

It is a sour sort of comedy, with Martin's disillusioned view of reality lending gloom to the atmosphere, and yet there is a real humour in the contrast between the hard-working smith intent on his business and the lazy self-pitying ex-beggar.

It may seem astonishing to modern readers that reviewers of the first production of *The Well of the Saints* found in it evidence of Synge's obsession with sex. Yet for Dublin in 1905, the treatment of Martin Doul's feeling for Molly Byrne must have appeared shockingly explicit. ...

The second act ends like the first in humiliation for Martin, a humiliation if anything more intense because more intimately personal. The renewed blindness which comes on at the very moment when Mary Doul enters and the outraged Molly Byrne turns on him makes for a moment of terrible depth and anguish.

MARTIN DOUL: [*turns round, sees* MARY DOUL, *whispers to* MOLLY BYRNE *with imploring agony*] Let you not put shame on me, Molly, before herself and the smith. Let you not put shame on me, and I after saying fine words to you, and dreaming ... dreams ... in the night. [*He hesitates, and looks round the sky.*] Is it a storm of thunder is coming, or the last end of the world? [*He staggers towards* MARY DOUL, *tripping slightly over tin can.*] The heavens is closing, I'm thinking, with darkness and great trouble passing in the sky. [*He reaches* MARY DOUL, *and seizes her left arm with both his hands – with a frantic cry.*] Is it the darkness of thunder is coming, Mary Doul? Do you see me clearly with your eyes?
MARY DOUL: [*snatches her arm away, and hits him with empty sack across the face*] I see you a sight too clearly, and let you keep off from me now.

Molly's shaming of him represents the destruction of his world, the fantasy-world of his imagination of which she was the centre. The apocalyptic imagery gives resonance to a return to blindness which is more than merely physical. With Mary Doul's fierce rejection, Martin's isolation is complete.

All three acts of *The Well of the Saints* have a similar movement: beginning on the level of detached ironic comedy, the action develops to a point of all but complete identification with the protagonists. At the start of Act III, as with the opening scenes of the other acts, we are back in a predominantly comic mode. Martin's 'soliloquy', overheard by Mary Doul, makes for a moment of broad humour when he tries to flee in terror:

Oh, merciful God, set my foot on the path this day, and I'll be saying prayers morning and night, and not straining my ear after young girls, or doing any bad thing till I die –
   MARY DOUL: [*indignantly*] Let you not be telling lies to the Almighty God.

However, the reunion between the two in which they rebuild their relationship on the basis of a new illusion is one of the most subtle and delicate scenes in the play in its combination of irony and understanding. Mary and Martin must each find their own means to a restored self-belief before they can meet on equal terms. Martin is admiring when Mary announces the fiction of her long white hair, but she ruthlessly refuses to help him towards a similar fiction. ... There is no quarter given in this battle of competing egos, and it is only when Martin discovers the possibilities of a long white beard to match Mary's long white hair that mutual satisfaction is achieved.

The return to illusion on the part of the beggars has met with stern disapproval from some critics who feel that Synge could not have endorsed such escapism.[1] But the play is not conceived in the black and white moralistic terms of truth and its opposite. Martin and Mary are to some extent professional liars: 'a priest itself', says Martin, 'would believe the lies of an old man would have a fine white beard growing on his chin'. When Martin congratulates Mary on her discovery, it is with admiration for her inventiveness: 'you're a cute thinking woman, Mary Doul, and it's no lie'. What they create with their new vision of beauty is something midway between the conscious lies they tell priests and passers-by and their former illusion in which they fully believed. They know at some level that it is false, as we can see when they are threatened with sight again: 'what good'll our gray hairs be itself, if we have our sight, the way we'll see them falling each day, and turning dirty in the rain?' Yet Synge demands our sympathetic feeling for the need for this degree of illusory self-respect. As Martin and Mary enjoy the spring sounds and smells of the countryside, there is a real and moving suggestion of emotional renewal.

It is for this reason that the prospect of a second cure seems to us, as to them, persecution by the Saint and the villagers. We feel for them in their pathetic and hopeless attempts to hide themselves away. In the opening scene of the play the beggars' suspicion of the sighted was viewed as comic inversion – 'they're a bad lot those that have their sight' – but now they seem justified: 'the lot of them young girls, the devil save them, have sharp terrible eyes, would pick out a poor man I'm thinking, and he lying below hid in his grave'. The deepest irony of all is that, to express their dissent from the values of the Saint and the villagers, they have only the language in which those values are implicit. 'The Lord protect us from the saints of God', cries Mary Doul. Synge often gave comic pointing to the miscellaneous Irish invocation of the Deity ... but nowhere more significantly than here. Who but the Lord *is* there to rescue Martin and Mary from the blessing of sight brought by His saint? They are caught uncertainly between prayer and blasphemy: 'who'd know rightly if it's good words or bad would save us this day from himself?'

Everything in the play builds towards the climax of the second attempted cure by the Saint. It was the scene Synge worked hard to revise for the revival of the play in 1908 and which he most wanted to see well performed in the theatre. His aim in the revisions was to add depth and clarity to both the Saint's arguments and Martin's, and to orchestrate the reactions of the people. He was conscious of the dangers of the Saint appearing an unsympathetic preacher and he added a stage direction to suggest a more kindly tone in his eloquent speech to Martin.

> SAINT: [*coming close to* MARTIN DOUL *and putting his hand on his shoulder*]
> Did you never hear tell of the summer and the fine spring in places where the holy men of Ireland have built up churches to the Lord, that you'd wish to be closed up and seeing no sight of the glittering seas, and the furze is opening above, will soon have the hills shining as if it was fine creels of gold they were, rising to the sky?

But equally he took great care with Martin's alternative blind man's vision:

I'll say it's ourselves have finer sight than the lot of you, and we sitting abroad in the sweetness of the warmth of night [SAINT *draws back from him*] hearing a late thrush, maybe, and the swift flying things do be racing in the air, till we do be looking up in our own minds into a grand sky, and seeing lakes and broadening rivers and hills are waiting for the spade and plough.

The crowd's reaction at first is one of more or less neutral enjoyment of the dispute, but as Martin definitely rejects the Saint's offer of sight, they become more aggressive. The suggestion that Mary should be cured and Martin left blind is in some sense an attack on him, as he himself feels: 'Would you have her looking on me and saying hard words to me till the hour of death?' They will not tolerate the idea of the couple deliberately remaining blind.

If it's choosing a wilful blindness you are, there isn't anyone will give you a hap'worth of meal, or be doing the little things you do need to keep you living in the world at all.

They put forward shrewd arguments to tempt Mary to forsake Martin and accept her sight. When revising the scene, Synge steadily increased the violence of the people's reaction against Martin and gave them lines enthusiastically dragging him away at the Saint's bidding: 'That's it. That's it. Come forward till we drop him in the pool beyond'. With Martin's final blatant and scandalous defiance of orthodoxy in the spilling of the holy water, they are prepared to stone the beggars out of the village.

The ordinary people's reality in *The Well of the Saints* lives between two worlds of imagination, that of Martin and Mary on the one hand, and of the Saint on the other. The Saint insists that if one has the vision to see 'the Spirit of God . . . shining out through the big hills, and steep streams falling to the sea', then the body can be forgotten, ignored. His is an aesthetic which glorifies the poor, the mean, the underfed as the inheritors of spiritual grace; it is the spirit of the Sermon on the Mount. But the Saint makes little contact with an everyday world of reality, with the Timmy the smiths and the Molly Byrnes, who do value strength of body, beauty, comfort. These *are* their realities. The inner life of imagination of the blind beggars is constructed by an interiorization of these ordinary realities. Their values are those of Timmy and Molly; they have no more time for the humble pride of spiritual self-abnegation than the villagers have. But their passionate egotism in clinging to the illusion of vanity separates them from those whose sensibilities are deadened by daily contact with the ugliness and superficiality of the actual. They set new standards for self-satisfaction – impossible standards which trouble because they cannot be satisfied. They re-make, and then Martin has fiercely to defend, their imaginary life. They reject the Saint's ascetic vision because what it means in fact is living with the reality of the Timmys and Mollys.

What was it I seen my first day, but your own bleeding feet and they cut with the stones, and my last day, but the villainy of herself you're wedding, God forgive you, to Timmy the smith.

It would be possible to give a schematic interpretation of *The Well of the Saints* in terms of three sorts of vision: the ordinary vision of the villagers, the spiritual vision of the Saint, and the poetic vision of Martin Doul. But though the play has its origins in parable, its dramatic images are not reducible to this sort of abstract pattern. The mood and meaning of the final scene, for instance, work by implicit suggestion rather than any direct symbolic significance. As the beggars leave, with the violent hostility of the crowd, Synge is careful to qualify the tone of defiant triumph in Martin's speeches with more sceptical views. Mary goes off with him to the south, but without his enthusiasm. ... Even more disturbing, because of its very casualness, is Timmy's remark after they leave:

There's a power of deep rivers with floods in them where you do have to be lepping the stones and you going to the south, so I'm thinking the two of them will be drowned together in a short while, surely.

Do the beggars go out to an almost certain death, or is this only a callous parting shot from Timmy, a brutal good riddance? T. R. Henn comments in words which brilliantly suggest the ambiguity of the play's effect:

Synge's reticence gives no symbolism, as a lesser poet might have done, to sloughs or rivers or winds. Only what Martin creates will – for this verbal moment – remain; for here illusions can be recreated, and perhaps maintained, in the gallant security of blindness.[2] ...

SOURCE: extracts from 'Introduction' to *The Well of the Saints* (Gerrards Cross and Washington, 1982), 14–22.

NOTES

[Reorganized and renumbered from the original. – Ed.]

1. For example, Donna Gerstenberger, *John Millington Synge* (New York, 1964), p. 55.
2. T. R. Henn (ed.), *The Plays and Poems of J. M. Synge* (London, 1963), p. 56.

Toni O'Brien Johnson The Well of the Saints and Waiting for Godot: Stylistic Variations on a Tradition (1984)

In their linguistic theories, both John Synge and Samuel Beckett are concerned with revitalization. Synge believed that this could best be achieved through using a 'living language' as the basis for literature, and acknowledged his own linguistic debt to the richness and imagination of the Irish country people whose language offered him an alternative to the 'modern literature of the towns [which was] far away from the profound and common interests of life' and was written in 'joyless and pallid words'.[1] Although Beckett's urban sympathies are greater than those of Synge, he found English to be a language 'abstracted to death' as early as 1929, when he rejoiced at Joyce's attempts to 'desophisticate' it.[2] Synge's use of Hiberno-English syntax can be shown to result in an increased sense of the concrete and the specific, which is *de facto* a refusal of abstraction. Beckett's use of French initially for the writing of *Waiting for Godot* is a refusal of the particular kind of abstraction to which he found English prone; and both the French version and his English translation of it make use throughout of markedly oral linguistic forms.[3] However, the sceptical and solipsistic disposition of Beckett towards language *per se* differs from that of Synge, which might be described as one of faith in its usefulness for both documentary and monumental purposes.[4]

The Well of the Saints and *Waiting for Godot* invite comparison because they each make use of a roadside setting, tramps, blindness and interdependence, which combination originates in the French medieval drama known to both the Irish dramatists.[5] The oldest extant French farce, *Le Garçon et l'aveugle* (late 13th century), portrays a blind old man and a young boy who acts as his servant and ultimately robs him. The use of an interdependent pair, one of whom is blind, was taken up two centuries later (1496) by André de la Vigne for his play *La Moralité de l'aveugle et du boiteux*. This play has all the characteristics of a medieval French farce, and belongs more properly with that genre than with the moralité.[6] In de la Vigne's play, a blind man, claiming at the opening to have been robbed by his servant, encounters a fellow-beggar who is a cripple. The two disabled beggars join forces: the blind man carries the cripple, whose eyes serve to guide them on their way. Finally, they are both cured by a miracle brought about by the corpse of the recently dead St Martin. This play, according to Synge's avowal to both Yeats and Padraic Colum, was the source for *The Well of the Saints*.[7]

The use of tramps 'on the road' allows the dramatist to introduce an exterior and somewhat indeterminate setting, thus releasing him from the distractions, trivia, and conventions of enclosed domestic life, and allowing him to give prominence to the needs and functions of the body. It also permits him to credibly attribute a crude, earthy, unpolished dialogue to characters reduced to the lowest social level. Besides, blindness can be exploited for both comic and pathetic purposes, and can be a means of realizing dependence on the stage.

In addition to setting, tramps, blindness and interdependence, there are some minor features in the two modern plays which have precedents in the French plays: there is the futile hiding of the beggars in de la Vigne's play,[8] which is taken up both at the opening of the third act of *The Well*, when Martin and Mary hide from the approaching saint, and in the attempt to hide Estragon from his imagined persecutors behind the tree in *Godot*.[9] In all four plays, a sense of desire nags at one character at least. In each case, there is also an increased sense of individual vision which hinges on the characters' blindness; and the problem of loneliness is made particularly evident. Besides, in both *The Well* and *Godot* long white hair and bald heads are used significantly. The body's needs and functions are prominent in various ways in all four plays; and both de la Vigne's play and Beckett's go so far as to involve characters in excretary activities and discussion of them.[10]

For the first decade of this century, the relative frankness of Synge's play with reference to the body is worthy of note, although it is considerably more subdued than Beckett's and bodily functions are not so concretely presented as they are in his. The speech of Synge's characters indicates that consciousness of themselves and of each other is rooted in their bodies. The first six pages of the text yield more than three references per page to parts of the body in the following order: hair, head, hands, skin, neck, brows, face, legs, eyes, ears, heart, mouth, feet, and knee. But the interest of these references lies not merely in their frequency, but in their nature: they function as a focus for the tension between ugliness and beauty which contributes to the basic structure of the play. [11]

Synge's conception of ugliness and beauty in tension with each other is revealed even in his listing of characters: Martin and Mary Doul are designated as weather-beaten, blind, ugly, and nearly fifty, whereas Molly Byrne is 'a fine-looking girl with fair hair', and Bride is 'another handsome girl'. At the opening of the play, the blind couple immediately reveal the illusion they share that Mary is beautiful, and when Martin expresses his longing for sight just for one hour 'the way we'd know surely we were the finest man, and the finest woman, of the seven counties of the east', the glaring contradiction between what the audience sees and hears becomes emotionally charged. [12] From this moment on, actual physical ugliness is maintained in tension with the illusion or desire of beauty.

Before the audience has actually seen Molly Byrne, she is implicitly an object of desire for Martin when he muses on her sweet voice and decides 'It should be a fine soft, rounded woman, I'm thinking, would have a voice the like of that'. This first indication of his longings draws the following rebuke from Mary: 'Let you not be minding if it's flat or rounded she is, for she's a flighty, foolish woman ...'. [13] In the second act, Martin's desire is directly voiced to young Molly in his lyrical invitation to her to go with him where she would not 'set down the width of your two feet and not be crushing fine flowers, and making smells in the air ...'. [14] The sense of the actual body is conveyed here by the graphic reference to Molly's 'two feet', the stylistic significance of which will be indicated later. Here, and throughout the play, desire for beauty is offset by the actuality of the 'old, shabby stump of a man' who is 'a pitiful show' and 'a raggy-looking fool', and by the numerous conceptions of ugliness which the characters express, such as 'old women rotting for the grave'; 'When the skin shrinks on your chin'; and 'them that's fat and flabby do be wrinkled young'.[15] Martin sets against the sheltered, illusory world of his blindness the 'big slobbering mouth', wrinkles, big red nose, and bleary eyes of Timmy the Smith, as well as the bleeding worn feet, big head, and welted knees of the ascetic saint.[16] Beautiful Molly gloats over Mary's disappointment in Martin's 'fat legs on him, and the little neck like a ram'.[17] And Mary ruthlessly reminds Martin of the time when his head will be 'as bald as an old turnip you'd see rolling round in the muck', in addition to saying to him 'I can't help your looks, Martin Doul. It wasn't myself made you with your rat's eyes, and your big ears, and your griseldy chin'.[18]

Such continual reference to the body as Synge makes here maintains attention on what he calls the 'common interests of life' and clearly operates against abstraction. In the case of Beckett, not only are there frequent references to the body, but there is also far greater physical expression in the various routines with boots, hats, and embracing, as well as the frequent opposition between word and action. Besides, the body functions as a metaphor for language in the play. . . . The run-down state of the body of language is endorsed by concentration on inferior bodily functions. . . . It is clear that the manner in which Beckett uses the body operates on multiple levels, but they are all directly related to his disposition towards language. First, opting for clowning routines and techniques reminiscent of the *commedia dell'arte*[19] shows a displacement of language by bodily gesture compared with the methods of Synge, who pays maximum and undivided attention to the words uttered, and was avowedly seeking to produce 'literature first – drama afterwards'.[20] And then the use of the body as metaphor for language reveals a more intense preoccupation with the subject than Synge's. . . .

The living, non-standard dialect which Synge used as a basis for his language allowed him to achieve a number of specific effects because of its peculiar syntactical structures. Hiberno-English structures arise from direct translation from their Irish originals. Irish is a noun-centred language, highly resistant to abstract neologisms, with few complex sentences owing to the scarcity of adverbs and relative pronouns. Thus the increased substantival weighting of Hiberno-English syntax results in a semantic emphasis which produces a greater sense of the concrete, the specific, and the presence of the speaker.[21] ... Through their patterns of emphasis, these structures create an intensified sense of the actual, and present a world which is almost tangible to the audience. Besides, the characters using these structures take each other's queries, replies, and statements seriously. They treat words as if they had meaningful reference, so that language is for them a useful social instrument. In addition to being an effective means of communication for them, it is also adequate for expressing their emotions, for instance Martin's joy, anger, and longing, as well as Mary's pride and disdain. The confidence with which these characters use language reflects the author's confidence in it.

The opposite, however, is true of Beckett's play. Because of 'advances' in linguistic theory and in the philosophy of language, as well as the growth of partly-inhibiting critical activity in the intervening years (and maybe also for reasons of individual temperament and experience), Beckett undertook the writing of *Godot* with grave doubts about the capacity of language *per se*, that is of any language, to convey meaning.[22] The variety of explanations he has offered over the years for his curious change to French yield, on analysis, the indication of an ascetic drive away from the temptations of the richness of English to rhetoric and virtuosity.[23] Above all, he wished to write '*sans style*', and by the time he came to translate *Godot* into English, the Hiberno-English style which had served Synge so well in the first decade of the century had become mannered. Therefore, there are few Hiberno-English structures to be found in the English version, compared with *All that Fall* the style of which has been described as a 'piece of self-indulgence'.[24]

Beckett's self-conscious approach to language is evident not only in his use of the body as metaphor for language, but also in his extensive use of old or worn linguistic forms which draw attention to themselves. Quotation and misquotation, cliché and platitude are all survivals of linguistic forms from the past which abound in *Godot*. ... Lucky's speech is a pastiche of a fragmented philosophical argument in the rationalist mode, with two 'objections';[25] and Pozzo's grandiloquence swings between the lyrical and the prosaic modes. Vladimir gives a version of high rhetoric when Pozzo calls for help, and he begins the 'narrative' of the two thieves to pass the time.[26] Numerous verbal rituals are observed, such as the curses and courtesies between the two tramps, most strikingly illustrated in the scene where they move towards the tree having decided to attempt suicide:

VLADIMIR: Go ahead.
ESTRAGON: After you.
VLADIMIR: No, no, you first.[27]

The vacuousness of various conventional 'fillers' is brought out by the context in which they are used, e.g. Estragon says, surveying the desolate scene, 'Charming spot . . . inspiring prospects . . . Let's go'.[28] And Pozzo pauses from shouting orders to Lucky to say to the tramps 'Touch of autumn in the air this evening'.[29] Likewise, various formulaic expressions of a social nature serve to point up the contradiction between verbal refinement and grossness of feeling.

The play is structured on a basis of contradiction involving not only linguistic forms from the past, but also actions and words centred on the present. The most striking example of present contradiction is that between action and word at the end of each act, when first Estragon says 'shall we go' and Vladimir replies 'Yes, let's go', but '*They do not move.*' The repetition of exactly the same words and non-action, with the tramps simply swopping the lines, crystallizes the contradiction.[30] The obvious lie is another version of the immediately perceptible contradiction: Vladimir chides Estragon for his evident lack of interest in his story of the two thieves, whereupon Estragon says '(*with exaggerated enthusiasm*) I find this really most extraordinarily interesting'.[31] The two tramps are avowedly waiting for Godot; when Pozzo first arrives and introduces himself, Estragon mishears his name as 'Godot', and says so. Yet, when Pozzo says to him 'You took me for Godot', he replies 'Oh no, sir, not for an instant, sir'.[32] In addition to these simple contradictions between 'lie' and 'truth', a more complex sequence of contradiction occurs concerning Pozzo's identity at his second arrival. Both the audience and Vladimir recognize Pozzo and Lucky by sight; not so Estragon, however, who once again thinks he is Godot, despite the meeting of the previous day. This apparent contradiction is further borne out by the failure of memory which accompanies Pozzo's blindness, so that the confirmation which both the audience and Vladimir expect concerning Pozzo's identity is not forthcoming.[33] This, as well as the other occasions in the play when the characters contradict each other, contradict themselves, repeat themselves with variations and echo themselves or each other, all discourage the audience from 'believing' what it sees and hears: it encourages distrust in language.

By contrast, *The Well of the Saints* poses no problem for the audience in identifying which words confirm and which contradict what it sees. At the outset, it can readily identify the actual contradiction between the ugly physical appearance of the blind couple and the illusion of beauty which their words convey. It transpires that this 'beauty' is part of a fictional world created for them with words by their seeing fellow-men. This fictional world is destroyed when Martin and Mary regain their sight, since this newly acquired sense of sight identifies their perception of each other with the public one. However, when blindness returns, they are at liberty to create their own fictional world which is independent of their seeing fellow-men, and also of the audience. Thus Mary can envisage herself ageing as 'a beautiful white-haired woman'; Martin thinks 'I'll be letting my beard grow in a short while – a beautiful, long, white, silken, streamy beard'; and finally they leave the settled community saying 'we've seen too much of everyone in this place, and it's small joy we'd have living near them, or hearing the lies they do be telling from the grey of dawn till the night'.[34] The coexistence of two different worlds, visible and imaginary or public and private, is again accommodated in language at the end of the play.

Synge's use of contradiction is a relatively simple opposition of visible actuality with two imaginary fictional worlds of which only the private one is autonomous. Beckett's use of contradiction is both structurally more fundamental and more complex, and it depends on his attributing a degree of self-conscious linguistic activity to his characters. While Synge's blind couple are unconscious that they are creating a private fictional world out of the language they share, many of the linguistic games played by Vladimir and Estragon are consciously undertaken 'to pass the time'. Also, Synge makes some neglected contents of the mind almost tangible through the very concrete nature of the language of his characters, whereas much of the language of Beckett's characters is vacuous.

Synge's tramps, being nearer to an oral tradition, still confidently use language for representational purposes, whereas Beckett's grant it no such powers. Synge effects his revitalization of English by basing it on the spoken language of a people who had recently acquired it, primarily through oral transmission. Thus he boldly altered its syntax according to structural forms from a noun-centred language and accordingly reduced its tendency to abstraction, without, however, expressly including such an intention in his theory. Beckett's characters, by continually using language to misrepresent what patently exists or happens, sophistically mislead themselves, each other, and the audience, to a point where all personal responsibility to referents is absent.

SOURCE: extracts from essay in *The Irish Writer and the City*, ed. Maurice Harmon (Gerrards Cross & Totowa, N.J., 1984), 90–102.

NOTES

[Reorganized and renumbered from the original. – Ed.]

1. J. M. Synge, Preface to *The Playboy of the Western World* in *Collected Works* Vol. IV, ed. Ann Saddlemyer (London: Oxford University Press, 1968), p. 53.

2. Samuel Beckett, 'Dante ... Bruno. Vico ... Joyce,' in *Our Exagmination Round his Factification for Incamination of Work in Progress* (repr. London: Faber & Faber, 1972), p. 15.

3. For treatment of Synge's syntactical structures, see Toni O'Brien Johnson, *Synge: The Medieval and the Grotesque* (Gerrards Cross: Colin Smythe, and Totowa, New Jersey: Barnes & Noble, 1982), pp. 97–114. Beckett's stylistic features are discussed by Andrew Kennedy in *Six Dramatists in Search of a Language* (London: Cambridge University Press, 1975). The present article owes much to his chapter on Beckett.

4. The concept of the documentary and monumental uses of language is developed by Paul Zumthor in 'Document et Monument', *Revue des Sciences Humaines* (Lille, January–March 1960), pp. 5–19, and in *Langues et techniques poétiques à l'époque romane* (Paris: Librairie C. Klincksieck), especially pp. 32–4.

5. Synge studied French medieval literature with Professor Petit de Julleville in Paris, and Beckett studied and subsequently taught French at Trinity College, Dublin.

6. See Mario Roques (ed.), *Le Garçon et l'aveugle* (Paris: H. Champion, 1912); P. L. Jacob (ed.), *Receuil de Farces, sotties et moralités* (Paris: Garnier, 1882), pp. 211–30 for *La Moralité de l'aveugle et du Boiteux*; and Toni O'Brien Johnson, 'The Well of the Saints and the Question of Genre', in op. cit., pp. 29–53.

7. See Gertrude Schoepperle, 'John Synge and his Old French Farce' in *North American Review*, October 1921, pp. 503–13.

8. P. L. Jacob, op. cit., pp. 226f.

9. Samuel Beckett, *Waiting for Godot* (London: Faber & Faber, 1956, repr. 1979), p. 74. This edition of *Godot* will be referred to throughout.

10. Cf. P. L. Jacob, op. cit., pp. 219–21 (the cripple, who is heavy because he has not defecated for six days, is put down to do so by the blind man) and *Waiting for Godot*, pp. 16 and 35, where Vladimir leaves the stage to urinate.

11. J. M. Synge, *The Well of the Saints* in *Collected Works* Vol. III: *Plays* I, ed. Ann Saddlemyer (London: Oxford University Press, 1968; repub. 1982 by Colin Smythe), pp. 71–81. This edition of *The Well* will be referred to throughout.

12. Ibid., pp. 69 and 73.

13. Ibid., p. 73.

14. Ibid., p. 117.

15. Ibid., pp. 115, 121 × 3, and 117.

16. Ibid., pp. 81, 107, 111, 141, and 149.

17. Ibid., p. 97.

18. Ibid., pp. 129 and 131.

19. See the following on non-verbal aspects of Beckett's plays: D. H. Curnow, 'Language and Theatre in Beckett's "English" Plays', in *Mosaic*, Vol. II, 1968–69; John Fletcher, 'Action and Play in Beckett's Theater', in *Modern Drama*, Vol. IX, 1966; and Edith Kern, 'Beckett and the Spirit of the *Commedia dell'arte*', in *Modern Drama*, Vol. IX, 1966.

20. Letter to Frank Fay, April 1904, quoted by Ann Saddlemyer in her Introduction to Vol. III of *J. M. Synge: Collected Works*, p. xxvii.

21. The altered syntactic emphasis of Hiberno-English has been analysed by Colin Meir as Yeats uses it: see his *The Ballads and Songs of W. B. Yeats: The Anglo-Irish Heritage in Subject and Style* (London: Macmillan, 1974), 'Yeats's Debt to Anglo-Irish Dialect', pp. 65–90. P. L. Henry, in his *An Anglo-Irish Dialect of North Roscommon* (Zurich: Aschmann & Scheller, 1957), gives many examples of Synge's use of structures of Irish origin.

22. See Andrew Kennedy, op. cit., pp. 26f and 135–9.

23. Beckett's explanations for his switch to French are listed by Ruby Cohn in *Back to Beckett* (Princeton: Princeton University Press, 1973), pp. 58f.

24. The principal examples of Hiberno-English usage in *Godot* are lexical, e.g. 'blathering', p. 10, 'dudeen', p. 35. Even where it extends to phrasal length, there is no indication that the structures are being used for the purposes of shifting syntactical emphasis, e.g. 'Get up till I embrace you', p. 9, or 'Go and see is he hurt', p. 87. Rather, these phrases endorse the notion of characters using well-worn oral forms. The view of *All That Fall* as self-indulgence is put forward by D. H. Curnow, op. cit., p. 56.

25. See Anselm Atkins, 'A Note on the Structure of Lucky's Speech' in *Modern Drama*, Vol. IX, 1966, p. 309; and 'Lucky's Speech in *Waiting for Godot*: A Punctuated Sense-Line Arrangement' in *Educational Theatre Journal*, December 1967, pp. 426–32.

26. See *Godot*, pp. 79f and 12.

27. Ibid., p. 17.

28. Ibid., pp. 13f.

29. Ibid., p. 24.

30. Ibid., pp. 54 and 94. Also, see Vladimir's speech beginning 'Let us not waste our time in idle discourse', p. 79.
31. Ibid., pp. 12f.
32. Ibid., pp. 22f.
33. Ibid., pp. 77–89.
34. Ibid., pp. 129, 131, and 151.

PART FOUR

The Playboy of the Western World

The Playboy of the Western World

Première: 26 January 1907, by the National Theatre Society at the Abbey Theatre, Dublin.

First printed in what was described as a Theatre Edition (Dublin: Maunsel, 1907), being Volume X of the Abbey Theatre Series. Manuscript and typescript drafts are detailed by Ann Saddlemyer in Synge's *Collected Works*, Volume IV (London: OUP, 1968), 294–359.

1. COMMENT AND REVIEWS

I *Lady Gregory* *(1913)*

... He worked very hard at *The Playboy*, altering it a good deal as he went on. He had first planned the opening act in the ploughed field, where the quarrel between Christy and his father took place. But when he thought of the actual stage he could not see any possible side wings for that 'wide, windy corner of high, distant hills'. He had also talked of the return of the father being at the very door of the chapel where Christy was to wed Pegeen; but in the end all took place within the one cottage room. We all tried at that time to write for as little scene-shifting as might be, for economy of scenery and of stage-hands.

In October, 1906, he writes to Mr Yeats: 'My play, though in its last agony, is not finished, and I cannot promise it for any definite day. It is more than likely that when I read it to you and Fay there will be little things to alter that have escaped me, and with my stuff it takes time to get even half a page of new dialogue fully into key with what goes before it. The play, I think, will be one of the longest we have done, and in places extremely difficult. ...'

I remember his bringing the play to us in Dublin, but he was too hoarse to read it, and it was read by Mr Fay. We were almost bewildered by its abundance and fantasy, but we felt – and Mr Yeats said very plainly – that there was far too much 'bad language', there were too many violent oaths, and the play itself was marred by this. I did not think it was fit to be put on the stage without cutting. It was agreed that it should be cut in rehearsal. A fortnight before its production Mr Yeats, thinking I had seen a rehearsal, writes: 'I should like to know how you thought *The Playboy* acted. ... Have they cleared many of the objectionable sentences out of it?'

I did not, however, see a rehearsal and did not hear the play again until the night of its production, and then I told Synge that the cuts were not enough, that many more should be made. He gave me leave to do this, and in consultation with the players I took out many phrases which, though in the printed book, have never since that first production been spoken on our stage. . . .

SOURCE: 'Synge', *English Review*, 13 (March 1913), 562–3.

II *J. M. Synge* (1907)

. . . 'The Playboy of the Western World' is not a play with 'a purpose' in the modern sense of the word, but although parts of it are, or are meant to be, extravagant comedy, still a great deal that is in it, and a great deal more that is behind it, is perfectly serious, when looked at in a certain light. That is often the case, I think, with comedy, and no one is quite sure today whether 'Shylock' and 'Alceste'[1] should be played seriously or not. There are, it may be hinted, several sides to 'The Playboy'. 'Pat', I am glad to notice, has seen some of them in his own way.[2] There may be still others if anyone cares to look for them.

SOURCE: letter published in *Irish Times*, 31 January 1907.

NOTES

 1. Leading figures in Shakespeare's *The Merchant of Venice* and Molière's *Le Misanthrope*.
 2. 'Pat' was P. D. Kenny, drama critic for the *Irish Times*.

III *W. B. Yeats* (1924)

. . . When I had landed from a fishing yawl on the middle of the island of Aran, a few months before my first meeting with Synge, a little group of islanders, who had gathered to watch a stranger's arrival, brought me to 'the oldest man upon the island'. He spoke but two sentences, speaking them very slowly: 'If any gentleman has done a crime we'll hide him. There was a gentleman that killed his father, and I had him in my house six months till he got away to America'. It was a play founded on that old man's story Synge brought back with him. A young man arrives at a little public-house and tells the publican's daughter that he has murdered his father. He so tells it that he has all her sympathy, and every time he retells it, with new exaggeration and additions, he wins the sympathy of somebody or other, for it is the countryman's habit to be against the law. The countryman thinks the more terrible the crime, the greater must the provocation have been. The young man himself, under the excitement of his own story, becomes gay, energetic and lucky. He prospers in love, comes in first at the local races, and bankrupts the roulette tables afterwards. Then the father arrives with his head bandaged but very lively, and the people turn upon the impostor. To win back their esteem he takes up a spade to kill his father in earnest, but, horrified at the threat of what had sounded so well in the story, they bind him to hand over to the police. The father releases him and father and son walk off together, the son, still buoyed up by his imagination, announcing that he will be master henceforth. Picturesque, poetical, fantastical, a masterpiece of style and of music, the supreme work of our dialect theatre, his *Playboy* roused the populace to fury. We played it under police protection, seventy police in the theatre the last night, and five hundred, some newspaper said, keeping order in the streets outside. It is never played before any Irish audience for the first time without something or other being flung at the players. In New York a currant cake and a watch were flung, the owner of the watch claiming it at the stage door afterwards. The Dublin audience has, however, long since accepted the play. It has noticed, I think, that everyone upon the stage is somehow lovable and companionable and that Synge has described, through an exaggerated symbolism, a reality which he loved precisely because he loved all reality. So far from being, as they had thought, a politician working in the interests of England, he was so little a politician that the world merely amused him and touched his pity. Yet when Synge died in 1909 opinion had hardly changed, we were playing to an almost empty theatre and were continually denounced. . . .

SOURCE: extract from 'The Bounty of Sweden', reprinted in *Autobiographies* (London, 1955), 569–70.

IV *Padraic Colum* (1926)

... One winter day I remember walking across Phoenix Park with
him, and his telling me about a new play that he was planning. It
would be an extravagant comedy, and it would turn upon a story
that he had heard – the story of a man accused of killing his father
and who is given refuge in a West of Ireland village. The psychological action would lie in the rise to self-esteem of a sheepish young
man through the dread fascination that is given him by the story of
his deed. Synge did not yet know what was to happen in the play: he
had planned a scene in the first act – the young man, eating a raw
turnip, sidles up to the counter of a public-house to get a glass of
porter with the only penny he has – that was to be the opening
scene. ...

   The Playboy of the Western World was written at times when Synge
was really ill, and for all its sanity and healthfulness, there are – or
rather there were in the first production – lines and an incident that
reflected the violence of the sick man. To-day, as it is played, it is
one of the popular plays in the Abbey Theatre's repertoire. *The
Playboy of the Western World* dramatises what is most characteristic
in Gaelic life – the Gaelic delight in vivid personality. ...

SOURCE: *The Road Round Ireland* (London & New York, 1926),
   367–9.

V *J. M. Synge* (1907)

In writing *The Playboy of the Western World,* as in my other plays, I
have used very few words that I have not heard among the country
people, or spoken in my own childhood before I could read the
newspapers. A certain number of the phrases I employ I have heard
also among the fishermen of Kerry and Mayo, or from beggars
nearer Dublin, and I am glad to acknowledge how much I owe,
directly and indirectly to the folk-imagination of these people.

Nearly always when some friendly or angry critic tells me that such or such a phrase could not have been spoken by a peasant, he singles out some expression that I have heard, word for word, from some old woman or child, and the same is true also, to some extent, of the action and incidents I work with. The central incident of *The Playboy* was suggested by an actual occurrence in the west. ...

SOURCE: note printed in Abbey Theatre programme, 26 January 1907.

VI   *W. G. Fay*   (1935)

... 1907 [was] the year that proved as stormy in my fortunes as its predecessor had been prosperous, for it began with the historic uproar over *The Playboy of the Western World* and ended with the departure of the Fays from the Abbey Theatre and from Ireland.

I often hear it said that a really great artist is unmoved by the howl of the rabble and goes on producing his work as he pleases, confident that the future will vindicate him. This is true only with some qualification. Great artists have shown magnificent examples of courage in the face of popular hostility, but that is not to say that they have not felt deeply wounded by it, and their resentment is often reflected in their work. A classic case is that of Thomas Hardy, who after *Jude the Obscure* retired from the struggle and devoted the rest of his life to poetry. But not every author, certainly not many young ones, can take the course of dignity and silence. The temptation to hit back is strong, and among those who have yielded to it we find J. M. Synge. He could not forgive the crass ignorance, the fatuity, the malevolence with which *The Well of the Saints* had been received. He had given of his best in good faith, and offence had been taken where no offence had been intended. 'Very well, then,' he said to me bitterly one night, 'the next play I write I will make sure will annoy them.' And he did. As soon as I cast eyes over the script of *The Playboy of the Western World* I knew we were in for serious trouble unless he would consent to alter it drastically. Many and many a time I strove with him, using all the arguments I could muster, to get him to see that if you attack your audience you must

expect them to retaliate, that you might as well write to a newspaper
and expect the editor not to insist on the last word. The emotions
displayed on the stage are designed by the author and interpreted by
the players to give the audience a vicarious experience of them, and
if the audience reacts to them, that is the measure of the author's
and actors' success. Thus, laughter on the stage makes laughter in
the house and anger makes anger. But by laughter I mean straight
laughter, not wrath disguised in a grin which the average audience is
quick to see through and resent accordingly. Synge could never be
made to understand that. He was apt to think in the terms of Zola,
who got his effects by keeping all his characters in one key. He could
never see that Zola was a novelist, not a dramatist, and that there is
all the difference between a printed story that one reads to oneself
and the same story told as a play to a mixed audience of varying
degrees of intelligence. Frank [Fay] and I begged him to make
Pegeen a decent likeable country girl, which she might easily have
been without injury to the play, and to take out the torture scene in
the last act where the peasants burn Christy with the lit turf. It was
no use referring him to all the approved rules of the theatrical game
– that, for example, while a note of comedy was admirable for
heightening tragedy, the converse was not true. The things that we
wanted him to alter did not amount to five per cent of the whole
play. *The Well of the Saints* had suffered from too much anger. *The
Playboy of the Western World* was anger *in excelsis*. The characters
were as fine and diverting a set of scallywags as one could invent for
one story, but it was years too soon for our audiences to appreciate
them as dramatic creations.

Frank and I might as well have saved our breath. We might as
well have tried to move the Hill of Howth as move Synge. That was
his play, he said, and, barring one or two jots and tittles of 'bad
language' that he grudgingly consented to excise, it was the play
that with a great screwing up of courage we produced.

I gave the *Playboy* long and careful rehearsal, doing my best to
tone down the bitterness of it, and all the time with a sinking heart. I
knew we were in for trouble, but it was my business to get Synge's
play produced as nearly to his notions as possible in the circumstances and with the material at my disposal. All through the first
act the play went splendidly, and I was beginning to feel hopeful,
even cheerful. The second act, too, opened to plenty of laughter. We
had not got to the beginning of the 'rough stuff'. But with the

entrance of the Widow Quin the audience began to show signs of restlessness. Obviously they couldn't abide her; and when we came to my line about 'all bloody fools', the trouble began in earnest, with hisses and cat-calls and all the other indications that the audience are not in love with you. Now that word 'bloody' in the script had given me qualms, but Synge had insisted – and who was I to contradict him? – that in the West it was the casual mild expletive, like 'bally', or 'beastly', or 'bloomin''. Yet how was Dublin to know that? In Dublin, as for that matter all over England and Scotland in those days, it was a 'low' word, a pothouse word. Quite a lot of years later, even, it provided the theatrical sensation of the London season when Bernard Shaw's Eliza Doolittle rapped it out in *Pygmalion*. Nowadays, I understand, it is so much a young lady's expression that no he-man ever dreams of using it. Synge was in advance of his time. There was therefore some excuse for the audience's protest, though it was needlessly violent. Yet the queer thing was that what turned the audience into a veritable mob of howling devils was not this vulgar expletive, but as irreproachable a word as there is in the English dictionary – the decent old-fashioned 'shift' for the traditional under-garment of a woman. There is a point in the play where Christy (which in this case was poor me) says, 'It's Pegeen I'm seeking only, and what'd I care if you brought me a drift of chosen females standing in their shifts itself, maybe, from this place to the Eastern World'. You may say that the image – a magnificent one, mark you – must have been shocking to so unsophisticated an audience as ours, but it was not the image that shocked them. It was the word, for the row was just as bad when Pegeen Mike herself said to the Widow Quin, 'Is it you asking for a penn'orth of starch, with ne'er a shift or a shirt as long as you can remember?'

The last act opened with the house in an uproar, and by the time the curtain fell, the uproar had become a riot. Two or three times I tried to get them to let us finish for the sake of those who wanted to hear the play, but it was no use. They wanted a row and they were going to have one. There were free fights in the stalls. Mr Hillis, our conductor, got his face damaged, and at one time it seemed as if the stage would be stormed. It was lucky for themselves that the patriots did not venture as far as that, for our call-boy, who was also boiler attendant and general factotum, had armed himself with a big axe from the boiler-room, and swore by all the saints in the calendar that he would chop the head off the first lad who came over the footlights.

And knowing him, I haven't a shadow of doubt that he would have chopped.

This was on a Saturday night. Over Sunday the directors had to consider whether they would bow to the storm and withdraw the play, or face it out. Very properly they took the courageous course, and the company, though it was no joke for them, loyally supported their decision to go on playing at all costs. And so on the Monday night the curtain was rung up to a well-organised pandemonium, for the patriots had been busy over the week-end also. As it was impossible for any of us to be heard, I arranged with the cast that we should simply walk through the play, not speaking a word aloud, but changing positions and going through all the motions, so to speak. The noise was terrific, but we finished the play. It was not until the Thursday night that, in order to give a fair deal to those who had paid their money to hear, the directors had the police in the theatre. We also had taken the precaution to pad the floor with felt, which frustrated the rhythmic stamping that had been the opposition's most effective device. Thus we were able once more to speak the lines, but our reputation as an Irish national institution was ruined. Not content with libelling the saintly Irish people, we had actually called in the tyrant Saxon's myrmidons to silence their righteous indignation! Of course the root of the trouble was that Synge had written a brilliant play about the Irish peasantry without any of the traditional sentiment or illusions that were then so dear to the Irish playgoer. He was accused of making a deliberate attack on the national character, whatever that may be. Even William Boyle was among the angriest of angry, though he had to confess that he had not seen the play but had only read the reports of the hubbub in the newspapers. To mark his loathing of us he withdrew all his plays, which I think was ungrateful, considering all we had done for him.

The uproar, of course, was not confined to the theatre. It re-echoed, with terrific amplification, in the Press, and Dublin in those days was peculiarly rich in organs of public opinion which ordinarily made a discordant chorus, but now were enabled to bray all together in something that was almost harmony. One or two writers ventured to 'praise with faint damns', but damning of some sort was *de rigueur*. Arthur Griffith was particularly venomous, and incidentally managed to make an ass of himself. He declared that 'shift' and 'bloody' were not the worst of Synge's verbal offences, that he and several friends present with him would take their Bible oath that another word, a nauseating word, a cloacine word was used. On being confronted with the script he had to admit (which he did with a very ill grace) that, in his eagerness to hear evil, he had misheard a perfectly innocent and commonplace word that sounds a little like it. Even more discreditable than this flight of imagination was his attack on the Abbey Theatre as an anti-Irish institution financed by English money, which was his agreeable way of describing Miss Horniman's generosity. The strictures of the dramatic critics and the fulminations of the leader-writers were followed up by the hysterics of the correspondence columns. Most of the letters were incredibly funny, though at the time we could not be expected to appreciate their humour. There was, for example, 'A Girl from the West', from whom I cannot help quoting a sentence:

Every character uses coarse expressions, and Miss Allgood (one of the most charming actresses I have ever seen) is forced to use a word indicating an essential item of female attire which the lady would probably never utter in ordinary circumstances even to herself. . . .

SOURCE: extract from *The Fays of the Abbey Theatre: An Autobiographical Record* by W. G. Fay & Catherine Carswell (London & New York, 1935), 211–17.

VII   *Daily Express*   (1907)

. . . The characters in the play are drawn from the people of the West of Ireland, and their language and methods of expression are as simple, unadorned, and direct as those of the type which they purport to represent. The comedy is in three acts, which are neither long nor heavy, and the dialogue is in many parts sparkling and witty. It would, perhaps, be better for some slight revision here and there, particularly in the third act in which there is a sentence spoken by the hero, which gave rise to an emphatic expression of dissent from the gallery, and which nobody could say was not justified. . . . The first act is brilliant and witty in dialogue and it made an excellent impression on the audience. The two following acts did not, however, quite maintain the standard thus set up, and the final curtain descended leaving many persons dissatisfied with the denouement. The incident already referred to – the howl set up at the objectionable phrase given to Christy to speak – spoiled everyone's chance of appreciating the finish of what is, on the whole, a clever piece of writing, cleverly acted and appropriately staged.

SOURCE: anonymous review in the Dublin *Daily Express* (28 January 1907), 6.

VIII *J. M. Synge* (1907)

... He [Townsend Walsh, biographer and dramatic critic] is quite right that early work like 'Riders to the Sea' has a certain quality that more mature work is without. People who prefer the early quality are quite free to do so. When he blames the 'coarseness', however, I don't think he sees that the romantic note and a Rabelasian note are working to a climax through a great part of the play [*The Playboy of the Western World*], and that the Rabelasian note, the 'gross' note if you will, *must* have its climax no matter who may be shocked. ...

SOURCE: letter to John Quinn dated 5 September 1907.

IX *James Agate* (1917)

'He passes away under a cloud, inscrutable at heart ... unforgiven, and excessively romantic. Not in the wildest days of his boyish visions could he have seen the alluring shape of such an extraordinary success.' This closing sentence from Mr Conrad's indictment of the romantically minded might well serve as epilogue to Synge's tragedy. The novel may be called a justification *à rebours* rather than an indictment, and Synge could call *The Playboy of the Western World* a comedy. For these playboys of Synge's and Mr Conrad's are of a world in which plain things cease to have plain meanings, death transfiguring to new and strange kinds of life, and failure leaping to amazing success. 'There's a great gap between a gallous story and a dirty deed', says Pegeen, and it is the right-thinking citizen and not the artist who will be keen to echo her. It is a pity that the savagery of the burning of [the] Playboy's leg is softened on the stage, out of deference, one must suppose, to the feelings of people who might see in it only an unpleasant physical cruelty and fail to recognize the conscientious persecution, the petty inquisitions of the *bourgeois*. Pegeen, as she burns his leg, has a 'God help him so', much too beautiful to be thrown away. And this artist, this playboy, fails to win Pegeen – fails, lured on to success beyond the understanding of the plain people of the play, the vision of unending romance. He is the triumphant lover of the whole actual world. The boast of the Playboy, his vaunted murder, is actually accomplished by the despicable widow Quin. Only Christy makes a wonderful song about it, so that there ceases to be a murder, the glory of the song blinding us. The widow Quin destroys her man in the commonplace circumstances of *actual* murder, ignominious, trite. We imagine that Synge attributed a real murder to one of the characters, and conveyed it in a contemptuous half-dozen lines to show his indifference and the indifference of his Playboy to the actuality of their themes. This soaring away from facts is the very essence of the play. Even the Playboy's love-making is not love, but love of the words love uses. Christy in his last scene with Pegeen is more self-conscious than Romeo. He tortures himself to fresh images of beauty:

Let you wait to hear me talking, till we're astray in Erris, when Good Friday's by, drinking a sup from a well, and making mighty kisses with our wetted mouths, or gaming in a gap of sunshine, with yourself stretched back unto your necklace, in the flowers of the earth.

And then spurred on by Pegeen's awe and hush to:

If the mitred bishops seen you that time, they'd be the like of the holy prophets, I'm thinking, do be straining the bars of Paradise to lay eyes on the Lady Helen of Troy and she abroad, pacing back and forward, with a nosegay in her golden shawl.

The whole beauty of the scene lies in the Playboy's real indifference to Pegeen except as a theme for love, and in the interweaving of glamours, his for his words, hers for him. It is not simple malice on

the widow Quin's part that she calls Pegeen 'a girl you'd see itching
and scratching, and she with a stale stink of poteen on her from
selling in the shop'. Nor is it an irresistible Zolaesque impulse of
Synge's, the uncontrolled passion of people other than artists for
seeing things as they really are. The point is that Pegeen, or another,
will do for this lover. The Playboy goes away, defeated and glorious
in the end, heedless of her.

It is almost a pity that the part is played by Miss Maire O'Neill.
One would like to see Pegeen as a wild, ignorant, healthily good-
looking girl, *dans le vrai*, exactly as she may be supposed to be 'in
real life'. Miss O'Neill has glamour, radiance, and all the wonder of
Christy's Helen of Troy and the holy Brigid speaking to the infant
saints. Christy's glamour loses force when it becomes rational and
sincere. And once get sincerity into this little play and you turn it
into a perverse and curious horror. Bring it in contact with truth and
its miracles of shunning fade and its fine evasions are away. It is a
marvel of artificiality like its author's style. The Playboy bestrides a
dung-heap. In his prose Synge twisted and compelled the country
speech to his liking, shaping its common beauties into rare and
precious things. The Irish peasants talk Irish-English, certainly, but
not the Irish-English of Synge. Let us rid ourselves of stories about
listening, note-book in hand, through chinks in floors and walls.
That is a necessity of letters that writers should hide. Synge's writing
is so little Irish that Irish people have been known to ask the
meanings of sentences. It is, rather, an extraordinary mosaic made
up of very beautiful Irish things, but no more 'natural' than the most
careful and precious inlay.

And when it's dead he is, they'd put him in a narrow grave, with cheap
sacking wrapping him round, and pour down quick-lime on his head, the
way you'd see a woman pouring any frish-frash from a cup,

is the speech of a nervous, sensitive modern. 'Cheap sacking', the
definite horror of it, betrays the man of letters as sharply as does the
cricket-cap in the ballad of the man who was to be hanged. Synge is
definitely an artist, dealing in the humbug that the art of writing
must always appear to be – to plain people. 'He goes away from a
living woman to celebrate his pitiless wedding with a shadowy ideal
of conduct.' So the Playboy, and so too every writer. And this play is
the singularly perfect work of a singularly perfect writer, who
renounced real life for shadowy ideals and ideas of living, and gave

up real language for the realities of a more perfect beauty. It is conceivable, even probable, that Synge cared little about his peasants. It is certain that he cared passionately for his writing about them. . . .

SOURCE: extract from 'The Irish Players', *Buzz, Buzz! Essays of the Theatre* (London, 1917), 150–3.

X *Edward Thomas* (1907)

The fresh beauty of the speech appears with greater clearness in the book than on the stage. Mr Synge has used only one or two words which he has not heard 'among the country people of Ireland, or spoken in his own nursery before he could read the newspapers'. That might seem a needless handicap; but then he uses their arrangement of these words – their idiom, their directness, their fancy that seems to be partly a quality of the words themselves. Since *Lyrical Ballads* there has hardly been such a notable purification of the diction of English verse (and prose, too) as has come in the past generation, chiefly from Irishmen like Messrs Yeats and Synge. The best of the old ballads are not more direct. The quite unbookish phrases are like the speech of very young children of high courage, and yet have in them at times great subtlety and fitness to the moods of modern men. Mr Synge's play is a mine of those phrases. His characters being simple country people and not considerably moved, we need not expect a wide range or much subtlety. Yet when his innkeeper says: 'Where would I get a pot-boy? Would you have me send the bell-man screaming in the streets of Castlebar?'; when Christy says: 'It's well you know it's a lonesome thing to be passing small towns with the lights shining sideways when the night is down, or going in strange places with a dog noising before you and a dog noising behind, or drawn to the cities where you'd hear a voice kissing and talking deep love in every shadow of the ditch, and you passing on with an empty, hungry stomach failing from your heart', or: 'If the mitred bishops seen you that time, they'd be the like of the holy prophets, I'm thinking, do be straining the bars of Paradise to lay eyes on the Lady Helen of Troy, and she abroad, pacing back and forward, with a nosegay in her golden shawl', when the Widow Quin speaks of 'Looking out on the schooners, hookers, trawlers is sailing the sea, and I thinking on the gallant hairy fellows are drifting beyond, and myself long years living alone' we relish speech as a really thirsty man does water. Not many writers can hope to mend their writing by listening to Irish peasant girls through a thin floor, but a comparison of Mr Synge's prose with the leading article or literary criticism of today will perhaps knock some young men off their stilts before it is too late. By nature or by art, we must achieve a speech something like this which corresponds with the thought almost onomata-poetically, or fail. . . .

SOURCE: *Bookman* (London), August 1907.

2. CRITICAL STUDIES

W. B. Yeats 'Mischievous Extravagance' (1910)

... *Riders to the Sea* has grown into great popularity in Dublin, partly because, with the tactical instinct of an Irish mob, the demonstrators against *The Playboy* both in the Press and in the theatre, where it began the evening, selected it for applause. It is now what Shelley's *Cloud* was for many years, a comfort to those who do not like to deny altogether the genius they cannot understand. Yet I am certain that, in the long run, his grotesque plays with their lyric beauty, their violent laughter, *The Playboy of the Western World* most of all, will be loved for holding so much of the mind of Ireland. Synge has written of *The Playboy*: 'Any one who has lived in real intimacy with the Irish peasantry will know that the wildest sayings in this play are tame indeed compared with the fancies one may hear at any little hillside cottage of Geesala, or Carraroe, or Dingle Bay'. It is the strangest, the most beautiful expression in drama of that Irish fantasy which overflowing through all Irish literature that has come out of Ireland itself (compare the fantastic Irish account of the Battle of Clontarf with the sober Norse account) is the unbroken character of Irish genius. In modern days this genius has delighted in mischievous extravagance, like that of the Gaelic poet's curse upon his children: 'There are three things that I hate: the Devil that is waiting for my soul; the worms that are waiting for my body; my children, who are waiting for my wealth and care neither for my body nor my soul: O, Christ, hang all in the same noose!' I think those words were spoken with a delight in their vehemence that took out of anger half the bitterness with all the gloom. ...

SOURCE: extract from 'J. M. Synge and the Ireland of his Time', *Essays and Introductions* (London, 1961), 337.

Frank O'Connor 'Male Myth' (1939)

... [Daniel] Corkery dislikes *The Playboy of the Western World* and goes to great pains to explain and justify the riots it caused. Again it is Synge's inability to understand the deepest spiritual emotions of the Irish countryman. Shauneen Keogh's cry, 'O St. Joseph and St. Patrick and St. Brigid and St. James, have mercy on me now!' shows, he tells us, that Synge's idea of the religious consciousness of the people was that of an outsider; 'for in that consciousness there is a vast chasm between the attributes of the Almighty and those of the saints'. From which one gathers that the author of the great lament for Patrick Sarsfield was a Protestant, since he distinctly says, '*Mo ghuidhe-se fein is guidhe Mic Mhuire leat!* – My own prayer too and the prayer of Mary's son'.

But Professor Corkery seems to have come skew-ways at *The Playboy*, for doesn't he assume that the theme is that of Beatrice and Dante:

> The indescribable, here it is done,
> The ever-womanly leads us on.

as he quotes from *Faust*? As there seems to be some doubt about the matter, it is as well to point out that the theme of *The Playboy* is – as we would expect – far simpler. It is almost mythological; we develop, Synge says, in imaginations of ourselves; 'Praise youth and it will prosper', the Irish proverb puts it; and so he shows us Christy Mahon, a half-idiot kept down by a tyrannical father, and who, as even half-idiots will, strikes out one day, and then flies in horror, under the impression that he is a parricide. He flies to a primitive community in the west, where outlaws are still admired, as they are in every primitive community. At the first touch of their respect Christy begins to respond; we see him becoming first loquacious, then a little vainglorious at the monstrousness of his own deed; yet not so much but that a knock at the door will send him scurrying for protection. We see that, after all, the 'dirty stuttering lout' needs only a little affection and praise to turn into a likely lad. When Pegeen and the widow dispute for his affections he grows by leaps and bounds, and the curtain falls on the first act while he is murmuring, 'Wasn't I a foolish fellow not to kill my father in the years gone by?'

Conscious roguery, says Professor Corkery, who seems to go wrong whenever he mentions *The Playboy*. An actor who spoke the curtain line with anything but earnestness and simplicity wouldn't know his job. At any rate, Professor Corkery denounces the whole thing. The theme, he says, is 'hardly even possible . . . the falling of a whole countryside at the feet of a self-declared parricide . . . is an assumption to which we cannot give more than grudging acceptance'. Not perhaps unless we have a deep sense of folk-life and approach it without that middle-class censoriousness which Synge abominated. Imagine trying to sing *Jesse James* with 'the word "conscience", the question of right and wrong, looming up before one's mind'.

> Jesse James was a lad that killed many a man,
> He robbed the Danville train,
> But a dirty little coward shot Mr. Howard
> And laid Jesse James in his grave.

'The impulse to protect the criminal', Synge says in *The Aran Islands*, 'is universal in the west. It seems partly due to the association between justice and the hated English jurisdiction, but more directly to the primitive feeling of these people, who are never criminals yet always capable of crime, that a man will not do wrong unless he is under the influence of a passion which is as irresponsible as a storm of the sea. If a man has killed his father and is already sick and broken with remorse, they can see no reason why he should be dragged away and killed by the law.'

Professor Corkery is right when he says the second act is weak. It is, shockingly weak, but not for the reason he suggests. The fact is that when Corkery criticizes the handling of Pegeen he is following Synge up the blind alley of the play. Pegeen is not a major character at all; she has not been acted upon by the dramatic machinery, and when she usurps the principal scenes in rivalry with the Widow Quin, she introduces an atmosphere of French farce which is always in conflict with folklore. Because the two characters essential to the myth are of course Christy and his father, and from the moment we become aware of the myth we know that inevitably old Mahon is still alive and are impatient for the necessary scene when the two characters who have been directly acted on by the dramatic machinery will resume their tussle on the new terms. There lies the real weakness of the second act. Nothing in it prepares us for the entrance of old Mahon, and the scenes with the young girls, with Pegeen, with Shauneen Keogh and the Widow Quin, which show us what Corkery calls 'the ascending graph' of Christy's development, are perilously close to being quite irrelevant. How different to the first act, where at every instant we are made aware of old Mahon, his family, and his home! 'And before I'd pass the dunghill, I'd hear himself snoring out – a loud lonesome snore he'd be making all times the while he was sleeping, and he a man would be raging all times the while he was waking, like a gaudy officer you'd hear cursing, and damning and swearing oaths.' 'Providence and mercy spare us all!' sighs Pegeen ecstatically, as well she might, and Christy continues, 'It's that you'd say surely if you seen him, and he after drinking for weeks, rising up in the red dawn or before it maybe, and going out into the yard as naked as an ash tree in the moon of May, and shying clods against the visage of the stars till he'd put the fear of death into the banbhs and the screeching sows'.

It is old Mahon's spiritual presence which keeps the whole first act so taut, and from the rise of the curtain on the second, we should be made ready for his entrance, should see that bandaged, raging man crawling up through Ireland, drawing ever nearer – perhaps it is he, surely it is; here he comes. It is the same prentice hand which, as in *The Well of the Saints*, invokes drastic dramatic machinery and then fails to exploit it.

And yet in spite of its faults, *The Playboy* is a play to which one gives one's heart. It is spontaneous, brilliant, full of joy; the myth when it transcends the clumsy intrigue has the power which only myths have of moving us profoundly. . . .

SOURCE: extract from 'Synge' in *The Irish Theatre*, ed. Lennox Robinson (London, 1939), 44–9.

Cyril Cusack A Player's Reflections on *Playboy* (1961)

I write primarily as an actor, which must at once set up a suspicion that what I say will be considerably coloured with ego and possible bias. So be it: I write out of my experience of playing Synge, and in particular the role of Christopher Mahon, which I have played over a period of just on twenty years – from 1936 to 1955 – ranging from Dublin, through the Irish provinces, to London and Paris. It is the one of all his characters through which, to my mind, almost to the point of identification a player may reach closest to the essential Synge, the playwright in search of himself.

When first I joined the Abbey Theatre, at its old Marlborough Street house, in 1932, the Synge repertoire was staling into a collection of museum pieces. No longer did *The Playboy of the Western World* conjure up a popular reaction of any kind. (I can recollect only a sentimental salute of applause for the love-scene – at the height of the tourist season.) Its audiences sat, thin and depressingly inert, present, as it were, behind a stifled yawn, some from a dutiful habit of play-going, some out of academic or literary interest, others from sentiment or curiosity – a wordless contradiction of the wordy tales of riots and ructions in the Abbey's early years.

Within the Theatre itself, however, amongst both directors and players *Playboy* still could arouse enthusiasm, occasionally even tempers, but referring mainly to the manner in which the play should be presented and acted, rather as if they were holding up the mirror to some far glory that was past. Introduced as 'prentice-player to the Synge drama I was at once made aware it required a 'traditional' style of acting, with a strong insistence from the 'traditionalists' on special rhythms and emphases in speech-delivery. It is true to say that already there existed in the Abbey, though a comparatively young theatre in the history of drama, a sense of tradition, but there was a tendency with some to hug it to death, forgetful of the fact that tradition, in order to remain vital, must draw upon the present as well as from the past. I approached my initiation with all due reverence.

Having myself, as a child-actor, emerged from the school of

155

melodrama associated with Boucicault and the despised 'stage-Irishman' – which, from Lady Gregory's pronunciamento, the Abbey was pledged to replace with indigenous theatre – I recognized the true theatrical quality of Synge. At the same time, instinctively I felt the necessity of relating the work to reality – as I knew it – and what I then understood as 'reality' was drawn from my observation of Irish speech and character through a touring childhood. So, though I was ignorant of the fact that the dramatist had, as he tells us, composed his dialogue in phrases culled directly from the mouths of the people, without being fully conscious of what I was doing I set out to play in a 'style' compounded of the purely theatrical with a form of naturalism perilously near to being simply representational, two apparently conflicting elements which nevertheless are present and compatible in the work of Synge. Needless to say, there was no great novelty in this, as I was to discover in my subsequent association abroad with many of the first generation Abbey players, of whose work in exile, even through an overlay of commercial theatre, I have had privileged glimpses; I would see that already had been achieved that fine balance of naturalism with the theatrical which was the ideal of Irish acting but which had fallen away, on the one hand into the near vaudevillian method demanded of the Irish actor by foreign commercial managements, and, on the other, into the false convention contrived by some of the later resident disciples of the Abbey tradition, or the pseudo-naturalism, later still, of younger reactionaries.

With the early disappearance from the Irish stage of Frank and W. G. Fay, who might be termed the Theatre's actor-founders, and – because of aims and views conflicting with those of its literary founders – with the general exodus from Ireland of such as Kerrigan and Digges, who left for America, and Sinclair, O'Rorke, Maire O'Neill and Sarah Allgood, who went to Britain, the unity of the company was temporarily broken and the acting tradition, so early flowering, was interrupted. Notwithstanding the arrival of individually great actors, like Barry Fitzgerald and F. J. McCormack, the succeeding company, though eventually an effective team, as a unit of personalities was less colourful. I should add that, while throughout its short history a number of highly competent and versatile players has remained with the Theatre, the general quality of the company has, however, from time to time taken on a different tone and emphasis.

My period with the Abbey Theatre, from 1932 to 1945, lay somewhere midway between the second group and the arrival of what I might describe as the Theatre's Gaelic-speaking era under the management of Mr Ernest Blythe. From then on, many of the players were recruited from rural Ireland, instead of, as had occurred heretofore, from Dublin; and for a time this latest period bore the bruise of crude behaviourism on the stage. Happily, there are signs now of some artistic rejuvenescence.

To return to my early experience: while allowances were made by the 'traditionalists' for my tentative and more exploratory renderings of Synge in some of the smaller roles – Bartley in 'Riders to the Sea', Owen in *Deirdre of the Sorrows*, even the Tramp in 'In the Shadow of the Glen' – when it came for me to play the major roles, of Christy in *The Playboy of the Western World* and Martin Doul in *The Well of the Saints*, murmurings were heard. On the opening night of a revival of the former play, with special settings and costume designs by the artist, Sean Keating, the late F. R. Higgins, poet and, at the time, managing-director of the Theatre, came to my dressing-room in a state of indignation:

'No Mayo man ever spoke like that!' he said.

'Why would he speak like a Mayo man?' I asked, in some bewilderment. 'Isn't he from Kerry? Doesn't he say ... "I'm thinking Satan hasn't many have killed their da in Kerry and in Mayo too"?'

Contrarily, the objection was concerned not so much with authenticity of dialect or the character's whereabouts as with the fact that in speaking the speech 'trippingly on the tongue' I had broken with a convention, one which, to my way of thinking, had set a manner of delivery altogether remote from human communication; much as that which, in style of speech, stance, and movement, down to the slightest inflection, the smallest gesture – until revitalized by the modern approach – had mummified the Shakespearean theatre. My heresy hunted out, I pleaded, defending a rather open position, that never had I heard human being speak so, as this convention demanded, and I disclaimed it as alien to both author and audience. To my relief, the performance was generally accepted as a revival in the literal sense and thence forward I saw myself as a protagonist of Synge, with a responsibility to communicate his language to the audience as living speech. ...

From my first playing of Christopher Mahon, which, erring on the side of naturalism, I related to myself, I became aware, as the play draws further away from the area of comedy towards its very much less comedic denouement, of some inadequacy, which for many years I attributed to the performance. Only latterly have I formed the opinion, however much it may smack of actor's vanity, that the inadequacy is in the play itself. This becomes evident as, with recurring anti-climax, it moves to its ending. Anti-climax is in the air when Christy, having chased Old Mahon with the loy, returns to the kitchen, alone, to be joined in a moment by Widow Quin who, with the girls, vainly tries to effect his escape. Again he is alone. (In the production with my company both in Dublin and Paris I had Christy flee the stage leaving it bare for the entry of the men.) Later comes the re-entry of Old Mahon, 'coming to be killed a third time . . .'; at the last there is the Playboy's speech after which, by the author's direction, 'he goes out', no more – a speech which, however rendered, only tolls a bell for the dead.

Christy, moving through a world of make-believe in which his listeners indulge with relish, reaches towards reality and self-discovery; as they accept, so he accepts his story, only here and there touching it with the shadow of positive mendacity; he assumes its central character as an actor identifying himself with the part he plays; but, unfortunately, at the play's ending reality disappears in a balloon-burst of disillusionment and the person of Christopher Mahon suddenly resolves itself into a dew. It is here that, as an actor, I find the part less than satisfying; here, where the playwright in search of himself is confronted with a void which is made the play's resolution. It is liberation, but a false one, of the artist in flight from reality; whom again we are invited to pursue into the mists in 'In the Shadow of the Glen' and *The Well of the Saints*. This may be acceptable as a poetic reality within the experience of the playwright but it falls short of universality. . . . Nevertheless, in his craftsmanship, in his sense of theatre, in his imagination and observation, in his desire and striving for identification with reality Synge is the greatest of the Irish dramatists. . . .

SOURCE: extracts from article in *Modern Drama*, 4 (December 1961), 300–4.

Robert Bechtold Heilman   'Sturdiest Comedy'   (1978)

... If we go back half a century [from Brendan Behan's *The Hostage* of 1960], cross Ireland westward to the 'wild coast of Mayo', moving from urban 'brockel' [one of Behan's character's name for a brothel] to rural seaside 'shebeen' or pub, we come across a similar range of personalities – from the naive to the knowing, from the spontaneous to the calculating, the extremes sometimes merging contradictorily – and a working community in which daily discords are all absorbed into the local way of life. In Synge's *The Playboy of the Western World* (1907), however, there is a real outsider: Christy Mahon comes from afar into a County Mayo village to excite longings and stir people at deeper levels usually not active in day-to-day life. The twenty-four-hour crisis – a remarkable feat of compression by the dramatist – turns on no political or societal problems, but unpretentiously goes to the heart of never wholly resolvable human desires and needs, and Synge is correspondingly closer to comic greatness than Behan. Christy Mahon is the mysterious visitant who sets people together by the ears or stands the local world on its head. He is potentially a demonic disturber or a new divinity. Thus Synge starts with an ancient archetype of community experience.

By reporting that he has murdered his father, whom he describes as a cruel and oppressive monster, Christy becomes a local idol. Patricide works with something of mythic force; kill the old king or priest or god and introduce a new and more vital order. Christy is an exciting medley of Hercules and potential Don Juan, fascinating to the women and hence subtly alarming to the men. As a hero he represents a break-through, daring, and the greatest liberty of all, that which recklessly subverts (the goal of all Ibsen characters who deride, or yearn to override, the 'sickly conscience'). Again, what goes on can be described in terms of Mann's dualism: the bohemian has charmed the bourgeois almost out of its usual caution and safety regulations. Christy is the liberating artist; there are various references to his poetic speech. Yet he himself does not wholly understand what psychic currents he has set up; pleasurably surprised at the warmth of his reception, he keeps repeating the murder story

159

rather mechanically – tediously to some – like a comedian with a sure-fire gag.

The hero has to be tested by further experience. It looks as if Christy will be done for when his supposedly dead father, furious over the filial blow on his still-bandaged head, shows up. For a while, though, he is held off by the Widow Quin ('about 30'). The one calmly pragmatic person in the community, she sees a good thing in Christy; she would gladly snatch him as a husband from Pegeen Mike, the lively, sharp-tongued, emotional young woman whom he really wants, and, failing the snatch, the widow is willing to help him for her own pecuniary advantage (with her balance and her sense of reality, she could be almost a Molière restabilizer of a situation). Her attitude really establishes Christy for us as more than a flash in the pan. We now see the naturalization of the hero – on the one hand the reduction of mystery in a packed Act III, on the other his earning of a more substantial local status: he wins various events in a local Olympic games. We infer that hitting his father, though Christy is still frightened of him, was itself a liberating experience that made it possible for him to discover latent abilities: this is the old myth of the late-developing hero who has been overlong oafish or inept. Christy's triumph ('such poet's talking, and such bravery of heart') completes his conquest of Pegeen Mike, who throws over her local swain Shawn Keogh ('a scarecrow, with no savagery or fine words in him at all'), and even wins her father's approval of a quick marriage to 'a daring fellow' who 'split his father's middle with a single clout'. Re-enter the father, unsplit and contemptuous: Pegeen Mike, who embodies a community's fickleness, turns against Christy; desperate to recover lost ground, Christy again lays his father out with a 'loy' (spade). Shock: the whole community turns against its erstwhile hero; only Widow Quin and a girl try to help him escape a new animosity – that of Pegeen Mike and all the men – which threatens him with hanging for his brutal crime. Resurrected a second time, his father rescues Christy: now in high spirits – Christy feeling himself a new masterful man, and his father delighted by his son's new manhood – they go off, declaring the local air uninhabitable, ridiculing Mayo, and anticipating a lively future elsewhere.

Synge's comedy achieves magnitude by giving play to some deeper human motives that stir up a community and could even shatter it. Beneath the villagers' attraction to the hero and to the spirit of romantic adventure which he embodies, Synge spots a strong inclination to violence ('savagery') and disorder, matters to which comic acceptance does not often extend. Synge's genius, however, is to present this anarchic, primitivistic passion in terms of the villagers' response to a deed marvellously conceived for its ambiguity and hence double utility. The father-'murder' happens twice, and Synge's big stroke is that the two events seem wholly different to the local audience. The first violent act is distant and narrated instead of present and actual. The villagers' admiration is called forth by a tale, a work of imagination; the exciting, envied breach of piety, of a fundamental bond of community, is a symbolic one. The catharsis is literary; the id roars, but there is no price. Then Synge brilliantly replaces the symbolic 'murder' by a literal, present, public one, and the 'clever, fearless' hero becomes a scoundrel worthy of hanging. Symbol and imagination are permitted what the actual is not; literary life has no limits, but literal life has to be limited. Synge now shows the community doing what it cannot fail to do, however unheroic and craven it may look as it condemns its once glorious hero. Pegeen Mike voices the issue: '. . . there's a great gap between a gallous [great, noble] story and a dirty deed'. 'Story' and 'deed': a fine summation of one of the dualisms that belong to the ways of the world. Back the town moves to the superego; to propriety and property, which, tame though they be, reaffirm stability; the bohemians go merrily on the way, and the bourgeois rules take over again, as they have to, even though they cause the sad sense of diminishment that always accompanies the resumption of ordinary life after a romantic escapade, a plunge into the forbidden, an imaginative adventure into new, gratifying, and frightening experience. The travelling minstrels depart, glory yields to safety, the spirit of bugle and drum to the humdrum.

The world that Synge leads us into is rich in meaning. The bohemians are outside the community and yet they, too, constitute a community with dynamics that hold for the village itself. The young hero finds himself, and the old order rejoices that he has done so, accepting the new possessor of manhood as a welcome companion. The new man establishes himself by a kind of initiation: demonstrating the ability, not to bear pain, but to inflict it; practising, not the unconscious cruelty of childhood, but the conscious ruthlessness that at the right times must coexist with pity if the adult world is not to go sentimental. The old order cries out at being hit, but it also sees the blow as a symbolic act; its absence would be worse than its presence. To the village the hero is a paradoxical fellow: he is liberating, but he is dangerous, an implicit critic of the nonheroic on which daily life depends. The community loves him but also fears and hates him; it enacts the perennial enthronement-followed-by-dethronement by which the sociopolitical body gratifies itself, that successive exercise of reverence for a hero and righteous indignation against him by which the public assures itself of its possession of opposite virtues – looking up to and looking down upon. At a different level the community knows what art may do and life may not. Let the libertinism embraced in art break out in the village square, and the villagers combine fear, right judgement, and self-righteousness in one confused, ambivalent, but vigorous response.

Yet, while he sees what the common feeling is, Synge does not make the village too homogeneous. It docs what it cannot help doing, but it has a healthful diversity. Even after the second 'murder' of Mahon, Sr., the Widow Quin and Sara Tansey are with Christy, wanting to save him from the mob; some women have an instinctual fidelity to the hero, a daring that answers to daring, a spontaneous affinity for the Juan in the strong man who pushes aside the code. Another energy besides that of convention and commandment is still active. We may wonder that Pegeen Mike is with the men, but we should not. She is essentially a nonsubversive child of the village, but, with her strong and quick feeling, she is a jump ahead of the community in its characteristic actions, either embracing the new hero or fearing and repudiating him. Yet Synge does not limit her to that, either, for he makes her also capable of the fine line that closes the play: 'I've lost the only Playboy of the Western World'. She does not disparage him to keep her self-image untarnished, or blame the community as if she were its victim. She acknowledges both that she has suffered a loss, and that the losing was hers. Instead of falling into sour grapes or recrimination or stoical nonexpression, she cries out with the pain of loss.

It has been said that the cry of anguish goes outside the bounds of comedy. On the contrary, it is the identifying mark of the sturdiest comedy that strains at conventional limits to include an unexpected range of the ways of the world. Comedy includes pain; it characteristically accepts pain as fact. To clarify: its business is not the pain of guilt, which is tragic, or the pain of hopeless suffering, which creates the drama of disaster, or of the stifling or barely salvable life, which is the material of black comedy. It is not the pain from which there is no escape and for which there is no remedy. It is simply the pain of things as they are and for the most part have to be; most frequently it is the pain of getting only what one is up to. The gently ironic notation of that pain is the apex of Synge's drama, which, without finger-pointing or side-taking, has genially accepted the ambiguous interplay between generations, between the hero and society, between different voices in society, between the symbolic and the literal forms of subversive action, between the realm of imagination with its libertine leaping and bounding, and the realm of workaday living with its inevitable walking and even trudging. ...

SOURCE: extract from *The Ways of the World: Comedy and Society* (Seattle & London, 1978), 159–63.

Augustine Martin Christy Mahon and the Apotheosis of Loneliness (1972)

Agreement is general among critics that *The Playboy of the Western World* is a masterpiece. But there is still a curious diversity of opinion about the precise nature of its excellence. Those among its first audience who were not infuriated by the play were puzzled by it. Those who did not condemn it in sociological terms as a libel or a travesty of Irish life wondered what else it might be. Synge himself hastily called it an 'extravaganza'[1] and swiftly withdrew the label. Yeats, arguing with a judge in court, preferred to call it an 'exaggeration'.[2] Even when critics took the debate beyond the cockpit of affronted patriotism they could not reach agreement either on its dominating theme or on the allied problem of its dramatic category.

Una Ellis-Fermor called it a 'tragi-comedy' which took for its main theme 'the growth of fantasy in a mind or a group of minds'.[3] Ann Saddlemyer expands this insight when she suggests that 'in *The Playboy* we see the power of the myth to create a reality out of the

dream or illusion itself'.[4] Professor Henn in his Introduction to the
Methuen edition of the *Plays and Poems* outlines seven possible
readings of the play. He suggests that it might be seen as a 'semi-
tragedy'; as a 'free comedy', in which moral issues are reversed,
transcended or ignored in the desire for 'energy'; as a 'Dionysiac
comedy'; as a 'satire' in which Christy becomes a 'comic Oedipus';
as 'mock-heroic' in which Christy becomes a 'comic Odysseus'; as 'a
tragi-comic piece with the Widow Quin as Nausicaa'; and finally, a
reading he seems to favour, as a tragedy with Pegeen as the 'heroine-
victim',[5] Norman Podhoretz in a persuasive essay suggests that the
play has 'the myth of rebellion against the father as its basis'.[6] P. L.
Henry sees Christy as the 'Playboy-Hero' and finds parallels to him
in *Beowulf* and the heroic Irish sagas.[7] Stanley Sultan finds in
Christy's person 'a pervasive, sincere and full-fledged analogue to
Christ'.[8] Alan Price sees it primarily as a play in which 'Christy's
imagination transforms the dream into actuality'.[9] Ann Saddlemyer
believes that '*The Playboy of the Western World* deals with the actual
creation of myth'.[10] Synge himself has remarked that 'there are, it
may be hinted, many sides to *The Playboy*';[11] the critics continue to
bear him out. Clearly the play is capable of yielding a wide diversity
of valid readings, depending what 'side' one approaches it from. But
where is its centre? What basic myth or fable does it enact? What
theme is embodied in that fable? What kind of play is it? These are
still questions worth asking.

More than one critic has complained that the end of *The Shadow
of the Glen* is unconvincing. The reconciliation between Daniel
Burke and Michael Dara – who after all had been planning to
supplant him as Nora's husband – has been seen as too sudden, too
much of a *volte-face*. 'I was thinking to strike you, Michael Dara,'
Burke says, 'but you're a quiet man, God help you, and I don't mind
you at all.' The point of course is that they are two of a kind; they are
settled men, householders. They want a world in which they can
have their drinks in peace. Michael Dara is no longer a threat once
Nora and the Tramp, the people of passion and poetry, have been
expelled. With their expulsion society has righted itself and can get
on with its quotidian business. The pattern is central to Synge's
comedies. As the curtain falls on *The Well of the Saints* the freebooters, Martin and Mary Doul, have departed, and the Saint leads
in the settled man, Timmy the Smith, and his bride to be married.
In *The Tinker's Wedding* the Priest is left 'master of the situation'

while the tinkers retreat into their vagrant irresponsibility. The end of *The Playboy* gives a richer, more complex, version of the same basic pattern. Michael James remarks with relief that 'we'll have peace now for our drinks', while a disconsolate Pegeen laments, too late, the loss of her only playboy. She realizes that Christy's visitation had presented her with a vivid possibility of passion and poetry, and that she has failed to grasp it. With the exit of Christy, launched on his 'romping lifetime', the spirit of Dionysus has departed. She is back where we had found her at the first curtain, in the world of Shawn Keogh and the papal dispensation and the trousseau that must be ordered from Castlebar.

The two life-views offered by the play may usefully be called Dionysiac and Apollonian. Dionysiac is the more easily acceptable: Daniel Corkery was perhaps the first to apply it when he rejected the term 'extravaganza' – 'Dionysiac would have served him better, meaning by that word the serving of the irresponsible spirit of natural man'.[12] Northrop Frye, on the other hand, describes Apollonian comedy as 'the story of how a hero becomes accepted by a society of gods'.[13] If we take the definition at its 'low mimetic'[14] level we can see that *The Playboy*, for a good deal of its action, shapes like this kind of comedy, only to swerve into Dionysiac triumph in its final resolution. It is clear from the early drafts[15] of the play that Synge considered and rejected many different kinds of ending: he contemplated a possible marriage between Christy and the Widow Quin, a *menage à trois* involving the two Mahons and the Widow Quin, even a wedding between Christy and Pegeen. But it became increasingly clear to him that his material demanded that Christy refuse membership of the settled community, and also that the discovery of his own nature involved the discovery and recognition of his real father and the rejection of the pseudo-Dionysian Michael James. For despite his recklessness at the wake, despite his willingness – at least while he is drunk – to have Christy as a son-in-law, Michael James ends up with a pathetic anxiety to protect our 'little cabins from the treachery of law'. On the other hand Old Mahon's final 'Is it me?' and 'I'm crazy again' betoken his delighted recognition that Christy is really his son, instinct with the same savagery, energy and *braggadocio*.

Indeed one can discern three groups of characters in the play, and distinguish them in terms of the Dionysiac and Apollonian postures. Old Mahon from the beginning and Christy towards the end embody the Dionysiac freedom, energy and excess. Shawn Keogh and the offstage but influential Father Reilly, at their low mimetic level, represent a version of the Apollonian – the rational, the settled, the well-ordered existence. The latter attitude finds expression not only in character and social pattern but in a sort of ritual invocation of 'the Holy Father and the Cardinals of Rome', of 'St. Joseph and St. Patrick and St. Brigid and St. James'. In between is a group – one might call them the 'pseudo-Dionysians' – who waver between the two positions. Michael James, Philly and Jimmy rejoice in the Bacchantic excess of Kate Cassidy's wake, but when their security is threatened they opt for the domestic pieties. They salute the Dionysiac vigour and daring; in the person of Christy they try to accommodate it, even to use it. But their ambivalence is patent, and it provides a good deal of the play's comic incongruity, as with Jimmy's remark before leaving for the wake: 'Now, by the grace of God, herself will be safe this night, with a man killed his father holding danger from the door'.

Pegeen is torn between the two attitudes. Her intended marriage to Shawn clearly implies no acquiescence to his values. When he asserts that 'we're as good this place as another, maybe, and as good these times as we were forever', she replies with scorn:

As good, is it? Where now will you meet the like of Daneen Sullivan knocked the eye from a peeler, or Marcus Quin, God rest him, got six months for maiming the ewes, and he a great warrant to tell stories of holy Ireland till he'd have the old women shedding down tears about their feet. Where will you find the like of them, I'm saying?

The irony of her situation is, of course, that when she does encounter the likes of them in Christy she proves unequal to the challenge thus presented. She recognizes in Christy a kinsman of the poets – 'fine fiery fellows with great rages when their temper's roused' – and approves. But she tries to domesticate him, to tame his fire. When she is presented in the final scenes with the full reality of his fiery nature she fails. As Norman Podhoretz puts it, she 'can perceive greatness but cannot rise to it'.[16] She is the tragic figure of the play. But that is not to agree with Professor Henn that the play is a tragedy, her tragedy.

The play is Christy's. It is about his escape to freedom between the Scylla and Charybdis of loneliness on the one hand and domination on the other. It is about his collision with settled society and his victorious rejection of it in favour of a new triumphalist attitude to the world. If the collision with society had resulted in his destruction the play would have been a tragedy. As it celebrates the victory of the aggressive individual will over the immoveable forces of society it must be deemed a Dionysiac comedy – the only great one of its kind that I know.

The core of this comedy is Christy's loneliness. Synge went to great pains to enunciate this theme, to build it up gradually till it achieves full expression half-way through the play. In the early drafts[17] Christy's loneliness is dwelt on at length in his conversation with Pegeen in the first act; but much of the material is later struck out with the marginal note – 'Reserve this lonesome motif for II'.[18] Eventually it is towards the middle of Act II that the theme gets its full orchestration. There, when Pegeen threatens to send him away Christy replies with bleak realism, 'I was lonesome all times and born lonesome, I'm thinking, as the moon of dawn.' This is the crux of his condition. How is he to heal the wound of his lonesomeness? Can he do so without exchanging one kind of domination for another? Because it seems at this point that he can only have Pegeen on her own overbearing terms. At this point he is willing to accept those terms; as yet he knows no better, he has not fully discovered himself. When she relents ('Lay down that switch and throw some sods on the fire. You're pot-boy in this place, and I'll not have you mitch off from us now') his relief is painful:

CHRISTY: [*astonished, slowly*]. It's making game of me you were [*following her with fearful joy*], and I can stay so, working at your side, and I not lonesome from this mortal day. . . .

The story of his domination by his father unfolds alongside the theme of his lonesomeness. In his description of Old Mahon in the horrors of drink the full Dionysiac chord is struck:

It's that you'd say surely if you seen him and he after drinking for weeks, rising up in the red dawn, or before it maybe, and going out into the yard as naked as an ash tree in the moon of May, and shying clods against the visage of the stars till he'd put the fear of death into the banbhs and the screeching sows.

The presence of Old Mahon in Christy's life had in itself been ferocious and formidable. It became unbearable, we are told in the second act, when he tried to force Christy into marriage with the woman who had suckled him as a child. It is this that rouses his

spirits to 'a deed of blood'. When Norman Podhoretz suggests that
the play's underlying myth is 'rebellion against the father'[19] he gives
us, I believe, precisely half the story. The other half is the recognition and acceptance of the father, and this is enacted in the reversal
at the end, after the second and deliberate 'killing'. In the meantime
Christy must discover and reject an alternative and different father
in Michael James, a different form of female domination in Pegeen
Mike. It is significant that Pegeen is the first person to offer him
violence when first he enters the Flaherty cabin, and that she
behaves towards him with the most surly possessiveness (*seizing his
arm and shaking him*) when the Widow Quin makes her play for him
towards the end of Act I. Before she leaves, the Widow Quin warns
him that 'there's right torment will await you here if you go
romancing with her like'. Therefore, though Christy may be in-
genuously happy with his 'great luck and company', the audience
watching the first curtain fall has its own well founded reservations.

At the opening of Act II we find Christy transformed with the
prospects of companionship which his new life seems to hold for
him. He can henceforth spend his days 'talking out with swearing
Christians in place of my old dogs and cat'. Immediately he has an
audience of young girls to whom he retells the story which has now
grown to heroic proportions.[20] He is praised for his eloquence as
well as for his daring. The toast proposed to him and the Widow
Quin by Sara Tansey compares them – both killers, and loners – to
the 'outlandish lovers in the sailor's song' and goes on to invoke the
extravagant Dionysiac values to which Christy now aspires in his
imagination but which he has yet to embody and realize in life and
action. . . . It is at this moment that Pegeen returns, drives them
from the house, and turns on Christy with quite gratuitous cruelty.
Here we see some of the 'torment' that the Widow Quin had
predicted for him. And it is here that the theme of loneliness is given
its full expression. Christy is forced to choose between an obedient
security with Pegeen on the one hand and the lonesome roads on
the other. One could argue that this is Christy's first failure: he
hasn't grown sufficiently into his new self to make the choice
appropriate to his nature. As Synge seems to have worked harder on
this than on almost any other scene in the play it is worth examining
at length:

> CHRISTY: [*loudly.*] What joy would they [the neighbour girls] have to
> bring hanging to the likes of me?

PEGEEN: It's queer joys they have, and who knows the thing they'd do, if it'd make the green stones cry itself to think of you swaying and swiggling at the butt end of a rope, and you with a fine, stout neck, God bless you! the way you'd be a half an hour, in great anguish, getting your death.

CHRISTY: [*getting his boots and putting them on.*] If there's that terror of them, it'd be best, maybe, I went on wandering like Esau or Cain and Abel on the sides of Neifin or the Erris Plain.

PEGEEN: [*beginning to play with him.*] It would, may be, for I've heard the Circuit Judges this place is a heartless crew.

CHRISTY: [*bitterly.*] It's more than judges this place is a heartless crew. [*Looking up at her.*] And isn't it a poor thing to be starting again and I a lonesome fellow will be looking out on women and girls the way the needy fallen spirits do be looking on the Lord?

PEGEEN: What call have you to be lonesome when there's poor girls walking Mayo in their thousands now?

CHRISTY: [*grimly.*] It's well you know what call I have. It's well you know it's a lonesome thing to be passing small towns with the lights shining sideways when the night is down, or going in strange places with a dog nosing[21] before you and a dog nosing behind, or drawn to the cities where you'd hear a voice kissing and talking deep love in every shadow of the ditch, and you passing on with an empty hungry stomach failing from your heart.

PEGEEN: I'm thinking you're an odd man, Christy Mahon. The oddest walking fellow I ever set my eyes on to this hour to-day.

CHRISTY: What would any be but odd men and they living lonesome in the world?

Two points are worth making here. Christy talks in the language and imagery of an outsider. It is the moving imagery of a traveller looking in at the settled world, wondering what it is like, certain that it alone holds the answer to his deprivation. Furthermore the warmth of this settled world is continuously seen in terms of sexual love. The one implies the other; his choice is between Pegeen Mike and exterior darkness. They slowly work towards a reconciliation, almost a declaration of love. But Pegeen's final remark before the entry of Shawn Keogh establishes her dominance in the relationship:

I'm thinking you'll be a loyal young lad to have working around, and if you vexed me while since with your leaguing with the girls, I wouldn't give a thraneen for a lad hadn't a mighty spirit in him and a gamey heart.

His 'wildness' is approved, so long as it dances to her tune.

Meanwhile the forces of society are working for his expulsion. Shawn Keogh, ambiguously abetted by the Widow Quin, tries to bribe him with a suit of clothes and a ticket for America. He fails, and the plot seems set fair for a romantic resolution, when Old Mahon appears. There is savage dramatic irony in the scene where Christy cowers behind the door and listens to his past being rehearsed for the Widow Quin in his father's contemptuous vision. . . . It is now evident that Christy must defeat or outwit his father if he is to realize his expectations. For the first time we find a genuine, if impotent, anger rising in him; and this anger is embodied in rhetoric that becomes more vivid and fearless as the play proceeds . . . The second act ends therefore with Christy poised between a past that holds only humiliation, impotence and loneliness, and a future that seems to offer him the vivid things – love, companionship, admiration and, more problematically, freedom.

When Old Mahon reappears at the opening of Act III the resemblances between him and Christy are deftly emphasized. . . . Furthermore, like his son, he is constantly described in the language and imagery – whether his own or Christy's – as an outsider, a wanderer. Though he owns a farm he never appears as a householder; he is consistently evoked in terms of the open air, the roads, the taverns, the prisons and asylums. . . . It is also notable that Old Mahon's descriptions of Christy present him in terms of the hills, the fields and the road – never of the house. These clear indications of an elemental kinship between them tend subtly to offset their mutual antagonism throughout and help to prepare us not only for their reversal of roles, but also their reconciliation in the recognition scene at the end. This recognition is hinted at when Old Mahon, watching the races on the strand, sees his own son carrying all before him. But he is not ready yet for the real recognition – that Christy is truly his son, an even greater 'playboy' than himself. This insight can only be reached when Christy recognizes Mahon as his real father, thereby rejecting the men of Mayo and their law-fearing timidity, and by transcending his infatuation for Pegeen.

But first, in that remarkable love scene with Pegeen in Act III, we are permitted to see Christy in full possession of his powers of eloquence, passion and tenderness playing for 'the crowning prize' and winning. Here Christy carries Pegeen triumphantly into his outdoor world: the language in which he wooes her is redolent of movement, of the outdoors, of 'Neifin in the dews of night'. She baulks coyly for a moment at his 'poacher's love', but cannot help yielding to it. . . . Christy for the first time seems to be winning on his own terms. The play seems to be moving towards the resolution of traditional romantic comedy, with a wedding between Christy and Pegeen, and a possible second between Old Mahon and the Widow Quin – a victory for Apollo. But Pegeen is not Nora Burke; and the play turns swiftly towards a different and altogether more satisfactory conclusion.

Christy is now 'mounted on the spring-tide of the stars of luck'; Pegeen swears to wed him 'and not renege'; Michael James – not without fumbling reservations – gives them his drunken blessing. It seems the moment of extreme felicity: Christy has found status, love, a new father. But it is a false felicity, because his real father is still alive. The sudden appearance of Old Mahon changes everything. Immediately Pegeen reneges. Her reason is the social one: she thinks it bad 'the world should see me raging for a Munster liar and the fool of men'. Christy now goes through a series of traumatic insights. First he tries to deny Old Mahon. He then appeals vainly for help to the two women. Then a vision of his past loneliness drives him to desperation. ... Now Old Mahon threatens him; the crowd jeers him; he begins to see the truth of his situation, the folly of his desire to be one of them. ... His second insight comes after he has 'killed' Old Mahon the second time. He thinks that Pegeen will take him back now, will 'be giving me praises the same as in the hours gone by.' But he must transcend this vanity. She rejects him more emphatically: for her there is 'a great gap between a gallous story and a dirty deed'. Again invoking the social ethic she urges the Mayo men to take him to the peelers 'or the lot of us will likely be put on trial for his deed to-day'. As she prepares a lighted sod to 'scorch his leg', he realizes the foolishness of his love for her. Now he is utterly alone, and it is significant that now his terror disappears. His true nature emerges in all its fierceness. His language rises to a fine reckless crescendo:

> CHRISTY: You're blowing for to torture me? [*His voice rising and growing stronger.*] That's your kind, is it? Then let the lot of you be wary, for if I've to face the gallows I'll have a gay march down, I tell you, and shed the blood of some of you before I die.
>
> SHAWN: [*in terror*]. Keep a good hold, Philly. Be wary for the love of God, for I'm thinking he would liefest wreak his pains on me.
>
> CHRISTY: [*almost gaily*]. If I do lay my hands on you, it's the way you'll be at the fall of night hanging as a scarecrow for the fowls of hell. Ah, you'll have a gallous jaunt I'm saying, coaching out through Limbo with my father's ghost.

SHAWN: [*to* PEGEEN]. Make haste, will you? Oh, isn't he a holy terror, and isn't it true for Father Reilly that all drink's a curse that has the lot of you so shaky and uncertain now.

CHRISTY: If I can wring a neck among you, I'll have a royal judgment looking on the trembling jury in the courts of law. And won't there be crying out in Mayo the day I'm stretched up on the rope with ladies in their silks and satins snivelling in their lacy kerchiefs, and they rhyming songs and ballads on the terror of my fate? [*He squirms round on the floor and bites* SHAWN'S *leg.*]

SHAWN: [*shrieking*]. My leg's bit on me! He's the like of a mad dog, I'm thinking, the way that I will surely die.

CHRISTY: [*delighted with himself*]. You will then, the way you can shake out hell's flags of welcome for my coming in two weeks or three, for I'm thinking Satan hasn't many have killed their da in Kerry and in Mayo too.

It is now that Old Mahon comes in again, 'to be killed a third time', and the two father figures, representing two different life-views, confront each other. Michael, sobered and diminished, pleads 'apologetically' for the safety of his little cabin and his daughter's security while Old Mahon rejoices in a future of bravado and adventure in which his son and he will 'have great times from this out telling stories of the villainy of Mayo and the fools is here'. It is here that Christy has his final insight and his ultimate victory. He now knows that he not only has mastered himself but subdued his father as well. He will go, but the roles will be reversed; he will be 'master of all fights from now'. He has at last discovered his true Dionysiac nature, and in discovering it he has shaken off all domination and transfigured his lonesomeness into a posture of gay, predatory adventure. In the parting speech the wildness of the father is elevated and transformed in the poetry and passion of the son:

CHRISTY: Ten thousand blessings upon all that's here, for you've turned me a likely gaffer in the end of all, the way I'll go romancing through a romping lifetime from this hour to the dawning of the judgment day . . .

So the freebooters take to their proper element, the road, and the timid people of Mayo take to their drinks, their hopes, their lamentations. The astringent light of comedy has clarified each role, defined each relation.

SOURCE: extracts from essay in *Sunshine and the Moon's Delight: A Centenary Tribute to John Millington Synge 1871–1909*, ed. S. B. Bushrui (Gerrards Cross & Beirut, 1972), 61–73.

NOTES

[Reorganized and renumbered from the original – Ed.]

1. Quoted by Green and Stephens, *Synge*, p. 240.

2. *Freeman's Journal*, 31 January 1907, p. 8.

3. *The Irish Dramatic Movement* (London, Methuen, 1954), p. 175.

4. *J. M. Synge and Modern Comedy* (Dublin, Dolmen Press, 1967), p. 23.

5. *The Plays and Poems of J. M. Synge* (London, Methuen, 1963), pp. 57–8.

6. 'Synge's *Playboy*: Morality and the Hero', *Essays in Criticism*, III, 3, July 1953, p. 337.

7. 'The Playboy of the Western World', *Philologic Pragensia*, Rocnik VII, Číslo 2–3, 1965.

8. 'A Joycean Look at *The Playboy of the Western World*', *The Celtic Master*, ed. Maurice Harmon (Dublin, Dolmen Press, 1969), p. 51.

9. *Synge and Anglo-Irish Drama* (London, Methuen, 1961), p. 162.

10. *Op. cit.*, p. 21.

11. *Synge*, p. 244.

12. *Synge and Anglo-Irish Literature* (Cork University Press, 1931), p. 185.

13. *Anatomy of Criticism* (Princeton University Press, 1957), p. 43.

14. *Ibid.*, p. 366. Low mimetic; a mode of literature in which the characters exhibit a power of action which is roughly on our own level, as in most comedy and realistic fiction.

15. *C.W.*, IV, p. 295 *et seq.*

16. 'Synge's *Playboy*: Morality and the Hero', *loc. cit.*, p. 344.

17. *C.W.*, IV, p. 82, notes 1–7.

18. *Ibid.*, note 1.

19. 'Synge's *Playboy*: Morality and the Hero', *loc. cit.*, p. 337.

20. The heroic motif in this play is treated thoroughly and perceptively by P. L. Henry, 'The Playboy of the Western World', *loc. cit.*

21. In the Methuen (Henn, *op. cit.*) and in all other previous editions I have consulted the word is 'noising'. Professor Saddlemyer changes it to 'nosing' but provides no textual note on the emendation.

Ann Saddlemyer 'Women in *The Playboy*' (1983)

Maurya of *Riders to the Sea*, Pegeen Mike of *The Playboy of the Western World*, Deirdre of the Sorrows, all are acknowledged leading figures in the hierarchy of twentieth-century drama. What has less often been observed (although more so recently)[1] is that in nearly all of Synge's plays the women are not only more clearly defined than most of the men but also treated with a sympathetic complexity which frequently determines plot, mood and theme. Even the jaunting, joy-ridden Christy Mahon is delineated and nourished by the two women who battle for possession, Pegeen and the Widow Quin. That very parricide which catapults him into mythic glory is initiated by his father's wily attempts to mate him with the fearsome Widow Casey – half-horror, half-nurse, surely in herself a veiled parody of the hag-goddess of sovereignty, the 'loathly lady', with a touch of insatiable Medbh thrown in for good measure:

A walking terror from beyond the hills, and she two score and five years, and two hundredweights and five pounds in the weighing scales, with a limping leg on her, and a blinded eye, and she a woman of noted misbehaviour with the old and young . . . He was letting on I was wanting a protector from the harshness of the world, and he without a thought the whole while but how he'd have her hut to live in and her gold to drink . . . 'I won't wed her,' says I, 'when all know she did suckle me for six weeks when I came into the world, and she a hag this day with a tongue on her has the crows and seabirds scattered, the way they wouldn't cast a shadow on her garden with the dread of her curse.'[2]

As the Mayoites learn to their cost, Christy Mahon escapes this gruesome Oedipal fate (to kill a father and marry with a mother); he also escapes finally from dependency, when, thanks to one woman, he is freed from hiding behind the skirts of another.[3] There is a fittingly heroic analogue in Old Mahon, himself vividly described in the midst of delirium tremens 'shying clods again the visage of the stars', recognizing Christy the new-found Playboy, 'I'd know his way of spitting and he astride the moon'. But it is Woman who has made that heroism possible through the act of recognition.

It is Pegeen who raises the broom and calls forth the beginning of a tale till then existing in the delighted curiosity of Christy's inquisitors alone, who can only reflect their private meaner, darker inclinations:

> PEGEEN: He's done nothing, so. If you didn't commit murder or a bad nasty thing, or false coining, or robbery, or butchery or the like of them, there isn't anything would be worth your troubling for to run from now. You did nothing at all. . . .
> CHRISTY: [*offended*]. You're not speaking the truth.
> PEGEEN: [*in mock rage*]. Not speaking the truth, is it? Would you have me knock the head of you with the butt of the broom?
> CHRISTY: [*twisting round on her with a sharp cry of horror*]. Don't strike me . . . I killed my poor father, Tuesday was a week, for doing the like of that.

It is Pegeen too who turns round Christy's self-image:

You should have had great people in your family, I'm thinking, with the little small feet you have, and you with a kind of quality name, the like of what you'd find on the great powers and potentates of France and Spain.

And, with the Widow Quin's eager collusion, it is Pegeen who reinforces 'such poet's talking, and such bravery of heart':

Up to the day I killed my father, there wasn't a person in Ireland knew the kind I was, and I there drinking, waking, eating, sleeping, a quiet, simple poor fellow with no man giving me heed. . . . Well, . . . It's great luck and company I've won me in the end of time – two fine women fighting for the likes of me –, till I'm thinking this night wasn't I a foolish fellow not to kill my father in the years gone by.

Act II of *The Playboy* replaces the chorus of sly male inquisitors with an equally curious but far more joyous and imaginative chorus of young girls, led by Sara Tansey, 'the one yòked the ass cart and drove ten miles to set [her] eyes on the man bit the yellow lady's nostril on the northern shore'. Fired by tales from the papers of 'the way murdered men do bleed and drip', Sara is philosophical enough to hide her initial disappointment at not finding Christy at home by making off with his boots: 'There's a pair do fit me well, and I'll be keeping them for walking to the priest, when you'd be ashamed this place, going up winter and summer with nothing worth while to confess at all'. Nor, when the meek murderer does finally appear, is she as easily overwhelmed as the men in the shebeen the night before:

Is your right hand too scared for to use at all? [*She slips round behind him.*] It's a glass he has. Well I never seen to this day, a man with a looking-glass held to his back. Them that kills their fathers is a vain lot surely.

And, despite the foolery of her toast to 'the wonders of the western world, the pirates, preachers, poteen-makers, with the jobbing jockies, parching peelers, and the juries fill their stomachs selling judgements of the English law' (in itself showing a remarkably clear vision of the ambiguities of justice, culled no doubt from her avid reading of newspapers), it is Sara Tansey who realistically but fruitlessly alongside the Widow Quin tries to help Christy escape from the paradox of justice he has created for himself in the last act.

If Sara Tansey is the leader of the day-time chorus, goading Christy into honing and refining his image as the giant-killer, and Pegeen is the fiery image of romance which culminates in the superb love-duet of Act III, transforming both sweating jockey and itching barmaid into sweet singers of the rude pastoral, it is the Widow Quin who serves as the arch linking the 'romantic' with the 'Rabelaisian' (Synge's own defensive terms for the balance of tension in the play). For in the creation of this witty, worldly, thirty-year-old widow, Synge encourages us to enter a world of harmless (though brutal) make-believe and sweet (though bitter) romance while effectively preventing us from resting comfortably within that golden pre-lapsarian world. The Widow is, after all, summoned out of the dark by Father Reilly himself, and bidden serve as chaperon and guardian to the unfolding of the entire play. Through her sympathetic, affectionately scornful eye, we are invited to take note not only of the making of the playboy but of our own eager contribution to that imaginative joy Synge celebrated as peculiar to the locality and the richness of peasant nature. For she too is carved of heroic stuff, though the deed itself is so close to home as to win but 'small glory with the boys itself'. Therein lies a further key to Pegeen's later denunciation of the marvel of a strange man 'with his mighty talk' of 'a gallous story' which becomes 'a dirty deed . . . a squabble in your back-yard and the blow of a loy'. Marcus Quin, hit with a rusty pick so that he never overed it, was also 'a great warrant to tell stories of holy Ireland till he'd have the old women shedding down tears about their feet'. And if Marcus Quin is both *in* mythology, lamented as a lost hero, and *outside* of it, felled in his own backyard so that his 'murder' is rejected as accidental and therefore commonplace, his Widow too is set apart, 'looking on the schooners, hookers, trawlers is sailing the sea', from her little houseen 'far from all sides' above. Like Christy, yet unlike, her isolation has created a breadth of sympathy and realistic appraisal not granted her fellow villagers. She acts as foil to both Christy and Old Mahon in her lusty humour and materialism, and as counterbalance to Pegeen and the village girls in her experience and longings. Significantly it is the widow who tags Christy 'the walking playboy of the western world', with all the irony that complex title – hoaxer, humbug, mystifier, role-player and play-maker – implies. Through her eyes the west of Ireland dissolves and expands, by way of 'foxy skippers from France' and one-way tickets to the western states, to the wonderful world of make-believe, the mysterious west as opposed to the mystic east, the far side of the moon: 'when it's the like of you and me you'd hear the penny poets singing in an August fair'. Yet constantly she brings the audience back to the very border between fantasy and realism with which Synge flirts, reminding us of the transitory nature of what is being played out before us. No wonder she almost toppled the delicate balance of the play's structure more than once in earlier drafts, forcing Synge to tone down her powerful sympathies and zest for life. In the completed text, she must be given her own rejection scenes with Christy and be swept offstage before we can take full note of Pegeen's hurt. But in the reverberations of Pegeen's final lament, 'Oh my grief, I've lost him surely. I've lost the only playboy of the western world', we catch the earthy tones of the more experienced playgirl who remains behind in Mayo, rooted in that reality from which Christy has been liberated. . . .

SOURCE: extract from 'Synge and the Nature of Woman' in *Woman in Irish Legend, Life and Literature*, ed. S. F. Gallagher (Gerrards Cross, 1983), 58–61.

NOTES

1. See Andrew Carpenter, 'Synge and Women', *Etudes Irlandaises*, 1979; Joan Templeton, 'Synge's Redeemed Ireland: Woman as Rebel', *Caliban*, 1980; F. A. E. Whelan and Keith N. Hull, '"There's Talkin for a Cute Woman!"': Synge's Heroines', *Eire*, 1980; Almire Martin, 'On Synge's *Riders to the Sea*: Maurya's Passion', *Cahiers du Centre d'Etudes Irlandaises*, 1977; Ellen S. Spangler, 'Synge's *Deirdre of the Sorrows* as Feminine Tragedy', *Eire*, 1977.

2. J. M. Synge, *The Playboy of the Western World, Plays* Book II, ed. Ann Saddlemyer (Oxford University Press, 1968), pp. 101–3. All subsequent quotations from the plays are taken from this edition.

3. Insufficient critical attention has been paid to the ambiguous farce in
Act III when the Widow Quin attempts to dress Christy in a woman's skirt,
a far cry from the comic hubris of Shawn's loan of clothing in Act II.

Raymond Williams 'Poverty and Fantasy in *The Playboy of the Western World*' (1952)

... *The Playboy of the Western World* is a brilliantly successful
comedy which at last succeeds in integrating the range of language
with an action to which the range is relevant. T. S. Eliot's important
essay on Jonson contains passages which are highly relevant to the
method and substance of the play. We can say that the comedy is
satiric. But

> Jonson's drama is only incidentally satire, because it is only incidentally a
> criticism upon the actual world. It is not satire in the way in which the work
> of Swift or the work of Molière may be called satire: that is, it does not find
> its source in any precise emotional attitude or precise intellectual criticism
> of the actual world. ... The important thing is that if fiction can be divided
> into creative fiction and critical fiction, Jonson's is creative.

Eliot's definition can be applied as it stands to *The Playboy*.
Perhaps the most important way in which Synge's play is to be
distinguished from the main stream of English comedy is its attitude
to character. The lively gang in the shebeen do not form a gallery of
individual portraits, displayed to us by the normal process of
revelation; neither is the record of the interplay the process of the
comedy.

> Whereas in Shakespeare the effect is due to the way in which the
> characters *act upon* one another, in Jonson it is given by the way in which
> the characters *fit in* with each other.

For it is not simply the fantasy of Christy Mahon, trailing the
awesome (and bogus) glory of 'a man has killed his da', with which
Synge is concerned; but with the fantasy of the whole community
who are equal makers of his illusion. The characters are an

individual world rather than a representative group; the individual existence of each is less important than the common emotional process within which their world is circumscribed. It is, of course, a small world, what Grattan Freyer called 'the little world of J. M. Synge'. Eliot again made the essential point.

But small worlds – the worlds which artists create – do not differ only in' magnitude; if they are complete worlds, drawn to scale in every part, they differ in kind also. And Jonson's world has this scale. His type of personality found its relief in something falling under the category of burlesque or farce – though when you are dealing with a *unique* world, like his, these terms fail to appease the appetite for definition. It is not, at all events, the farce of Molière; the latter is more analytic, more an intellectual redistribution. It is not defined by the word 'satire'. Jonson poses as a satirist. But satire like Jonson's is great in the end not by hitting off its object, but by creating it; the satire is merely the means which leads to the aesthetic result, the impulse which projects a new world into a new orbit.

In modern drama, the point can be made again by reference to *Peer Gynt*, with which Synge's play has several correspondences. Ibsen satirizes the folk-fantasy of the Norwegians in much the same mood as does Synge that of the Irish. And as in the case of Peer Gynt, Christy Mahon's illusion of greatness is nourished and raised to the heights by a community where the mythology of force (compare the tales they spin of Red Jack Smith and Bartley Fallon) is dominant; Christy – 'a man did split his father's middle with a single clout' – is the familiar tale of a giant. But when the revengeful father comes on his trail, the collapsed hero is as quickly turned to sacrifice. And when the hero does the famous deed in apparent truth, his shocked spectators learn 'that there's a great gap between gallous story and a dirty deed'.

But again the deed is not completed:

Are you coming to be killed a third time, or what is it ails you now?

Finally Christy realizes that it is not the deed which made him glorious, but the telling of the deed, that 'poet's talking'. And this he retains. He goes out from the community confident in his new strength, but acknowledges that it is the community which made him:

Ten thousand blessings upon all that's here, for you've turned me a likely gaffer in the end of all, the way I'll go romancing through a romping lifetime from this hour to the dawning of the judgement day.

It is not only Christy who is transformed; the community itself has made something. Their 'hero' may go from them, but he is their creation – 'the only Playboy of the Western World'. A starved community – and this is the irony but also, unconsciously, the cruelty of the action – has at once alienated and launched its destructive and confusing fantasy. The fantastic deception is separated from them; lost to them; gone out into romance. It is a bitter comment on the poverty, which required other experience and other actions. It is also a bitter comment, as we now look back, on the real relation between the Irish drama and the Irish people of this period. What the writers found, in their own medium, was 'richness', but the richness was a function of a more pressing poverty, and this was at times idealized, at times compounded; in *The Playboy* faced but then confidently superseded: the poverty and the fantasy, always so closely related, seen now as bitterly nourishing each other; grasped and projected into an exiled orbit. . . .

SOURCE: extract from *Drama from Ibsen to Brecht* (London, 1968), 146–8. The essay on Synge is unchanged from its first appearance in *Drama from Ibsen to Eliot* in 1952.

Robert Welch 'Synge's Strange Translation' (1986)

. . . *Cathleen ni Houlihan* [by W. B. Yeats] is still a disturbing play, so strong a charge of life does it carry. The same can be said about J. M. Synge's masterpiece *The Playboy of the Western World*, first produced at the Abbey Theatre in 1907.

> And that enquiring man John Synge comes next,
> That dying chose the living world for text . . .

So Yeats wrote of Synge in 'In Memory of Major Robert Gregory'. Yeats is linking Synge with Gregory, and both with his ideal of that to which the artist should aspire, to be 'life's epitome'. Synge, in Yeats's view, had the 'discipline' necessary to be an artist, to be someone capable of making a world which would be complete in its variety, a 'second nature' in Sydney's phrase. The 'living world' became his text, which he enquired into, elaborated, and interpreted in his work.

It is the quality of interpreted life, of life opened up, that strikes us in the *Playboy*. Time and again, in reading the *Playboy* one is struck by the uncanny way in which Synge has carried into his text the way Irish country people speak, talk and think. In my own, limited, experience I have heard West Cork people come out with locutions just as strange, feelings just as wild and terrifying, as anything in the *Playboy*. This is not a world that Synge has invented out of nothing.

In the *Playboy* we recognize the life presented to us as arising out of modes of speech and patterns of behaviour which are Irish, but the way in which they are presented to us, in the elaborate and brilliant language, makes us think about them even as we recognize them, makes us feel them strange despite our closeness to them. In a sense the riots the *Playboy* caused were a true reaction to the play's method and technique.

A Dublin audience, seeing the *Playboy*, in 1907, would realize that this was how they themselves were, or how they had been not long since. Practically everyone in that Dublin audience of 1907 would have had a relative or would have known someone living in the traditional, and, to an urban way of thinking, in the backward, way of life Synge's play re-enacts. Synge was enquiring into exactly what they were attempting to escape from into a modern world of new suburbia, where the old ways and the old codes and the old language could become a fit object of sentimental attention, but nonetheless dead. This is one of the themes of Joyce's short story 'The Dead'. The last thing most of them would have wanted was an epitome of Western life as Synge gave it.

The trouble with the *Playboy* was that Synge's play is an extraordinarily accurate reflection of Western Irish life, unsentimental, undignified, unmediated by any considerations other than the creation of that world in and for itself. His craft is so sure, his technique so perfect, his involvement with his material so total that the play becomes an entirely convincing world. All the parts interlock. Formally it is a masterpiece.

Take the language. Synge's language is vivid. It is based upon the English speech of the Irish country people of his time, with constructions and grammatical patterns taken from Irish. But the English speech of the Irish country people is itself dependent upon

the grammatical and syntactical forms of Irish. The syntactical
strangeness of the speech, its distance from standard English usage
draws our attention to it as a thing in itself: it is 'foregrounded' in the
Formalist use of that term. But the people of the play, like Irish
country people, take their language seriously. In the following
exchange Christy tells Pegeen, her father and his cronies that he's
killed his da. Just before this Christy has been saying that his soul is
damned and that he only has hanging to look forward to. Watch the
way the language draws attention to itself: words like 'speaking' and
'saying' are re-iterated; and when Christy tells them what he has
done Pegeen repeats what he says with an Anglo-Irish usage of the
copula, that derives from Irish, and has the effect of making the
players and audience think again about what Christy has said:

PEGEEN: [*with a sign to the men to be quiet*]: You're only saying it. You did
   nothing at all. A soft lad the like of you wouldn't slit the windpipe of a
   screeching sow.
CHRISTY: [*offended*]: You're not speaking the truth.
PEGEEN: [*in mock rage*]: Not speaking the truth is it? Would you have me
   knock the head of you with the butt of the broom?
CHRISTY: [*twisting round on her with a sharp cry of horror*]: Don't strike
   me. I killed my poor father, Tuesday was a week, for doing the like of
   that.
PEGEEN: [*with blank amazement*]: Is it killed your father?

In itself Pegeen's phrase is insignificant, but in the context the
Irishism 'Is it . . .' ('*An é gur mharáis t-athair?*') followed by the verb
'killed', has the effect of drawing to our attention the emphatic way
Irish people use speech and the strangeness of the act described.
Also advanced here, in the play of the language, is the whole notion
of the relationship between an actual thing and its 'likeness', which
is a major theme of the play and one totally involved with the use of
language and rhetoric: 'A soft lad *the like of you* wouldn't slit the
windpipe of a screeching sow', and: 'I killed my poor father,
Tuesday was a week, for doing *the like* of that'.

   Through the story Christy tells and re-tells of his killing his father
and in the way that story is received he discovers a new self, one that
he can hardly recognize, so 'unlike' his old self is it. He looks at his
likeness in the looking-glass at the beginning of Act II and remem-
bers the old piece of glass he and his father had down in Kerry:

CHRISTY: Didn't I know rightly I was handsome, though it was the divil's
   own mirror we had beyond, would twist a squint across an angel's

brow; and I'll be growing fine from this day, the way I'll have a soft lovely skin on me and won't be the like of the clumsy young fellows do be ploughing all times in the earth and dung.

It is through his story, his language, that Christy's self is reborn 'fine'. The medium of the play, to which Synge pays such close attention, is the mode of Christy's transformation into a new likeness. The *Playboy* plays with possibility and in doing so opens up a world which is formally orchestrated and one in which language is continually made strange. The story Christy tells is the means by which he comes into his new likeness, but at the same time we are invited to consider the difficult relationship between an actual thing and a rendition of it in language. This is what the play of the *Playboy* plays with. All the time the audience is being invited to consider the relationship between Synge's 'likeness' of Ireland and its own likeness of it, that one in its head. How good is our capacity for story telling? How good is our capacity for the life it can unfold? How good is our capacity to entertain the second nature art can bring forth?

Christy is reborn Christus Rex. But Old Mahon, St. Paul's old man, comes back. Formally, this is the most daring of all the play's devices. The story Christy tells is revealed as a story. What is to happen? In the end Christy tries to make his story good. He stretches his father with a loy a second time to find that the people who were enthralled by the tale are disgusted by the fact. The second felling takes place off stage, at which there is 'dead silence'. Pegeen says '. . . there's a great gap between a gallous story and a dirty deed', and Christy is bound and tortured. Again the Old Man arises, unvanquished, and comes in on all fours. Christy is himself on the floor and father and son confront each other on their knees. 'Are you coming to be killed a third time?' asks Christy. The son takes command and the two head off together. Christy, in his last speech, says to the Mayo people, 'you've turned me a *likely* gaffer in the end of all'. The likeness he has discovered for himself has not been annulled; it stays. The likeness to ourselves we see in the play's formal arrangements and reversals also stays. The likeness of the play is a likeness for our life, as it was for the people of Dublin in 1907. Too good a likeness, too formally confident and serene as it made its challenges and demands. So strongly integrated is the thing, so alive to its own motives and reverberations, so satisfyingly coherent in its arrangement of events, that we acknowledge it as something with its own life. The life that pervades it is like the life that arises in us, that cannot find expression but in the strange translation of art and drama. Again, we return to Yeats's 'First Principles' essay of 1904:

A feeling for the form of life, for the graciousness of life, for the moving limbs of life, for the nobleness of life, for all that cannot be written in codes, has always been greatest among the gifts of literature to mankind.

This is the kind of gift Synge made to Ireland in *The Playboy of the Western World*. In this play the Anglo-Irish drama has fully emerged.

SOURCE: extract from 'The Emergence of Modern Anglo-Irish Drama: Yeats and Synge', *Irish Writers and the Theatre*, ed. Masaru Sekine (Gerrards Cross & Totowa, N.J., 1986), 214–17.

Declan Kiberd 'Sharp Critique of Excess' (1980)

... Synge's work has often been interpreted as a study in Irish exaggeration, but in fact his plays and essays offer a sharp critique of excess. In an essay written as early as 1904, he rejected the braggadocio and feckless Stage Irishman of the past, but was no less critical of the anti-Stage Irishman of the present. He complained pointedly about the brogue of the Stage-Irish writers in whose idiom he found 'a familiarity that is not amusing'; and he wrote that, as a result 'a great deal of what is most precious in the national life must be omitted from their work, or imperfectly expressed'. When Frank Hugh O'Donnell went from door to door among the denizens of literary Dublin with his pamphlet attacking 'The Stage Irishman of Pseudo-Celtic Drama', he cannot have expected support from a leading playwright of the very theatre which he had denounced most bitterly. But Synge welcomed the pamphlet and wrote: 'A young literary movement is never the worse for adverse and candid criticism. It should never be forgotten that half the troubles of England and Ireland have arisen from ignorance of the Irish character, ignorance founded on the biased views of British and Irish historians and on the absurd caricatures which infest the majority of plays and novels dealing with Irish folk and affairs. Lever, Lover, Boucicault and *Punch* have achieved much in the way of making the Irish character a sealed book to Englishmen'.[1] This clear rejection of the Stage Irishman was accompanied in the same essay by an equally trenchant denunciation of the holier-than-thou anti-Stage Irishman of the present. He felt that men such as O'Donnell were so intent on avoiding any taint of Stage Irishness that they had ceased to be real – they had forgotten who they truly were in their endless campaign not to be somebody else. Synge therefore insisted that 'the rollicking note is present in the Irish character – present to an extent some writers of the day do not seem to be aware of – and it demands, if we choose to deal with it, a free rollicking style' (p. 376). For this reason Synge was as anxious to expose the pretensions of the O'Donnells of this world as he was keen to explode the original Stage Irishman, for both prevented the honest depiction of the realities of rural Irish life. He praised the Abbey Theatre which had offered a solution to this problem: 'it has contrived by its care and taste to put an end to the reaction against the careless Irish humour of which everyone has had too much'. That sentence shrewdly implies a criticism not only of the careless humour of the past, but also of the excessive reaction against such caricature in the present. Synge noted with some asperity that 'the effects of this reaction are still perceptible in Dublin, and the Irish National Theatre Society is sometimes accused of degrading Ireland's vision of herself by throwing a shadow of the typical Stage Irishman across her mirror' (p. 398).

Just such an accusation was made against *The Playboy of the Western World* three years later; and it is clear from the 1904 essay that Synge had always anticipated this type of criticism. Far from being another travesty of the national character, however, his play is an attack on the lyric gush, pugnacity and violence popularly associated with the Stage Irishman. It is also, though covertly, an assault on the anti-Stage Irishman of Wilde and Yeats. In *The Decay of Lying* Wilde had constructed an elaborate defence of the mask or anti-self, which took the form of an ingenious justification of lying. Conceding that the mask was founded on a lie, he asserted that lying was no shame: 'After all, what is a good lie? Simply that which is its own evidence'. This is the datum of *The Playboy* where Christy

Mahon became great by believing himself so, winning the acclaim of the community, as Pegeen acidly remarks, 'by the power of a lie'. The whole play is simply an investigation of the validity of Wilde's initial observation: 'Many a young man starts in life with a natural gift for exaggeration which, if nurtured in congenial and sympathetic surroundings, or by imitation of the best models, might grow into something really great and wonderful'. Much later, Yeats would describe his own cultivation of the anti-Stage Irish pose as the strategy of a man not so very different from Christy Mahon:

> One that ruffled in a manly pose
> For all his timid heart.

In *The Player Queen* Yeats followed Wilde in his explanation of the underlying idea: 'To be great . . . we must seem so. . . . Seeming that goes on for a lifetime is no different from reality'. Synge was not so sure. In *The Playboy* he offered his criticisms of Wilde's theory, of fine words divorced from real action, of gestures struck rather than deeds done – in short, of the fatal Irish gift for blarney. He voiced his own doubts in Pegeen's grief-stricken complaint that 'there's a great gap between a gallous story and a dirty deed'. Synge suspected that, at bottom, the mask of the elegant anti-self purveyed by Wilde and Yeats was merely a subtle latter-day version of ancient Irish blarney.

In portraying an Irish hero who is acclaimed by village girls for a deed of violence, Synge offered what Maxim Gorki was later to describe as 'a subtle irony on the cult of the hero'. His play shows that the so-called fighting Irish can only endure the thought of violence when the deed is committed elsewhere or in the past. But when a killing occurs in their own backyard, then they become suddenly aware of that gap between poetic stories and foul deeds. Far from being another attempt to pander to the British notion of Ireland, Synge's play was an honest attempt to express the nation to itself, to reveal to his own countrymen the ambiguity of their own attitude to violence. He foresaw how Pearse and the heroes of 1916 would evoke only the jeers of an apathetic Dublin populace. He foresaw only too well how generations of Irishmen would sing ballads of glamorized rebellion and offer funds for the freedom-fighters – so long as the fighting took place at a safe distance in past history or at the other side of a patrolled political border. He believed that a writer's first duty may be to insult rather than to humour his countrymen, to shock his compatriots into a deeper self-awareness of their own dilemmas. He exploded forever the strange myth of the fighting Irish and, like Joyce, revealed to his country-men an even more distressing truth – the fact that their besetting vice was not pugnacity but paralysis.[2] ...

SOURCE: extract from 'The Fall of the Stage Irishman', *The Genres of the Irish Literary Revival*, ed. Ronald Schleifer (Norman, Okl., and Dublin, 1980), 46–9.

NOTES

[Reorganized and renumbered from the original – Ed.]

1. J. M. Synge, *Collected Works: Prose* (Oxford, 1966), p. 397.
2. This was also the diagnosis offered by Pearse in his essays of 1914, where he argued that Ireland had lost the right to nationhood because her people had grown decadent and supine. The rising which he led just two years later proved just how true that diagnosis was, as Dubliners mocked and the rest of the country failed to join in the rebellion. Although today the Irish yet retain the reputation for pugnacity and aggression, there is even less basis than ever to the myth. The fact remains that since 1798 the nation has not fought a war, the much-vaunted risings of 1848, 1867 and 1916 being more in the nature of skirmishes which only a few had the courage to join. Even today, when the twenty-six counties possess a sizeable army of their own, the official soldiers of the state polish their superb hardware and mount displays of gymnastics, while a handful of crazy idealists with meagre equipment wage a war of liberation in the six counties against the wishes of the majority on both sides of the border. Ireland has been occupied by foreign armies since 1169. It is now almost two hundred years since a disciplined national army resisted the forces of occupation. In the same period the English have fought literally dozens of wars and will in the future doubtless fight many more. And yet there are still Englishmen who believe that the Irish are bellicose. See P. H. Pearse, *Political Writings and Speeches* (Dublin, 1924).

PART FIVE

Deirdre of the Sorrows

Deirdre of the Sorrows

Première: 13 January 1910 by the Irish Players at the Abbey Theatre, Dublin.

First published in a limited edition, prepared for the press by W. B. Yeats, Lady Gregory and Molly Allgood (Dundrum: Cuala Press, 1910). Later that year it appeared in Volume II of *The Works of J. M. Synge* (Dublin: Maunsel, 1910) with a few minor alterations to the text. Manuscript and typescript drafts are detailed by Ann Saddlemyer in Synge's *Collected Works*, Vol. IV (London: Oxford University Press, 1968), 369–93.

1. COMMENT AND REVIEWS

I *J. M. Synge* (1908)

... I don't know whether I told you that I am trying a three-Act prose Deirdre – to change my hand. I am not sure yet whether I shall be able to make a satisfactory play out of it – these saga people when one comes to deal with them seem very remote; – one does not know what they thought or what they ate or where they went to sleep, so one is apt to fall into rhetoric. In any case I find it 'an interesting experiment', full of new difficulties, and I shall be the better, I think, for the change. ...

SOURCE: letter to John Quinn dated 4 January 1908.

II *Padraic Colum* (1926)

... I have a vivid memory of the occasion when I saw him for the last time. I met him in a street in Dublin. He was going out to Kingstown, and I walked with him to Westland Row Station and sat with him for a while on the platform. He had been in hospital: his face was hollow, and although he spoke quietly there was great intensity in his speech. He was working on *Deirdre of the Sorrows*, and he had, in spite of his illness, got down to the third act. He began to tell me about this act: there would be an open grave on the stage. I spoke doubtfully of the impression that this would make – would it not be a too obvious heightening of the tragic feeling? But he said that he had been close to death, and that the grave was a reality to him, and it was the reality in the tragedy he was writing. I knew how near he had been to death when he spoke to me in that way. ...

SOURCE: *The Road Round Ireland* (London & New York, 1926), 369–70.

III *Lady Gregory* (1913)

... [T]here could be a sharp edge to his wit, as when he said of a certain actress (not Mrs Campbell) whose modern methods he disliked, she had turned Yeats' *Deirdre* into 'the second Mrs Conchubor'. ... [H]is strength did not last long enough to enable him to finish *Deirdre of the Sorrows*, his last play. After he had gone, we took infinite trouble to bring the versions together, and we produced it early in the next year, but it needed the writer's hand. I did my best for it, working at its production through snowy days and into winter nights, until rheumatism seized me with a grip I have never shaken off. I wrote to Mr Yeats: 'I still hope we can start [the new year] with *Deirdre*. ... I will be in Dublin for rehearsals in Christmas week, though I still hope to get to Paris for Christmas with Robert, but it may not be worthwhile. I will spend all January at the Theatre, but I must be back on the first of February to do some planting; that cannot be put off'. And again, 'I am more hopeful of *Deirdre* now. I have got Conchubor and Fergus off at the last in Deirdre's long speech, and that makes an immense improvement; she looks lonely and pathetic with the other two women crouching and rocking themselves on the floor'.

For we have done our utmost for his work since we lost him, as we did while he was with us here.

SOURCE: 'Synge', *English Review*, 13 (March 1913), 556, 565–6.

IV *Lady Gregory & W. B. Yeats* (1910)

Mr Synge began writing this play about two years before his death, but it was often put aside because of illness, and was left at the last unfinished. He had brought in a new character, Owen, and had meant to make more use of him, and he would have enriched and elaborated the dialogue, working it over and over again according to his custom. We are giving it as he left it, putting in not more than a half-dozen words and taking out here and there a sentence that did not explain itself.

SOURCE: note printed in Abbey Theatre programme, 13 January 1910.

V   W. B. Yeats   (1910)

It was Synge's practice to write many complete versions of a play, distinguishing them with letters, and running half through the alphabet before he finished. He read me a version of this play the year before his death, and would have made several more always altering and enriching. He felt that the story, as he had told it, required a grotesque element mixed into its lyrical melancholy to give contrast and create an impression of solidity, and had begun this mixing with the character of Owen, who would have had some part in the first act also, where he was to have entered Lavarcham's cottage with Conchubor. Conchubor would have taken a knife from his belt to cut himself free from threads of silk that caught in brooch or pin as he leant over Deirdre's embroidery frame, and forgotten this knife behind him. Owen was to have found it and stolen it. Synge asked that either I or Lady Gregory should write some few words to make this possible, but after writing in a passage we were little satisfied and thought it better to have the play performed, as it is printed here, with no word of ours. When Owen killed himself in the second act, he was to have done it with Conchubor's knife. He did not speak to me of any other alteration, but it is probable that he would have altered till the structure had become as strong and varied as in his other plays; and had he lived to do that, 'Deirdre of the Sorrows' would have been his masterwork, so much beauty is there in its course, and such wild nobleness in its end, and so poignant is an emotion and wisdom that were his own preparation for death.

SOURCE: preface to *Deirdre of the Sorrows: A Play by John M. Synge* (Dublin, 1910).

2. CRITICAL STUDIES

Ann Saddlemyer   *Deirdre of the Sorrows*: Literature First . . . Drama Afterwards   (1972)

'My next play must be quite different from the *P. Boy*. I want to do something quiet and stately and restrained and I want you to act in it.' When Synge wrote these words to his fiancée Molly Allgood early in December 1906 he was ill, on the verge of disillusionment with the Abbey Theatre, and thoroughly fed up with Christy Mahon and the myth-making Mayoites. He was just recovering from his bitterest quarrel with Molly and was facing an even greater crisis with his mother, to whom, from a safe distance in England, he was at last breaking the news of his engagement. . . .

It is impossible to say with any certainty when he decided to turn to ancient saga material for his next play, although it is apparent from his notebooks and published writings that he had been interested especially in the Deirdre story for at least five years. Even before he enrolled in de Jubainville's course in Old Irish at the Sorbonne in the spring of 1902 he had attempted his own translation of 'The Sons of Usnach' during a visit to Aran. When he reviewed Lady Gregory's book *Cuchulain of Muirthemne* Deirdre's lament was cited as one of its finest passages, and he may well have had this story in mind when he wrote to Lady Gregory herself, 'What puny pallid stuff most of our modern writing seems beside it!'[1] A few years later he again singled out passages from the Deirdre story when reviewing A. H. Leahy's *Heroic Romances of Ireland*; but this time the translation was criticized as a 'deplorable misrepresentation of the spirit of these old verses' and the author was sternly advised to study Andrew Lang's translation of the medieval French *conte-fable*, *Aucassin and Nicolette*, a book he also recommended to Molly as 'filled with the very essence of literature and romance'.[2]

Following Lady Gregory's lead, other Abbey Theatre dramatists were exploring Ireland's past for fresh material. AE's only play, *Deirdre*, was well-known and frequently revived by amateur companies throughout the country. In November 1906 Synge and Molly observed with some misgivings Yeats's one-act *Deirdre*; the same month he sent her *Aucassin and Nicolette* (which became their favourite book) and also recommended Lady Gregory's 'charming' translation of 'The Sons of Usnach'. Now, in March 1907 after the *Playboy* fracas, Yeats's earlier 'Cuchulanoid drama'[3] *On Baile's Strand* was revived, with Molly playing one of the musicians, followed two weeks later by Yeats's revised *Deirdre*, Molly again in the cast. At the same time, she was rehearsing the title role of W. S. Blunt's *Fand*, based on 'The Only Jealousy of Emer', another story from Lady Gregory's *Cuchulain*. Spurred by this renewal of interest in saga material, and encouraged no doubt by his reading of Walter Scott, Synge revised an early poem, 'Queens', and drafted an essay entitled 'Historical or Peasant Drama'. . . . The essay concluded that historical fiction was now impossible and insincere, that modern poetry apart from a few lyrics was a failure, and again ended with a question: 'Is the drama – as a beautiful thing a lost art? . . . For the present the only possible beauty in drama is peasant drama, for the future we must await the making of life beautiful again before we can have beautiful drama'.[4]

But if Synge was not yet ready to accept 'the drama of swords', he could not deny the magnificence and tenderness of Ireland's popular imagination, which he had eloquently praised in the preface to *The Playboy* and out of which the saga material had grown. Other aspects of theory had also matured, for by now, too, he had reconciled the role of the artist with an earlier role, the lonely sensitive observer of nature's moods. . . .

Synge had recognized in the twilights of Wicklow and the grey mists of Aran that nature too has a psychic memory, that time and place in turn range beyond the hours and seasons to include incidents from the distant past and hints of the future. His one-act tragedy *Riders to the Sea* had revealed this layering of events within the story of one family through the experiences of old Maurya, whose grief became at the same time personal and universal, encompassing the loss of three generations while centring on the last of six strong sons. Her final lament is for all mothers, everywhere, and for all who mourn, have mourned and will mourn the coming of death: 'No man at all can be living forever, and we must be satisfied'. Now he delved deeper into Ireland's past in an effort to identify and capture what is richest and most lasting in life, nature and time, and came at last to that meeting-place where man's story becomes part of the universal experience, to the fountainhead of all literature – folk history and primitive knowledge. In *The Well of the Saints* Synge had examined man's need for a myth out of which to carve the reality of his dreams; in *The Playboy of the Western World* he had explored the process of myth-making and celebrated its dangers and glories; now he turned to his most difficult task yet, the re-creation, in terms significant to modern man, of the myth itself. It was to lead him back through the unsophisticated peasant of Wicklow, Aran, and Kerry into the Irish folk spirit of legend, to the mingling of the immediacy of passion with those unyielding constants, Death and Time.

The starting-point on this journey must be the artist's personality and individual experience. For the first time the joy of a love returned matched Synge's exultation over beauty in the natural world, and his letters to Molly illustrate a fresh awareness of the sharp pain of intense emotion:

All that we feel for each other is so much connected with this divine world, that our particular affection, in a real sense, must be divine also.

You feel as fully as anyone can feel all the poetry and mystery of the nights we are out in – like that night a week ago when we came down from Rockbrook with the pale light of Dublin shining behind the naked trees till we seemed almost to come out of ourselves with the wonder and beauty of it all. Divine moments like that are infinitely precious to both of us as people and as artists . . . I think people who feel these things – people like us – have a profound joy in love, that the ordinary run of people do not easily reach. They love with all their hearts – as we do – but their hearts perhaps, have not all the stops that you and I have found in ours. The worst of it is that we have the same openness to profound pain – of mind I mean – as we have to profound joy, but please Heaven we shall have a few years of divine love and life together and that is all I suppose any one need expect.

Illness and exile had forced him also to a profound awareness of the brevity of man's span within the universal cycle:

There is nearly a half moon, and I have been picturing in my mind how all our nooks and glens and rivers would look, if we were out among them as we should be! Do you ever think of them? Ever think of them I mean not as places that you've been to, but as places that are there still, with the little moon shining, and the rivers running, and the thrushes singing, while you and I, God help us, are far away from them. I used to sit over my sparks of fire long ago in Paris picturing glen after glen in my mind, and river after river – there are rivers like the Annamoe that I fished in till I knew every stone and eddy – and then one goes on to see a time when the rivers will be there and the thrushes, and we'll be dead surely.

Long before he had begun to write, Deirdre's lament at leaving Alban was part of his own experience.

But it would be a mistake to suggest that morbidity led Synge to the story of Deirdre. His first fears in tackling the theme were that 'the "Saga" people might loosen my grip on reality'. Diffidently, he expressed doubts as to his ability to write a satisfactory play. 'These saga people, when one comes to deal with them, seem very remote', he complained to John Quinn; 'one does not know what they thought or what they ate or where they went to sleep, so one is apt to fall into rhetoric.' But he admitted it was an interesting and challenging experiment, 'full of new difficulties, and I shall be the better, I think, for the change'.

Many of those difficulties were inherent in the material itself, for the tale of Deirdre and the Sons of Usnach was the most familiar of all legends of the heroic cycle of Cuchulain and the Red Branch. Although manuscripts might differ in details, the general outline, the beginning and the end, were well known and the facts with which Synge worked were common to most versions. Even before Deirdre was born it was prophesied, so the story goes, that she would grow to be of great beauty and thereby cause the ruin of Ulster, the downfall of the House of Usna, and the death of many men. Hearing this, the High King Conchubor took her for his ward and placed her in a secluded place in the charge of a nurse and a tutor; but before he could claim Deirdre as his bride, she met Naisi and persuaded him to elope with her. The lovers, accompanied by Naisi's brothers Ainnle and Ardan, fled to Scotland where they took service with the King and won great honour by their feats of valour. Eventually they were found by Fergus, who as Conchubor's emissary brought pledges of forgiveness and a safe return to their beloved Ireland. Naisi, despite Deirdre's dreams foretelling disaster, agreed to return, but Conchubor had arranged to separate Fergus from his charges. With the help of magic, Naisi and his brothers were killed; Fergus sought revenge by pillaging and burning Emain, the seat of kings for many generations; and Deirdre, having fulfilled her unhappy prophecy, killed herself.[5]

But the problem remained: how to express the reality of this well-

used myth 'in a comprehensive and natural form'? Yeats had chosen
to concentrate on the last scene of the drama, using a chorus of
musicians to explain events of the past and illuminate Conchubor's
treachery. His two proud lovers remain frozen in their eagle-like
passion until released by death. Synge followed AE's earlier example
and wrote his play in three acts, but with none of AE's mysticism or
unconscious bathos ('Thou art the light of the Ultonians, Naisi',
intones the druidess Lavarcham, 'but thou are not the star of
knowledge.'). From the beginning, although their story is foretold,
Synge's characters remain true to their own natures; the action is the
result of strong personalities clashing because they cannot do
otherwise and still be themselves. Although he retained a hint of
mysticism until very late drafts, eventually he rejected all dependence on prophecy or premonition; similarly the Sons of Usna meet
their death not through druidic incantations but because they are
tricked and outnumbered. But Synge's greatest originality remains
the blending of theme and character, the shifting of emphasis
and climax, in keeping with his developed theory of art and drama.
He would not be satisfied until all was strengthened, 'made personal', simple, intense, charged with his own vision of the world. In
this experiment 'chiefly to change [his] hand', he moves from the
bright sunlit world of comedy and the melodramatic exaggeration
necessary for the vividness of the amoral, to the moonlit world of
tragedy and the patient anatomization of passion against a stark
background of death and time. He wrote in his notebook, 'Sudden in
the romance writer a real voice seems to speak out of their golden
and burning moods, it is then they are greatest'.[6] He sought this
same greatness in his dramatization of the saga of Deirdre of the
Sorrows.

Synge completed his first draft of the play in November 1907. The
ninth and final draft of Act I was completed four months later; but
Act III, which ran to eleven drafts, was not in a finished state until
mid-January 1909, and the second act was still unsatisfactory in its
fifteenth draft, when Synge entered Elpis Nursing Home for the last
time. During the fifteen months he was at work on the play there
were many interruptions, but all contributed to his development of
the story: theatre responsibilities – directing, managing, and
coaching – made him more aware of heightened dramatic effect;
publication of his poetry forced him to clarify further his thoughts on
language and the artist; bouts of illness sharpened his sense of the

beauty of this world and the urgent need to 'play all the stops'; comradeship with Molly intensified his belief in the purity of the passions; his mother's final illness served to remind him of the untidiness of a lingering old age and the reality of death. It is always intriguing to contemplate what might have been, but even in its unfinished state, with additional help from the notebook drafts, it is possible to see how closely Synge wove themes developed out of his personal view of the world through the framework of the established myth and, beyond the established text, to glimpse the shadowy pattern of the planned masterpiece. Had he lived to complete the play I believe it would have retained the same shape, but colour and theme would have been infinitely enriched through character and mood, the lyrical romanticism balanced by a tough fibre of the grotesque.

As it now stands, *Deirdre of the Sorrows* is a twilight play beginning in the darkness of storm clouds and ending in the stillness of death.[7] Twilight for Synge, especially in Ireland, was a time filled with 'vague but passionate anguish', when 'moments of supreme beauty and distinction' are possible, tinged with suggestions of death and loneliness. On such a night an ageing king will feel conscious of empty days and time passing, a young princess will become aware of her destiny, joyous young princes of their moment of triumph. It is the romantic hero Naisi who voices the tension already evoked by the forces of nature: 'At your age you should know there are nights when a king like Conchubor would spit upon his arm ring and queens will stick their tongues out at the rising moon. We're that way this night, and it's not wine we're asking only . . .'. Distant thunder and threat of the worst storm in years are an appropriate background to the rare moment when the young child of nature sheds the duns and greys of her peasant world, lays aside nuts and twigs from the hillside, to don the jewels and robes and destiny of a queen. For Deirdre will be no ordinary queen, one rather who will be 'a master, taking her own choice and making a stir to the edges of the seas'. A woman of her like cannot deny the natural impulses within her, must in fact reach out and grasp what is hers, 'the way if there were no warnings told about her you'd see troubles coming'. She dreads Emain, the Dun of an ageing High King, because it is an unnatural resting place for one who has learned to be at one with the woods, the birds, the rivers, sun and moon. The threat of death holds less fear, being a natural part of nature's law; 'All men have age coming and great ruin in the end'. Just as nature has schooled Deirdre in the wisdom of time, so nature unites the two lovers: 'By the sun and moon and the whole earth, I wed Deirdre to Naisi . . . May the air bless you, and water and the wind, the sea, and all the hours of the sun and moon'. It is significant that Lavarcham, learned wise woman that she is, cannot wed them; she is committed to the rule of the High King, who is at war with time, careless of nature, and ambiguous in his feelings towards Deirdre. It is Ainnle, 'who has been with wise men and knows their ways', yet is fellow huntsman and comrade-in-arms to Naisi, who performs the ceremony and thus initiates the Fate of the Children of Usna.

Seven years in Alban are happy and bright, with love as pleasing as 'the same sun throwing light across the branches at the dawn of day'. But it is at the beginning of the darkness of winter that the lovers choose to leave, 'the time the sun has a low place, and the moon has her mastery in a dark sky'. Twilight now is the foreshadowing of death and the end of love: 'It's this hour we're between the daytime and a night where there is sleep forever'. Earlier the woods promised fulfilment of love; now they deny hope of safety, for independently both lovers confess their awareness that in the course of nature nothing can stand still. 'There are as many ways to wither love as there are stars in a night of Samhain, but there is no way to keep life or love with it a short space only'. The quiet woods below Emain Macha hide the promised grave, open to receive them 'on a dark night'. When Deirdre at last mourns the death of Naisi and prepares for her own death, she bequeathes the strange dignity of her loneliness to the little moon of Alban, left 'pacing the woods beyond Glen Laid, looking every place for Deirdre and Naisi, the two lovers who slept so sweetly with each other'. Lavarcham's final speech underscores this sympathy with the natural world, but at the same time assures the permanence of a universe in which their story can be told forever: 'Deirdre is dead, and Naisi is dead, and if the oaks and stars could die for sorrow it's a dark sky and a hard and naked earth we'd have this night in Emain'.

Against this background of the natural passage of time, Deirdre and Naisi's decision to return to Emain becomes much more significant and meaningful. Just as they had earlier chosen life in the woods and exile from Ireland, now they choose to accept the harsh facts of nature and go gladly forward to meet fate in an effort to

retain the fullness and freshness of their love. 'Isn't it a better thing
to be following on to a near death, than to be bending the head
down, and dragging with the feet, and seeing one day a blight
showing upon love where it is sweet and tender?' For seven years
they have had perfection of love and comradeship; but the dread of
the natural course of life and love, heretofore unspoken, has now
fallen like a shadow across that perfection of passion. Unlike
Lavarcham, who speaks for the unfolding of the full course of nature,
they prefer to cut their time short. Nor do they wish to fight off or
distort the true course of nature like Conchubor, who sees Deirdre as
surety against old age and death, or Owen, who attempts to seduce
Deirdre from her natural mate. But their decision has far-reaching
implications, for Ainnle and Ardan, who have been satisfied with
comradeship and fraternal loyalty, are pulled along with them; 'four
white bodies' will share the grave chosen by Deirdre and opened by
Conchubor.

But if the lovers' decision prepares the way for joy and triumph in
myth, where love reigns supreme over death, it introduces a
contrasting leitmotif, the pain of love in the real world, with the
ultimate irony of the grave's victory. As the moment of nature's
perfection can never be isolated, so the dream of perfect love in this
life proves impossible. The climax of their story occurs not in Act II,
at the decision to return to Emain – that is a continuation of their
acknowledgment of the inexorable laws of nature –, but here in Act
III at the edge of the grave prepared for Naisi by Conchubor.
Panicking at the realization of what they must lose to retain their
place in the saga, Deirdre reneges on that pact in the woods and
seeks an unnatural compromise with Conchubor. She pleads for the
very right to age and withering mortality that she had earlier
rejected: 'I'll say so near that grave we seem three lonesome people,
and by a new made grave there's no man will keep brooding on a
woman's lips, or on the man he hates. It's not long till your own
grave will be dug in Emain and you'd go down to it more easy if
you'd let call Ainnle and Ardan, the way we'd have a supper all
together, and fill that grave, and you'll be well pleased from this out
having four new friends the like of us in Emain'. But it is too late, for
Conchubor is helpless to break the chain of events earlier forged by
the two lovers; Ainnle and Ardan are attacked. Now Deirdre, for the
first time, forces Naisi to choose between his brothers in battle and
complete absorption in her love. Because he can no longer follow his

whole nature (foreshadowed in the brothers' quarrel at the end of Act II), Naisi breaks under the strain and bitterness erupts, cracking the perfection he and Deirdre had risked everything to attain. Hurt by the threat of loss, the lovers quarrel and in a stroke of painful irony lose the safety of the grave.

But Naisi's death in the shadow of Deirdre's mockery heightens his role at the end of the play; Deirdre's grief is intensified by the memory of their quarrel: 'It was my words without pity gave Naisi a death will have no match until the ends of life and time'. The story told forever threatens to be one of pain, not comfort; not only have they lost their love – their own choice – but they have lost their triumph as well, and Deirdre is left truly desolate. The only way to retain the fullness of their story and thus preserve their love is for Deirdre to grow even further in stature, until Conchubor becomes 'an old man and a fool only', and a greater High King, Death, marks her for his own. To regain a sense of her own strength and retrieve the dignity of her loss, she must turn her thoughts back from this night 'that's pitiful for want of pity' to the splendour of their life in the woods. Her lament must embrace not only the glory of the past but also the future, where palaces fit for queens and armies become again the haunts of weasels and wild cats, crying on a lonely wall below a careless moon. Finally, sorrow itself must be cast aside to make room for the cold pity of prophecy and the impersonal triumph of the myth. Only then, by giving up all claims to this world, can Deirdre be assured of her joy with Naisi forever. Exulting in her loneliness, she stands imperious and triumphant over the grave of the Sons of Usna, free at last of all demands both of man and time itself:

I have put away sorrow like a shoe that is worn out and muddy, for it is I have had a life that will be envied by great companies. It was not by a low birth I made kings uneasy, and they sitting in the halls of Emain. It was not a low thing to be chosen by Conchubor, who was wise, and Naisi had no match for bravery. . . . It is not a small thing to be rid of grey hairs and the loosening of the teeth. . . . It was the choice of lives we had in the clear woods, and in the grave we're safe surely.

Not only do the characters represent various stages on the spectrum of choice and reaction to time, they also indicate the full range of the passions of love and loneliness. While on Aran Synge had observed the simplicity of primitive man's judgement, 'that a man will not do wrong unless he is under the influence of a passion which is as irresponsible as a storm on the sea'. Now, using material 'filled with the oldest passions of the world', he set out to construct through his various characters a chord which would sound all the notes of love and longing, ranging from Naisi's romantic defiance of destiny to Lavarcham's wise acceptance of the passing of love. In contrast to the character development of his comedies, here he must start with persons already fully developed, infinitely themselves, 'types' in a special sense. It might not be too fanciful, in fact, to trace this simplification of character and emphasis on individual ruling passions back to his earlier studies of music and French literature. The currents or leitmotifs of destiny (as well as the consuming fire at the conclusion) are expressed in a grand Wagnerian manner, while the starkness and grandeur of passion and the inevitability of its consequence are reminiscent of French classical theatre, in particular the dramas of Racine.[8]

When he reviewed Lady Gregory's *Cuchulain of Muirthemne*, Synge remarked,

Everywhere wildness and vigour are blended in a strange way with impetuous tenderness, and with the vague misgivings that are peculiar to primitive men. Most of the moods and actions that are met with are more archaic than anything in the Homeric poems, yet a few features, such as the imperiousness and freedom of the women, seem to imply an intellectual advance beyond the period of Ulysses.[9]

Now in the character of Deirdre, written especially for Molly, he sought to convey the same imperious freedom, strength of will, and maturity of passion. The full responsibility of action rests finally on Deirdre alone; the intensity and purity of her love must be above question, and matched by greatness of soul in both herself and her lover. But Deirdre must also be sufficiently realistic to be 'probable', perhaps like the young girl he admired on Aran: 'At one moment she is a simple peasant, at another she seems to be looking out at the world with a sense of prehistoric disillusion'.[10] By using nature not as atmospheric background only but as the living standard by which Deirdre determines her actions, Synge attempted to combine the present with the past and emphasize the inevitability of her decisions. The framework and scope of her personality are fully developed in the first act: although caught in the web of prophecy, she is eminently herself. Wild with the wildness of nature, she has spent her days on the hillside or alone in the woods, 'gathering new life . . . and taking her will'. It is 'wilfuller she's growing these two months

or three', Lavarcham complains to Conchubor, and Deirdre echoes
the warning: 'I'm too long watching the days getting a great speed
passing me by, I'm too long taking my will, and it's that way I'll be
living always'. The 'like of her' is not for Conchubor, blind to the
ways of nature, and careless of Deirdre's schooling in freedom,
greedy for a comrade to ease the weight and terror of time. In place
of nuts, twigs, birds and flowers, he offers her dogs with silver
chains, white hounds, grey horses, symbols of the constraints of his
role. However, Deirdre seeks not her opposite, but 'a mate who'd be
her likeness', whose high spirits will match her wildness, and who in
the violence of youth will wrench love from its hiding place and taste
'what is best and richest if it's for a short space only'.

   Like Deirdre, Naisi has been a long time in the woods and dreads
neither death nor the 'troubles are foretold'. Challenged by Deirdre,
he accepts his destiny, 'and it earned with richness would make the
sun red with envy and he going up the heavens, and the moon pale
and lonesome and she wasting away'. Perhaps he has more to lose,
for he and his brothers have 'a short space only to be triumphant
and brave'. A warrior as well as a hunter, he knows long before
Deirdre the untidiness of death, 'a tale of blood, and broken bodies
and the filth of the grave'. And in Act II, although Deirdre first
voices her dread of the passing of love, 'wondering all times is it a
game worth playing', it is Naisi who acknowledges responsibility for
that dread and tries to protect Deirdre from the advance of time. But
after seven years the safety he offers in the woods is as ineffective as
the security of Conchubor's High Chambers; reluctantly he must
acknowledge the justness of Deirdre's decision to return. Just as
Naisi had more to lose in their flight to Alban, now he has greater
troubles to bear: the prophecy foretells the ruin of the Sons of Usna,
while Deirdre's fate is left undetermined. He must carry with him
the memory of their love and the bitter possibility of being superseded by another; and he stands to lose not only Deirdre's love but
the perfect comradeship of his warrior brothers, a double loneliness
in the grave.

   On either side of the two young lovers stand Conchubor and
Lavarcham, representing two aspects of love tempered by age.
Again their characteristics are clearly identified in the first act.
Lavarcham, wise in the ways both of man and the natural world,
combines the function of chorus (in the Elizabethan sense) and the
tolerance of age. ... But in spite of her role as wise teacher,

Lavarcham is vulnerable in her love for Deirdre: anxiety gives way to insolence and bitter anger when the sons of Usna discover Deirdre's hiding-place in Act I; grief at the prospect of Deirdre's sorrow in Act II forces her again to defy fate in a desperate attempt to keep the lovers in Alban. Owen tells us that Lavarcham too has had her share of love and happiness, but in contrast to Deirdre, she has chosen to accept the limitations of old age. . . . Yet there is room in her pity for Conchubor as well; it is she who remains at the end to mourn the deaths of Deirdre and Naisi, and to offer comfort to the broken, desolate old king.

Conchubor on the other hand refuses to accept age and its consequences. Defying the course of nature, he claims Deirdre for his bride although his role in her upbringing makes him more father than lover. In Act III he remains stubbornly tied to the remnants of passion, asserting again his unnatural right: 'It's little I care if she's white and worn, for it's I did rear her from a child should have a good right to meet and see her always'. Bewildered, he at last recognizes he will never deserve the grief Deirdre holds for Naisi, and having lost the right to both love and kingship in his last desperate fight against time, he is led away by Deirdre's old nurse, a pathetic, broken old man. 'There's things a king can't have. . . .'

Conchubor's folly arises out of ignorance; alone and defeated, he deserves our pity at the end. But with Conchubor sole rival to Naisi the spectrum of love was not complete, nor despite the omnipresence of death was the reality of love sufficiently rooted in the clay and the worms. Almost desperately, Synge sought for a foil to Conchubor, for another aspect of the distortion of love. At first he contemplated developing Ainnle's role so that he became his brother's rival, but that would upset the delicate balance he had achieved through the lovers' quarrel. A harsher, grotesque element was necessary, underscoring the ugliness of time and the violence of unfulfilled, unseemly passion. Finally he introduced Owen, the ragged, wild messenger of Act II who rudely and brusquely reminds Deirdre of the passing of time and inevitability of old age. Coldly rejected by Deirdre, he returns to startle Naisi and finally commits suicide as first casualty of Deirdre's beauty. Synge died before he could work Owen fully into the fabric of his play, but from his notebooks and Yeats's diaries it is possible to ascertain the role this grotesque figure was to carry. In Act I, Yeats reported, 'He was to come in with Conchubor, carrying some of his belongings, and afterwards at the end of the act to return for a forgotten knife – just enough to make it possible to use him in Act II'. 'When Owen killed himself in the second act, he was to have done it with Conchubor's knife.'[11] Synge therefore intended Owen to serve as spy for Conchubor and, succumbing to the fatal charm of Deirdre, thus serve as contrast also to Conchubor's other servants, Lavarcham and Fergus. But here passion exceeds all restraint and form, introducing an entirely new note and emphasizing a different kind of loneliness. For Owen is an outsider, the freak or madman of nature, perhaps the fool. He may have his origin in Trendorn of the early saga, the stranger hired by Conchubor to kill Naisi; like Trendorn, Owen hates Naisi because Naisi killed his father. He has some affinity also with the tramp of Synge's earlier plays, especially Patch Darcy, the herd of *The Shadow of the Glen* who runs mad in the hills from loneliness. But in *The Aran Islands* we can find further clues. Standing on the shore of the south island Synge noticed among the crowd 'several men of the ragged, humorous type that was once thought to represent the real peasant of Ireland ... there was something nearly appalling in the shrieks of laughter kept up by one of these individuals, a man of extraordinary ugliness and wit'. Commenting on 'this half-sensual ecstasy of laughter', he reasoned,

Perhaps a man must have a sense of intimate misery ... before he can set himself to jeer and mock at the world. These strange men with receding foreheads, high cheek-bones, and ungovernable eyes seem to represent some old type found on these few acres at the extreme border of Europe, where it is only in wild jests and laughter that they can express their loneliness and desolation.[12]

Here I believe we have the source for Owen's disjointed passion, his wild fits of laughter and sudden action, perhaps even for the folly of his hopeless love for Deirdre. Had Synge finished the play, Owen would perhaps have taken on also more of the character of the Elizabethan fool, who speaks in riddles of great sense and carries with him a haunting reminiscence of another world. But here, in his unfinished state, Owen tells Deirdre nothing she does not already know, nor does the grotesqueness of his imagery rouse in her anything but momentary contempt and a slight uneasiness at the vehemence of his tone. Owen's impact is directed instead towards the audience, lest they overlook the seriousness of Deirdre's earlier confession to Lavarcham, require further assurance of the perfection

of the love Deirdre and Naisi have shared for seven years, or seek to
identify a climax of action too early in the play. The reality of old age
is already a threat to Deirdre, but we may not have grasped its full
horror: 'Well go take your choice. Stay here and rot with Naisi, or go
to Conchubor in Emain. Conchubor's a swelling belly, and eyes
falling down from his shining crown, Naisi should be stale and
weary'. And, in contrast to the lonesomeness of happiness fulfilled,
there is the loneliness of love unfulfilled: 'It's a poor thing to be so
lonesome you'd squeeze kisses on a cur dog's nose'. There is
something more terrible in this mad folly than in the mistaken folly
of Conchubor's solitude. Love can also lead to madness and an
undignified death.

Deirdre of the Sorrows was, Synge had claimed, chiefly an experiment to change his hand. In the range of character, depth of passion,
and evocation of atmosphere, the play even in its unfinished state
proved once again the originality of his genius. At the same time,
however, he remained true in treatment of subject and development
of theme to the task he originally set himself. As early as April 1904
he had written to Frank Fay, 'The whole interest of our movement is
that our little plays try to be literature first – i.e. to be personal, sincere, and beautiful – and drama afterwards'. And a later jotting in his
notebook unconsciously traces his own development as a dramatist:
'Dramatic art is first of all a childish art – a reproduction of external
experience – without form or philosophy; then after a lyrical interval
we have it as mature drama dealing with the deeper truth of general
life in a perfect form and with mature philosophy.'[13]. . .

SOURCE: extracts from essay in *J. M. Synge: Centenary Papers 1971*
   ed. Maurice Harmon (Dublin, 1972), 88–107.

NOTES

(Reorganized and renumbered from the original – Ed.]

All quotations concerning Synge's comments on *The Playboy of the Western
World* and the writing of *Deirdre of the Sorrows* are taken from my
introduction to *J. M. Synge Plays Book II* (Oxford University Press, 1968).
   1. From a letter dated April 1902 in the possession of Major Richard
Gregory.
   2. See *J. M. Synge Prose*, ed. Alan Price (Oxford University Press,
1966), p. 371; all quotations from Synge's letters to Molly are taken from

Letters to Molly: J. M. Synge to Maire O'Neill, ed. Ann Saddlemyer (Belknap Press of Harvard University Press, 1971).

3. In a letter to Stephen MacKenna, January 1904, Synge rejected the concept of 'a purely fantastic unmodern, ideal, breezy, springdayish, Cuchulainoid National Theatre', describing a recent production of Yeats's *The Shadowy Waters* as 'the most *distressing* failure the mind can imagine', see 'Synge to MacKenna: The Mature Years', *Massachusetts Review* (Winter 1964), p. 281. He wrote of Yeats to Molly on 21 August 1907: 'I saw a book copy of *Deirdre* at Roberts' yesterday at 3/6. There is an extraordinary note at the end giving a page of the play that he had cut out, and then found that it was necessary after all. He makes himself ridiculous sometimes'.

4. See *Plays Book II*, pp. 393–4, for the complete essay.

5. In addition to Lady Gregory's and Leahy's translation of the cycle, Synge was also familiar with a manuscript written about 1740 by Andrew MacCruitin, and published in 1898 by the Society for the Preservation of the Irish Language; with the work done on the legend by his professor at the Sorbonne, H. d'Arbois de Jubainville, and doubtless knew countless other recent translations, including the cantata by T. W. Rolleston and his friend the composer Michelle Esposito. See Appendix C of Maurice Bourgeois, *John Millington Synge and the Irish Theatre* (London: Constable, 1913), Adelaide Duncan Estill, *The Sources of Synge* (Folcroft Press, 1969), pp. 34–41, and Herbert V. Fackler's article on the Deirdre legend in *Eire-Ireland* (Winter 1969), pp. 56–63.

6. Notebook 47, in the possession of Trinity College Dublin.

7. William Empson in *Seven Types of Ambiguity* (London: Chatto and Windus, 1947), pp. 38–42, traces the imagery of the storm and the grave throughout the play.

8. As early as *Riders to the Sea*, Synge developed his themes musically; this can be seen more clearly in his later scenarios where 'current' or 'motif' is paralleled by character development and plot. Synge tended to choose examples from Elizabethan and French classical dramatists; there are among his papers scene analyses of both *l'Avare* and *Phèdre*, and he attended lectures on French literature by Petit de Julleville, whose monumental *Histoire du Théâtre en France* he knew well. Synge also acted as advisor for the Abbey Theatre productions of Lady Gregory's translations of Molière, even writing to the *Comédie Française* for copies of their prompt books.

9. See *Prose*, pp. 368–9, also his article 'La Vieille Littérature Irlandaise', ibid., pp. 352–5.

10. *Prose*, p. 114, also p. 143 note: 'They have wildness and humour and passion kept in continual subjection by their reverence for life and the sea that is inevitable in this place'.

11. W. B. Yeats, *Autobiographies* (London: Macmillan, 1955), p. 457 and Yeats's Preface to the published play, *Plays Book II*, p. 179.

12. *Prose*, pp. 140–2.

13. See *Plays Book I*, p. xxvii and *Prose*, p. 350.

William Empson 'Dramatic Irony in Deirdre of the Sorrows' (1930)

... Deirdre, we have been told, is uniquely beautiful; she is being brought up alone in the woods to be old Conchubor's queen; troubles have been foretold; she is wilful; she has seen Naisi in the woods; she prefers him to Conchubor. Conchubor visits her, says he will marry her in three days, and leaves her to return to his capital. She asks her nurse, who could help her against him, would the nurse herself, no, would this great man or that, possibly, more possibly, would Naisi, and there is a storm of denial:

> LAVARCHAM: In the end of all there is none can go against Conchubor, and it's folly that we're talking, for if any went against Conchubor it's sorrow he'd earn and the shortening of his day of life.
> [*She turns away, and* DEIRDRE *stands up stiff with excitement and goes and looks out of the window.*]
> DEIRDRE: Are the stepping-stones flooding, Lavarcham? Will the night be stormy in the hills?
> LAVARCHAM: The stepping-stones are flooding, surely, and the night will be the worst, I'm thinking, we've seen these years gone by.

Upon these words Deirdre 'tears upon the press and pulls out clothes and tapestries', robes herself as a queen, and prepares for the coming of the young princes.

This storm is dramatically effective for various reasons. As part of the plot it makes Naisi and his brothers come for shelter when she is wanting them; on the classical tragic model it makes the day of the action an unusual one, a day on which it seems fitting that great things should happen, and gives a sort of unity to the place by making it difficult to get there. Further, we are in doubt as to the position of Conchubor, and this allows of several implications. If we are to conceive that he has got across the stepping-stones already, then their flooding means that Deirdre's way of safety, to Conchubor and his palace and the life which is expected of her, has been cut off; that it is high time she behaved like the stepping-stones and isolated herself with Naisi; that what in the story is done heroically by her own choice is, in dumb show, either as an encouragement or as an ironical statement of the impotence of heroic action, done by the weather; and that all these troubles which she is bringing on herself have been foretold and are beyond her control. If we are to conceive that Conchubor has not yet got across the stepping-stones, she is in danger of being condemned to his company if he turns back, as, in fact, she is in any case, since he will marry her in three days; it is against a fatal and frankly alien heaven that she exerts her courage and her royalty; the weather is now one of the inevitable forces against which she is revolting, and is that one of those forces which makes it urgent she should revolt now. If we are to conceive that Conchubor is just getting across the stepping-stones, the weather is her ally, and there is some encouragement for revolt in the thought that he may be drowned.

For the storm to mean so much it must receive particular attention, and it is assured of this by marking a change in the tone of the conversation. The preceding series of questions has received the wrong answer at its climax; Naisi is the man who can help her, and her nurse says he can not. Since energy has accumulated towards this question, and is now dammed by the negative, it bursts out of the window into a larger world, and since we find there, instead of the indifference of external Nature, instead of the calm of accepting the statement that there is no hope, a larger release of energy and the crescendo repeated in the heavens, we compare the storm with the plot and are surprised into a Pathetic Fallacy. It is not that Nature is with her or against her, is her fate or her servant; the Fallacy here claims more generally that Nature, like the spectators, is excited into a variety of sympathies, and is all these four together. The operation is thus a complicated one, but it is normal, of course, to the crudest forms of melodrama. My point is that, for a Pathetic Fallacy to cause much emotional reverberation, it must be imposed upon the reader by an ambiguity.

Since the storm has been fixed, by all these devices, firmly in the spectator's memory, a slight reference at the other end of the tragedy can call it back to give another dramatic irony. Naisi has been killed and Conchubor left in possession.

DEIRDRE: Do not raise a hand to touch me.
CONCHUBOR: There are other hands to touch you. My fighters are set in among the trees.
DEIRDRE: Who'll fight the grave, Conchubor, and it opened on a dark night?

The *night* is *dark* enough now, and, of course, her main meaning is that she can't be fought after she has killed herself. But she herself could not *fight* against the impulses of the *night* at the beginning of the play, when she ran off with Naisi and *opened the graves* which are only now being filled; nor against the weariness which is the turning-point of the action, that sense that happiness could not last for ever which drove them back to Ireland and their enemy. This third *dark night* in a sense covers the other two; we are made, therefore, to feel that the unity of time, in spite of the lovers' seven years of happiness, has somehow been preserved. The *grave*, partly in consequence of this, is not that of Deirdre only, against which Conchubor cannot *fight*; she is hopeless because she herself cannot *fight* against the *grave* in which Naisi is lying; and there is thus a further dramatic irony of the heroic action that defeats itself, in that it is Conchubor, as well as Deirdre, who *opened a grave*, whether for her or for Naisi, by his actions on either *dark night*; that Conchubor, no more than Deirdre, can *fight* either of them; that after the way Conchubor has killed Naisi, Deirdre cannot live to endure Conchubor and Conchubor cannot hold Deirdre from her *grave*. Lastly, there is a threat from Deirdre against Conchubor, making the *grave* his as well as theirs; her choice of death, or the forces he has himself loosed against her, will kill him; as indeed he is led from the stage suddenly old and aimless and 'hard set to see the way before him'. The *grave* having been spread on to three persons now takes effect as a generalization, and names the mortality of all the protagonists, incidental soldiers included; 'all life is strangely frustrated, all efforts incalculable and in vain; we are all feeble beside the forces given to us and in the face of death all parties are on the same side'.

This implication, by the way, that all the characters are people subject to the same situation, that they all understand, though they may not take, the same attitude, is important to some types of play and often gets called their 'meaning'. However, it is less insisted upon than dramatic irony by critics because (being a less conscious form of that device) it does not need to be noticed to be appreciated, and, therefore, is at once a less likely and a less useful thing for them to notice. For the rather limited and doctrinaire pessimism exploited by Synge it is a powerful weapon; consider this piece of dialogue, when the lovers are wondering whether to go back to Ireland, where they will find death and their proper social position:

NAISI: If our time in this place is ended, come away without Ainnle and Ardan to the woods of the east, for it's right to be away from all people when two lovers have their love only. Come away and we'll be safe always.

DEIRDRE: There's no safe place, Naisi, on the ridge of the world. . . . And it's in the quiet woods I've seen them digging our grave, and throwing out the clay on leaves are bright and withered.

NAISI: Come away, Deirdre, and it's little we'll think of safety or the grave beyond it, and we resting in a little corner between the daytime and the long night.

DEIRDRE: It's this hour we're between the daytime and a night where there is sleep for ever, and isn't it a better thing to be following on to a near death, than to be bending the head down, and dragging with the feet, and seeing one day a blight showing on love where it is sweet and tender?

These may seem absurdly simple phrases for Deirdre to twist into her more gloomy meaning, but it was Naisi who first suggested the idea from which he is now trying to reassure her; it is because at the back of his mind he agrees with her that upon all phrases of comfort he can give her there lies the same shadow of the grave. . . .

SOURCE: extract from *Seven Types of Ambiguity* (London, 3rd edn, 1953), 38–42. The section on Synge is unchanged from the first edition (1930).

Eugene Benson 'Tragic and Human Dimensions' (1982)

. . . The open grave on stage in the third act is most fitting. Like the bundle of clothes in *Riders to the Sea*, the grave reinforces the play's intensity and adds a degree of suspense to the inevitability of the action. It is also used to bring about a surprising *rapprochement*. As the quarrel between Conchubor and Naisi progresses by the edge of the grave, Synge intensifies further the tragic character of the catastrophe by having Deirdre effect a reconciliation among lover, loved one and rival. The grave, she argues, is the ultimate reality which renders human emotions – love and hate – irrelevant:

DEIRDRE: I'll say so near that grave we seem three lonesome people, and by a new made grave there's no man will keep brooding on a woman's lips, or on the man he hates.

This reversal, which seems to offer escape, is followed by another even more powerful and harrowing reversal when Deirdre and Naisi quarrel by the grave immediately before Naisi's death. It is an astringently characteristic touch paralleling Maurya's refusal in *Riders to the Sea* to bless Bartley before he too goes to his death. 'And you'll have me meet death with a hard word from your lips in my ears?' Naisi cries out, aghast. Deirdre, in brutal language, goes on to denounce their seven years in Alban as 'a dream' and demands his death. This final quarrel, where Yeats felt the lovers lose all they had given their life to keep, has its parallels also in the scene where Martin curses Molly in *The Well of the Saints* and in the scene in *The Playboy* where Pegeen betrays and tortures Christy.

It was Synge's intention to make Act III of *Deirdre of the Sorrows* 'Rider-like' and there are obvious similarities. The final scene where Deirdre mourns the death of the Sons of Usna resembles Maurya's lament for the loss of her sons; both threnodies are delivered to the accompaniment of the *caoine*. There are a number of similarities too in the development of the threnodies. In speech after speech Deirdre moves from self-pity ('who'll pity Deirdre?') through affirmation ('It's you three will not see age or death coming'), elegiac remembrance ('It was the voice of Naisi that was strong in summer'), words of burial ('Let us throw down clay on my three comrades'), resolve to die ('I will not leave Naisi'), prophetic utterance ('because of me . . . there will be a story told of a ruined city and a raving king and a woman will be young forever'). The final note is tragic exaltation:

I have put sorrow away like a shoe that is worn and muddy, for it is I have had a life that will be envied by great companies. It was not by a low birth I made kings uneasy, and they sitting in the halls of Emain. It was not a low thing to be chosen by Conchubor, who was wise, and Naisi had no match for bravery. . . . It is not a small thing to be rid of grey hairs and the loosening of the teeth. [*With a sort of triumph*] . . . It was the choice of lives we had in the clear woods, and in the grave we're safe surely.

It is a magnificent closing speech – astonishingly crammed with details of the actress's business – but it should not distract us from the fact that the lovers, for all their heroic passions, have been defeated by life. Synge's austere and tragic view of life first drama-

tized in *Riders to the Sea* is reaffirmed in our final glimpse of King
Conchubor broken, like King Oedipus or King Lear, by the
slaughter of those near to him through kinship or desire:

> LAVARCHAM: I have a little hut where you can rest Conchubor, there is a
> great dew falling.
> CONCHUBOR: [*with the voice of an old man*]. Take me with you, I'm hard
> set to see the way before me.

It is difficult to resist the conclusion that in his last play Synge
glorifies a death-wish. The dominant *leitmotif* of the play is a horror
of life which brings ageing and which entails (for Deirdre) an
inevitable loss of beauty and a consequent blighting of love. The
motif of the first scene between Deirdre and Naisi was 'welcome to
destruction', and Synge characterizes the scene where Deirdre
commits suicide as 'defiance of life'. The quarrel scene with Naisi
parallels the scene in *Riders to the Sea* where Maurya refuses Bartley
her blessing; both women send their men to their deaths because, for
different reasons, they perceive death to be good. Life, in Synge's
final play, is often described in images of decay while death is
usually praised. Naisi's death 'will have no match'; 'It's you [the
sons of Usna] will not see age or death coming'; 'it was a clean
death was your share, Naisi'; 'Draw back a little from Naisi who
is young forever'; 'a woman will be young forever'; 'it is not a
small thing to be rid of grey hairs and the loosening of the teeth';
'in the grave we're safe surely'. In Act I Conchubor had offered
Deirdre Emain Macha as 'a place is safe and splendid'; in Act II
Naisi had offered her a refuge in nature – 'Come away into the safety
of the woods'; but in Act III Deirdre comes finally to realize that
only in the grave is she safe, just as Maurya was brought to the same
bitter realization: 'Bartley will have a fine coffin out of the white
boards, and a deep grave surely. . . . What more can we want than
that?'

There is, further, a striking resemblance between Synge's *Deirdre
of the Sorrows* and Wagner's *Tristan and Isolde* which he undoubtedly
knew from his musical studies. Both works memorialize the
doomed lovers of two famous Celtic legends; both express the
anguish of a personal hopeless love (Synge's for Molly Allgood,
Wagner's for Mathilde von Wesendonck); both celebrate the theme
of Love-as-Death (*Liebestod*) which brings the lovers an ultimate
freedom and an eternal youth. To Naisi's statement that the grave

puts 'a great space between two friends that love', Deirdre counters, 'maybe it's that grave when it's closed will make us one forever'.

It might seem, on first glance, that the epic story of Deirdre's tragic love for Naisi lay outside the scope and character of Synge's dramatic genius. *The Well of the Saints* and *The Playboy of the Western World* seem the very antithesis of an art that is 'quiet and stately and restrained'. In his poem, 'The Passing of the Shee', he had derided AE's mystical attraction to heroic Celtic figures like 'sweet Angus, Maeve and Fand', choosing instead the tough peasant note:

> We'll search in Red Dan Sally's ditch,
> And drink in Tubber fair,
> Or poach with Red Dan Philly's bitch,
> The badger and the hare.
> (*Poems*, p. 38)

. . . But if Synge dismisses AE so cavalierly it is because he felt that his art lacked a 'grip on reality'. In a series of notes written in 1908, Synge tried to solve the problems inherent in writing on historical or saga stories. He felt that with a very few exceptions historical plays and novels and poems ('Utopian work') were 'relatively worthless'. But there were methods by which one might avoid 'artificial retellings of classical or saga stories'. The first was to recognize that the place of religious art had been taken by 'our quite modern feeling for the beauty and mystery of nature. . . . Our pilgrimages are not to Canterbury or Jerusalem, but to Killarney and Cumberland and the Alps' (*Prose*, p. 351). *Deirdre of the Sorrows* surpasses any of Synge's plays in its evocation of 'the beauty and mystery' of Nature. Speech after speech is crammed with descriptions of nature which operate dramatically rather than merely poetically. Naisi's dread and relief after he has discussed his fear of seeing Deirdre grow old are vividly dramatized in images drawn from nature:

I've had dread, I tell you, dread winter and summer, and the autumn and the spring-time, even when there's a bird in every bush making his own stir till the fall of night. But this talk's brought me ease, and I see we're as happy as the leaves on the young trees and we'll be so ever and always though we'd live the age of the eagle and the salmon and the crow of Britain.

Deirdre, who has overheard Naisi's admission, poses the tragedy of their departure and death against poignant memories of their love amid the woods of Cuan:

There's no place to stay always. . . . It's a long time we've had, pressing the lips together, going up and down, resting in our arms, Naisi, waking with the smell of June in the top of the grasses, and listening to the birds in the branches that are highest. . . . It's a long time we've had, but the end has come surely.

When Ainnle weds the lovers it is in language drawn not from theology but from nature: 'By the sun and moon and the whole earth, I wed Deirdre to Naisi. . . . May the air bless you, and water and the wind, the sea, and all the hours of the sun and moon'. It was through the immediacy of such observations based on nature that Synge hoped to make his saga theme more real.

A second method was to demythologize his characters and forge for them a speech which would further humanize them. Synge's King Conchubor is less a king than an ageing father–lover. In Act I he enters accompanied only by Fergus, and his two scenes with Lavarcham and Deirdre portray him as a rather pathetic figure, stiff in the company of the servant, suppliant in his attitude to Deirdre. Deirdre, too, is first presented like any peasant girl – '*poorly dressed with a little bag and a bundle of twigs in her arms*'. With the exception of the scene in Act I where Deirdre dresses herself in the robes of a queen, she is presented as a child–woman doomed to a tragic fate rather than as a queen. The same process of demythologizing extends to Naisi who behaves less like a prince than a hunter and lover associated, like Deirdre, with the natural world. The many drafts of *Deirdre of the Sorrows* show Synge constantly seeking to re-create the remote world of Cuchulain and the Red Branch within the tragic and human dimensions of lover, loved one and rival. . . .

SOURCE: extracts from *J. M. Synge* (London and Basingstoke, 1982), 144–9.

Declan Kiberd 'Synge's *Deirdre* and Friel's *Faith Healer*' (1985)

Faith Healer by Brian Friel may well be the finest play to come out of Ireland since J. M. Synge's *Playboy of the Western World*. It is also, without a doubt, one of the most derivative works of art to be produced in Ireland this century – and this gives rise to a question. How can a play which is indebted so heavily to a number of previous works be nevertheless a work of profound and scintillating originality? And how can a play consisting of four separate monologues by characters who never openly confront each other be a fully *dramatic* work, in any real sense of that word?

We should first consider Friel's debts. *Faith Healer* might be called an intergeneric work where the forms of novel and drama meet, for it is a kind of dramatized novel. The idea of four contradictory monologues may have come to Friel from a reading of William Faulkner's most famous novel *The Sound and the Fury*. The method is identical, even down to the detail of having one of the monologues narrated by a witness of unstable mind, in Faulkner the lunatic Benjy, in Friel the shattered and suicidal Grace Hardy. This attempt to take an outstanding device of the modern novel, and redeploy it in the dramatic form is a characteristic modernist strategy, for modernism loves to mix genres – one thinks of Eliot's fusion of drama and poetry, Joyce's use of drama in the middle of *Ulysses*, Flann O'Brien's crazy blend of cowboy tale and Celtic lore in *At Swim-Two-Birds*. Although Faulkner's novel and Friel's play both challenge the audience to judge for itself the inconsistencies between the various monologues there is one crucial difference. The novel can be reread, the play cannot be rerun to some point of contention. To that extent, the dramatic form is even more baffling and unsettling in its effect on its audience.

Friel's other debt is even more striking. *Faith Healer* is clearly a remoulding of the legend of Deirdre of the Sorrows, a tale which has been dramatized by many leading Irish writers from George Russell to W. B. Yeats, from J. M. Synge to James Stephens. The idea of a well-brought-up girl, destined for a noble calling in the north of Ireland, but spirited away to Scotland by an attractive but feckless

217

man, to the great dismay of an elderly guardian – that, in a nutshell, is the plot of both Friel's and Synge's plays. In Scotland, the lovers live well enough for many years, supported by their manager Teddy, who discharges the same role in *Faith Healer* as that played by Naisi's brothers, Ainnle and Ardan, in Synge's play. Ultimately, however, their nomadic and rootless life is felt to be increasingly hollow and stressful. With some foreboding, they decide to return to Ireland, but in their nervousness and apprehensiveness, each lover attributes the decision to the other. Their worst fears are realized on arrival in Ireland. As Francis Hardy says: 'there was no sense of homecoming',[1] or as Synge's Naisi says, looking at the shabby rooms and open grave, which the King offers by way of greeting: 'And that'll be our home in Emain'.[2] Earlier, he gloomily remarks that 'it's little we want with state or rich rooms or curtains, when we're used to the ferns only, and cold streams and they making a stir'[3] – a sentence which could just as aptly describe the raw, open-air life of Francis, Grace and Teddy camping out by the fields and streams of Scotland.

   One of the great themes of Synge's play and of the original Gaelic legend is Deirdre's love of place. Before her final departure from Scotland, she lists the names of all the abandoned places with tender care. So it is with her laments for Glen Ruadh, Glen Laid, the Woods of Cuan and so on in Synge's play. In one of his less well-known essays on 'The People of the Glens', Synge had remarked on the 'curiously melodious names' to be found in Wicklow – Augha-vanna, Glenmalure, Annamoe[4] – and he built lilting lists of the names into his Wicklow plays. Friel self-consciously builds on the ancient Gaelic tradition in those passages where Francis and Grace recite the Scottish place-names, as the Faith Healer says, 'just for the mesmerism, the sedation, of the incantation'.[5] This is an ancient Gaelic device redeployed by Seamus Heaney, for example in poems such as 'The Tollund Man':

> Something of his sad freedom
> As he rode the tumbril
> Should come to me, driving,
> Saying the names
>
> Tollund, Grabaulle, Nebelgard,
> Watching the pointing hands
> Of country people,
> Not knowing their tongue.[6]

What is revealing in Friel's play, however, is the fact that Grace fouls up the order of her husband's incantation. She omits his third line from the list and, at the end of her monologue, is so distraught that she cannot get beyond the opening lines:

> Aberarder, Kinlochbervie,
> Aberayron, Kinlochbervie,
> Invergordon, Kinlochbervie . . . in Sutherland, in
> the north of Scotland . . .[7]

She trails off helplessly and this linguistic failure is the sure sign of her imminent collapse.

In *Faith Healer*, as in the Deirdre legend, the lovers return to Ireland with the premonition that it will be a return to disaster and even death for the hero. And this is what happens. Only at the very end does Friel depart radically from Synge's plot. Whereas Synge's Deirdre dies soon after Naisi in the romantic medieval versions, Friel follows the more hard-edged Old Irish rendition by having her live on for a year in misery, before her eventual suicide. . . .

SOURCE: extract from 'Brian Friel's *Faith Healer*,' in *Irish Writers and Society at Large*, ed. Masaru Sekine (Gerrards Cross, 1985), 106–8.

NOTES

1. Brian Friel, *Faith Healer* (London: Faber, 1980), p. 16.
2. J. M. Synge, *Collected Plays* 2, ed. A. Saddlemyer (Oxford: Oxford University Press, 1968), p. 249.
3. Ibid., p. 247.
4. J. M. Synge, *Collected Works: Prose*, ed. Alan Price (Oxford: Oxford University Press, 1966), p. 216.
5. *Faith Healer*, p. 11.
6. Seamus Heaney, *Winter Out* (London: Faber, 1972), p. 48.
7. *Faith Healer*, p. 27.

Hugh Kenner   The Living World for Text   (1983)

...The sixth play of Synge was *Deirdre of the Sorrows*, which the indefatigable first-nighter Joseph Holloway thought 'of little worth'.

'The ruck of muck', he wrote in his 1910 diary; and 'the loftiness of the theme was trailed in the mud'. True, this Deirdre is a girl who can be short with the High King of Ireland and men comparably exalted. Her 'Draw a little back with the squabbling of fools' is not a thing we'd hear from the Deirdre of Yeats, a poet's Queen, never less than lofty, even coquettishly lofty. Yet it hushes the stage for words she can speak in a low intent voice, and even spoken with no special emphasis they search the full register of Synge's rhetoric:

> DEIRDRE: Draw a little back with the squabbling of fools when I am broken up with misery. [*She turns round.*] I see the flames of Emain starting upward in the dark night; and because of me there will be weasels and wild cats crying on a lonely wall where there were queens and armies and red gold, the way there will be a story told of a ruined city and a raving king and a woman will be young for ever. [*She looks round.*] I see the trees naked and bare, and the moon shining. Little moon, little moon of Alban, it's lonesome you'll be this night, and tomorrow night, and long nights after, and you pacing the woods beyond Glen Laid, looking every place for Deirdre and Naisi, the two lovers who slept so sweetly with each other.

'Raving', 'naked', 'slept with each other': with an effort one can grasp what it was dismayed Holloway. Yet there is precedent for such descents of diction. 'A lass unparallel'd', wrote Shakespeare of his Cleopatra, in his one play to meld the subplot with the high plot and achieve this by language only. 'Lass' is a low word. So is 'dung':

> And it is great
> To do that thing that ends all other deeds,
> Which shackles accidents and bolts up change,
> Which sleeps, and never palates more the dung,
> The beggar's nurse, and Caesar's.

Wincers have not been lacking who'd emend 'dung' to 'dug'. And what of 'wretch', 'fool', and 'ass'?

> [*To an asp*] Come, thou mortal wretch,
> With thy sharp teeth this knot intrinsicate
> Of life at once untie. Poor venomous fool,
> Be angry, and dispatch. O, couldst thou speak,
> That I might hear thee call great Caesar ass,
> Unpolicied!

(The next words are 'O Eastern star!') And Deirdre:

I have put away sorrow like a shoe that is worn out and muddy, for it is I have had a life that will be envied by great companies. . . . It was the choice of lives we had in the clear woods, and in the grave, we're safe, surely.

One more speech ('. . . It is a cold place I must go to be with you, Naisi. . . .') and she has pressed a knife into her heart. It seems beyond doubt that Synge's model was the death-scene of Cleopatra, that he was not awed by its challenge, and that transposing such effects of scale and grandeur from Shakespeare's baroque Alexandria to a 'Tent . . . with shabby skins and benches' in barbaric Ireland was well within the grasp of a talent still extending its scope as he sank toward death. If 'grey hairs, and the loosening of the teeth' might be Nora Burke speaking, that is not because Synge is still fixed amid his phrases of 1903. It is one note merely on a long scale over which, in those last desperate months, he was gaining serene command. The resources of the Synge of Deirdre, unglimpsed by the Synge of Nora Burke and Pegeen Mike, include a new mastery of the single taut word: 'It was the choice of lives we had in the clear woods', where 'clear' condenses an outdoor starlit world, their one-time openness of vision, the freedom of the woods as against Emain with red gold on the walls, a moment's decisive clarity amid entanglements. Or test the ring of another understated phrase: 'It was not by a low birth I made kings uneasy. . . .' How finely indeterminate is 'uneasy'!

There is language here of such originality that Synge would be dead twenty years before anyone managed an articulate response to it. That was William Empson, who saw in 1929 that such words as the following force a critic to say something new:

DEIRDRE: . . . It should be a sweet thing to have what is best and richest, if it's for a short space only.
NAISI: And we've a short space only to be triumphant and brave.

'The language here seems rich in implications; it certainly carries much feeling and conveys a delicate sense of style. But if one thinks

of the Roman and mediaeval associations of *triumphant*, even of its
normal use in English, one feels a sort of unexplained warning that
these are irrelevant; the word here is a thin counter standing for a
notion not fully translated out of Irish; it is used to eke out that alien
and sliding speech-rhythm, which puts no weight upon its single
words'.[1]

Deirdre of the Sorrows is not a play Synge finished; Act II is
especially thin, and no one can say what he would have done to it all
in more months. In its provisional state it's still enough to show us
how his conception of tragedy had progressed from the steady
keening of *Riders to the Sea*, and his sense of language from the quick
comic contrasts of *The Playboy*. Old Mahon's 'It's Christy! by the
stars of God! I'd know his way of spitting and he astride the moon'
was minted by the same sensibility as 'I have put away sorrow like a
shoe that is worn out and muddy', but being comic it verges on
mannerism, and the *Deirdre* speech is beyond mannerism. So is this:

DEIRDRE: Do not raise a hand to touch me.
CONCHUBOR: There are other hands to touch you. My fighters are set
    round in among the trees.
DEIRDRE: Who'll fight the grave, Conchubor, and it opened on a dark
    night?

It was soon a commonplace that Synge wrote such speeches with
a mind absorbed by his own death. That he was dying all his short
working life – indeed 'dying chose the living world for text' – was a
necessary part of the myth Yeats made of him. Romantic ritual has
need of a stilled precursor: must canonize if need be even a
Chatterton, pathetic faker and Wordsworth's 'marvelous boy'. The
complex role Wordsworths or Yeatses play includes obligation
toward some void left by destiny, some body of unimaginable things
unsaid: what mute inglorious Miltons might have uttered, what
sweeter unheard melodies were lost with Keats. Such compensation
as the living can offer is all the more poignant in being forever
insufficient, since what can replace unique individual power?

Though we can never test such a myth for truth, it is tempting to
wonder how the Irish Renaissance would look had Synge lived, the
Psalmist's span, into the 1940s, and had it been Yeats who was
silenced instead, say by the nervous breakdown he suffered early in
1909. In losing much poetry, needless to itemize, we should have
gained a movement at whose centre was a great dramatist, inter-

nationally acclaimed. What we have, *The Playboy* even, is 'prentice work; he found his vocation late, and had but six years for it.

His death left Yeats to create a myth of noble isolation in a Tower, and left the other pole of the Irish literary future at the disposal of a 'lankylooking galoot' Synge had known in Paris, where, the hole being greater than the pants, he seldom took off his macintosh. That was James Joyce, 1902. Though Joyce, fresh out of college, argued heatedly that *Riders to the Sea* was too brief for canonical tragedy, he esteemed it enough to take trouble over an Italian translation the Synge estate wouldn't grant Triestinos leave to play. He even called Synge's art 'more original than my own' (1907), and though he made Buck Mulligan mock at Synge – Shakespeare, says the Buck, is 'the chap that writes like Synge' – in *Finnegans Wake* he slipped Synge's name into a list of Lord Mayors of Dublin, and in Trieste and Zurich and Paris sustained as did no one else in our century the principle that incessant labour and redrafting might elevate seeming trivia into greatness.

SOURCE: extract from *A Colder Eye: The Modern Irish Writers* (New York, 1983), 139–43.

NOTE

1. The reference here is to *Seven Types of Ambiguity* (London, 3rd edn, 1963), p. 5 (not included in the extract printed in the present Casebook). [*Editor's note*]

SELECT BIBLIOGRAPHY

Only the more important editions of Synge's writings and the more substantial studies of his work (in addition to those included in this Casebook) are listed here; for comprehensive checklists of critical material see Paul M. Levitt, *J. M. Synge: A Bibliography of Published Criticism* (Dublin: Irish University Press, 1974), E. H. Mikhail, *J. M. Synge: A Bibliography of Criticism* (London: Macmillan, 1975), Edward A. Kopper, *John Millington Synge: A Reference Guide* (Boston: Hall, 1979) and Edward A. Kopper, *Synge: A Review of the Criticism* (Lyndora, Pa.: Kopper, 1990). The largest archive of Synge manuscripts, typescripts and personal papers is located in the library of Trinity College, Dublin. Microfilms of these manuscripts (Brighton: Harvester Microform Publications, 1987), covering an exceptional range and variety of material, are available in a number of scholarly reference libraries.

EDITIONS

Ann Saddlemyer (ed.), *J. M. Synge: Collected Works*, Volumes III and IV (London: OUP, 1968; reprinted, Gerrards Cross: Smythe; Washington, D.C.: Catholic University of America, 1982). Contains definitive texts of all Synge's plays.

Ann Saddlemyer (ed.), *J. M. Synge: Plays* (London: OUP, 1969). Paperback edition of the major plays in the texts printed in Volumes III and IV of the *Collected Works* edition.

T. R. Henn (ed.), *The Plays and Poems of J. M. Synge* (London: Methuen, 1963).

Robin Skelton (ed.), *Four Plays and the Aran Islands* (London: Oxford University Press, 1962).

Robin Skelton (ed.), *Riders to the Sea* (London: Oxford University Press, 1969). Uses ms in Houghton Library, Harvard, that embodies several minor differences from other published texts.

Nicholas Grene (ed.), *The Well of the Saints* (Gerrards Cross: Colin Smythe; Washington: Catholic University of America Press, 1982). First edition of play to make use of all the major theatrical revisions of 1905 text.

T. R. Henn (ed.), *The Playboy of the Western World* (London: Methuen, 1961).

Malcolm Kelsall (ed.), *The Playboy of the Western World* (London: Ernest Benn Ltd, 1975), New Mermaids edition.

Ann Saddlemyer (ed.), *The Collected Letters of J. M. Synge: Volume I, 1871–1907* (Oxford: Clarendon Press; New York: OUP, 1983), *Volume II, 1907–1909* (Oxford: Clarendon Press; New York: OUP, 1984).

RECORDINGS

Riders to the Sea and *In the Shadow of the Glen*. Spoken Arts Recording no. 743. Radio Eireann Players Production.
The Playboy of the Western World. Angel recordings nos. 35357–35358. With Siobhan McKenna and Cyril Cusack.

BOOKS AND ARTICLES ON SYNGE

General

Maurice Bourgeois, *John Millington Synge and the Irish Theatre* (London: Constable, 1913; New York: Benjamin Blom, 1965).
Daniel Corkery, *Synge and Anglo-Irish Literature* (Dublin & Cork: Cork University Press, 1931; London & New York: Longman's Green, 1931; New York: Russell and Russell, 1965).
Anthony Cronin, *Heritage Now: Irish Literature in the English Language* (Dingle: Brandon, 1982).
Herbert V. Fackler, *The Tragic Queen: The Deirdre Legend in Anglo-Irish Literature* (Salzburg: Universität Salzburg, 1978).
David H. Greene and E. M. Stephens, *J. M. Synge 1871–1909* (New York: Macmillan, 1959; Collier Books, 1961).
Augusta Lady Gregory, *Our Irish Theatre* (New York & London: Putnam's, 1913).
Nicholas Grene, *Synge: a Critical Study of the Plays* (London: Macmillan, 1975; Totowa, N.J.: Rowman & Littlefield, 1976).
Robert Hogan and James Kilroy, *The Modern Irish Drama, III. Laying the Foundations, 1902–1904* (Dublin: Dolmen Press; Atlantic Highlands, NJ: Humanities Press, 1976).
Robert Hogan and James Kilroy, *The Modern Irish Drama, IV. The Abbey Theatre: The Years of Synge 1905–1909.* (Dublin: Dolmen Press; Atlantic Highlands, NJ., 1978).
Toni O'Brien Johnson, *Synge: The Medieval and the Grotesque* (Gerrards Cross: Colin Smythe; Totowa, NJ: Barnes & Noble, 1982).
Declan Kiberd, *Synge and the Irish Language* (London: Macmillan, 1979).
Mary C. King, *The Drama of J. M. Synge* (London: Fourth Estate, 1985).
Edward A. Kopper, Jr, *A J. M. Synge Literary Companion* (New York & London: Greenwood, 1988).
D. E. S. Maxwell, *A Critical History of Modern Irish Drama 1891–1980* (London & New York: Cambridge University Press, 1984).
Alan Price, *Synge and Anglo-Irish Drama* (London: Methuen, 1961).
Ann Saddlemyer, *J. M. Synge and Modern Comedy* (Dublin: Dolmen Press, 1968).
Robin Skelton, *The Writings of J. M. Synge* (London: Thames & Hudson, 1971).
Weldon Thornton, *J. M. Synge and the Western Mind* (Gerrards Cross, Bucks: Colin Smythe, 1979).

Riders to the Sea

David R. Clark (ed.), *John Millington Synge: Riders to the Sea* (Columbus, Ohio: Charles E. Merrill, 1970).
D. S. Neff, 'Synge's Hecuba', *Eire-Ireland*, 19 (1984), 74–86.

The Well of the Saints

Grace Eckley, 'Truth at the Bottom of a Well: Synge's *The Well of the Saints*', *Modern Drama*, 16 (1973), 193–8.
Anthony Roche, 'The Two Worlds of Synge's *The Well of the Saints*', *Genre*, 12 (1979), 439–50.

The Playboy of the Western World

Gail Finney. 'The "Playgirl" of the Western World: Feminism, Comedy and Synge's Pegeen Mike', *Themes in Drama 11: Women in Theatre*, ed. James Redmond (Cambridge, 1989), 87–98.
René Fréchet, 'Synge and Ireland: the Solitude of the Artist in *The Playboy of the Western World*', *Threshold*, 33 (1983), 60–73.
C. L. Innes, 'Naked Truth, Fine Clothes and Fine Phrases in Synge's *Playboy of the Western World*', *Myth and Reality in Irish Literature*, ed. Joseph Ronsley (Waterloo, 1977), 63–75.
James C. Pierce, 'Synge's Widow Quin: Touchstone to the *Playboy's* Irony', *Eire-Ireland*, 16 (1981), 122–3.
Thomas R. Whitaker (ed.), *Twentieth Century Interpretations of The Playboy of the Western World* (Englewood Cliffs, NJ: Prentice Hall, Inc., 1969).

Deirdre of the Sorrows

Ellen S. Spangler, 'Synge's *Deirdre of the Sorrows* as Feminine Tragedy', *Eire-Ireland*, 12 (1977), 97–108.
Robin Wilkinson, 'The Shadow of Deirdre: a Structuralist Approach to two plays by John Millington Synge', *Cahiers du Centre d'Études Irlandaises*, 4 (1979), 87–100.

NOTES ON CONTRIBUTORS

JAMES AGATE (1877–1947): drama critic of the *Sunday Times* for over twenty years. His many publications include books on the theatre and an autobiography (*Ego*) in 9 volumes; perhaps the best representative collections of his weekly reviews are *Brief Chronicles* (1943) and *Red Letter Nights* (1944).

RONALD AYLING: Professor of English at the University of Alberta, Canada. Literary adviser to the Sean O'Casey estate, his publications include a posthumous collection of the playwright's writings (1967) and, in collaboration with Michael J. Durkan, *Sean O'Casey: A Bibliography* (1978). His casebook on O'Casey's Dublin Trilogy was published in 1985.

SIR MAX BEERBOHM (1872–1956): critic, essayist and cartoonist, he succeeded Shaw as drama critic of the *Saturday Review* in 1898. His criticism was collected in *Around Theatres* (2 volumes, 1924).

EUGENE BENSON: Professor of English at the University of Guelph, Ontario, Canada. He has had considerable stage experience, has published widely on modern drama and was one of the editors for the *Oxford Companion of Canadian Theatre* (1989). His volume on Synge in the 'Macmillan Modern Dramatists' series was published in 1982.

PADRAIC COLUM (1881–1972): distinguished Irish poet, playwright and folklorist.

CYRIL CUSACK: noted actor and stage director, he worked with the Abbey Theatre from 1932 to 1945 and then formed his own company at the Gaiety Theatre in Dublin. Recorded *The Playboy of The Western World* in 1955.

SEAMUS DEANE: Professor of English at University College, Dublin. Author of two books of poetry – *Gradual Wars* and *Rumours* – he is a frequent contributor to *Encounter*, *Times Literary Supplement*, *Modern Language Review* and other journals. In 1973 he received the AE Award for Literature.

ERROL DURBACH: Professor of Drama at the University of British Columbia, specializing in Modern and Comparative Drama. Especially interested in tragedy he has published essays on Ibsen, Synge and other playwrights and edited *Ibsen and the Theatre: The Dramatist in Production* (1980).

SIR WILLIAM EMPSON (1906–1984): distinguished poet and critic; for many years Professor of English in the University of Sheffield, he earlier taught at Cambridge and in Japan and China. He was knighted in 1979.

WILLIAM G. FAY (1872–1947): leading actor and stage director in the formative years of the Abbey Theatre, Dublin, he took major roles in all Synge's plays first staged there.

DONNA GERSTENBERGER: Professor of English and former head of department, University of Washington, Seattle. Author of books and articles on American and English Literature, including *John Millington Synge* (revised 1990), *Iris Murdoch*, *The Complex Configuration: Modern Verse Drama* and *Richard Hugo*.

LADY GREGORY – *née* Isabella Augusta Persse (1852–1932): co-founder, with W. B. Yeats, of the Abbey Theatre, Dublin; prolific playwright and folklorist. *Our Irish Theatre*, a personal history, was published in 1913. Her *Journals 1916–1930* (2 vols, 1978–1987) are indispensable reading for an understanding of the Anglo-Irish literary movement.

NICHOLAS GRENE: Fellow and Director of Studies in Modern English at Trinity College, Dublin, his publications include *Synge: a Critical Study of the Plays* (1975), *Shakespeare, Jonson, Molière: the Comic Contract* (1980) and *Bernard Shaw: a Critical View* (1984). He has edited Synge's *The Well of the Saints* (1982) and is currently working on Shakespearean tragedy.

ROBERT BECHTOLD HEILMAN: formally Professor of English at the University of Washington, Seattle, and author of *This Great Stage: Image and Structure in King Lear* (1948), *Magic in the Web: Action and Language in Othello* (1956), *Tragedy and Melodrama* (1968), *The Ways of the World: Comedy and Society* (1978) and (with Cleanth Brooks) *Understanding Drama* (1948).

T. R. HENN (1901–74): Irish critic and poet, he taught at Cambridge; his publications include an edited edition of Synge's works, *The Lonely Tower* (1949) and *The Bible as Literature* (1970).

TONI O'BRIEN JOHNSON: lectures on English literature at the University of Lausanne: her publications include *Synge: the Medieval and the Grotesque* (1982), and she is currently working on a study of the grotesque in the Anglo-Irish dramatic tradition.

DENIS JOHNSTON (1901–87): distinguished Irish playwright (of the generation that followed O'Casey), broadcaster and journalist.

HUGH KENNER: Mellon Professor in Humanities, Johns Hopkins University, Baltimore; wide-ranging in his critical writings, his books on Irish subjects include *Dublin's Joyce* (1955), *The Stoic Comedians: Flaubert, Joyce and Beckett* (1962), *A Reader's Guide to Samuel Beckett* (1973), *Joyce's Voices* (1978), *Ulysses* (1980) and *A Colder Eye* (1983).

DECLAN KIBERD: Lecturer in Anglo-Irish Literature and Drama at University College, Dublin, he writes regularly on literature and politics in both the English and the Irish languages. His publications include *Synge and the Irish Language* (1979), *The Merchant of Venice: A Commentary* (1980) and *The Last Europeans* (1987), a general assessment of nine modern Irish writers from Wilde to Heaney.

THOMAS KILROY: playwright, novelist and critic, and Professor of English in University College, Galway. Best known for *The Death and Resurrection of Mr. Roche*, *The O'Neill*, *Talbot's Box* and *Double Cross*, plays which have been well received in Ireland and abroad.

AUGUSTINE MARTIN: Professor of Anglo-Irish Literature and Drama at University College, Dublin, and (since 1983) a member of the Board of Directors of the Abbey Theatre. He has served as a Senator of the Irish Republic (1973–80), as Director of the Yeats International Summer School at Sligo (1978–81) and as Vice-Chairman of the Irish Cultural Relations Committee of the Department of Foreign Affairs (1979–82). His publications include *Anglo-Irish Literature, a History* (1980), a critical study of James Stephens and a biography of William Butler Yeats.

D. E. S. MAXWELL: Professor of English in York University, Canada, and Master of Winters College, Toronto, 1969–79. His publications include *The Poetry of T. S. Eliot* (1952), *American Fiction* (1963), *Poets of the Thirties* (1969), *Brian Friel* (1973) and *Modern Irish Drama* (1984).

GEORGE MOORE (1852–1933): celebrated Irish novelist and man of letters, his autobiographical work *Hail and Farewell* (3 vols, 1911–14) is an indispensable if irreverent commentary on the early years of the Anglo-Irish literary movement.

MAIRE NIC SHIUBHLAIGH (MAIRE WALKER, 1888–1959): leading actress in earliest days of the Irish National Theatre Society and subsequent Abbey Theatre company, she created memorable roles in Yeats's early plays and was the original Nora Burke in Synge's *In the Shadow of the Glen* (1903).

FRANK O'CONNOR (pen-name of Michael Francis O'Donovan, 1903–66): distinguished Irish novelist and short story writer, he served on Abbey Theatre board for the last years of W. B. Yeats's reign there.

SIDNEY POGER: Professor of English in the University of Vermont; he has published studies on modern poetry and on Irish literature, including the plays of W. B. Yeats.

GEORGE ROBERTS (1873–1953): friend and publisher of many writers active in the early Abbey Theatre movement; his Dublin firm, Maunsel & Co., was the first to publish Synge's plays and the first collected edition of his works (4 vols, 1910). He performed in two premières of Synge's plays: as

Dan Burke, in *In The Shadow of the Glen* (1903), and Timmy the Smith in *The Well of the Saints* (1905).

ANN SADDLEMYER: Professor of English and Drama at the University of Toronto, a Fellow of the Royal Society of Canada and a former chairman of the International Association for the Study of Anglo-Irish Literature. Her publications include *Synge and Modern Comedy* and *In Defence of Lady Gregory Playwright*; her editions of Synge's plays (2 vols, 1968) and of his *Collected Letters* (2 vols, 1982 and 1983) are exemplary texts.

EDWARD THOMAS (1878–1917): English poet and journalist; his literary reputation has steadily increased since his death in battle in Flanders.

ROBERT WELCH: Professor of English and Head of the Department of English, Media and Theatre Studies in the University of Ulster. His publications include *Irish Poetry from Moore to Yeats* (1980), *The Way Back* (1982) and *A History of Verse Translation from the Irish: 1789–1897* (1986), and (in preparation) *A Companion to Irish Literature*, dealing with both of Ireland's literary languages.

RAYMOND WILLIAMS (1921–1988): formerly Fellow of Jesus College, Cambridge, and Professor of Drama there. A prolific scholar and one of the best-known English Marxist critics, he has written widely on drama and film and on English cultural traditions. His publications include *Drama from Ibsen to Eliot* (1952) – largely rewritten in 1968 as *Drama from Ibsen to Brecht*, though the Synge section is unchanged – *Drama in Performance* (1954), *Culture and Society 1780–1950* (1958), *The Long Revolution* (1961), *Communications* (1962) and *Modern Tragedy* (1966).

KATHARINE WORTH: formerly Professor of Drama and Theatre Studies in the University of London and Head of the Drama Department at Royal Holloway College. Her publications include *Revolutions in Modern English Drama* (1973), *The Irish Drama of Europe* (1978) and *Oscar Wilde* (1983); she also edited the symposium *Beckett the Shape Changer* (1975). She has made new productions, with the University of London Audio-Visual Centre, of Beckett's *Eh Joe*, *Words and Music*, *Embers* and *Cascando*.

W. B. YEATS (1864–1939): distinguished poet and critic and co-founder of the Abbey Theatre, Dublin.

INDEX

Figures in **bold type** refer to main entries in the present Casebook. Synge's plays are listed separately; for his non-dramatic writings, see under Synge, John Millington.